INTERVENTIONS

Queer Oz Folk is published on the land of the Wurundjeri People of the Kulin Nation. We acknowledge the Traditional Owners of country throughout Australia and recognise their continuing connection to lands, waters and culture. We pay our respects to their Elders past, present and emerging. Their land was stolen, never ceded. It always was and always will be Aboriginal land.

Graham Willett has been active in the gay and lesbian movement in Australia since 1979, in groups as diverse as the *Gay Community News* Collective, Stonewall 25, ACTUP and the Australian Queer Archives. He has researched and published widely on the history of queer activism in Australia, including *Living Out Loud* (2000), from which this book is extracted.

To all those who led the way, with thanks.

First published 2024 by Interventions Inc

This book was originally published as chapters 1 – 8 of Living Out Loud: A history of gay and lesbian activism in Australia, Allen and Unwin, 2000

Interventions is a not-for-profit, independent, radical book publisher. For further information:
> www.interventions.org.au
> info@interventions.org.au
> PO Box 24021
> Melbourne VIC 3001

Queer Oz Folk Series Vol 5
Series editor: Graham Willett
Queer Oz Folk publishes Australian queer history in good quality, affordable editions with an eye to the widest possible audiences.

Title: Before Mardi Gras: Lesbian and Gay Activism in Australia, 1969-1978
Author: Graham Willett

ISBN: 978-0-6486416-2-9 Paperback
ISBN: 978-0-6486416-3-6 Ebook

Front and back cover design and layout by Simon Strong
Interior design and layout by Viktoria Ivanova.
Front cover photo: Graham Willett
Back cover photo: Untitled, Ponch Hawkes, ©1973

© Graham Willett 2024

The moral rights of the author have been asserted.
All rights reserved. Except as permitted under the Australian Copyright Act 1968 (for example, a fair dealing for the purposes of study, research, criticism or review), no part of this book may be reproduced, stored in a retrieval system, communicated or transmitted in any form or by any means without prior written permission.

All inquiries should be made to the author: info@interventions.org.au

 A catalogue record for this book is available from the National Library of Australia

BEFORE MARDI GRAS: LESBIAN AND GAY ACTIVISM IN AUSTRALIA, 1969-1978

GRAHAM WILLETT

CONTENTS

Introduction (2024) — 1
Introduction (2000) — 9
Chapter 1: The Scene and the Unseen: Kamp Life in the 1950s — 15
Chapter 2: Liberalism and its Limits — 33
Chapter 3: CAMPing Out — 49
Chapter 4: The Challengers — 77
Chapter 5: Lobbing Eggs and Lobbying — 103
Chapter 6: The Three Pillars of Ignorance — 131
Chapter 7: Hastening Slowly, 1974-78 — 153
Chapter 8: Backlash, Resistance and the Community — 181
Endnotes — 209

ABBREVIATIONS AND ACRONYMS

ACT	Australian Capital Territory
ALP	Australian Labor Party
ANU	Australian National University
ANZCP	Australian and New Zealand College of Psychiatry
AQuA	Australian Queer Archives
ASIO	Australian Security and Intelligence Organisation
AUS	Australian Union of Students
BLF	Builders Labourers' Federation
CAMP	Campaign Against Moral Persecution
CCL	Council for Civil Liberties
DOB	Daughters of Bilitis
FOL	Festival of Light
GAA	Gay Activists Alliance
GLF	Gay Liberation Front
GTSG	Gay Teachers' and Students' Group
HGS	Homosexual Guidance Service
HLRS	Homosexual Law Reform Society
LCL	Liberal Country League
MCC	Metropolitan Community Church
NSW	New South Wales
SGL	Sydney Gay Liberation

INTRODUCTION (2024)

If this book provokes feelings of *déjà vu*, there is a reason. *Before Mardi Gras* is, in fact, a reprint of the first eight chapters of my earlier work, *Living Out Loud*. In 13 chapters, that book took the story of gay and lesbian activism in Australia almost up to its publication date – to about the year 2000. The chapters reprinted here stop in the immediate aftermath of Sydney's first Gay Mardi Gras (as it was called then) in 1978.

It is 45 years since that first Mardi Gras took to the streets. An exuberant, dressy celebration of pride was transformed by the police into a riot, as the poofters and lezzos asserted their right to be out and about. The next year, on the first anniversary, thousands gathered to march again, to defy and protest and celebrate. From then on, there was no holding back. Year after year, nothing could stop us: rainstorms and Christians, AIDS and Covid only fuelled our determination to show ourselves off – to each other, to Australia and to the world.

In the decades after 1978, laws that dated back to King Henry VIII were overthrown, professional opinion revisited and revised, public attitudes transformed. Queer people, with our friends and allies, profoundly reshaped Australia and the lives of all those who live here. New ways of living and being have emerged, creating an abecedarium of peoples demanding recognition, respect and rights.

It is not surprising, that so many people see the origins of that struggle for equality in 1978. But in this book, in these chapters from *Living Out Loud*, I am looking at the decade *before* 1978, at the emergence of a movement for the remaking of how we think about – and live – sex, sexuality and gender. The decade after 1969 laid the foundations for the eruption of 1978 and for all that came after. It is impossible to understand Australia today without some knowledge of what worked so well, so early.

In that decade, the first gay newspapers, radio programs and telephone advice services appeared. Action groups worked in trade unions, in universities and schools and in political parties of all stripes. The National Homosexual Conference in 1975 turned out to be the first of an annual series that lasted until the mid-1980s. Activism meant marches, lobbing eggs – and lobbying, and picnics. Holding hands in the street, dressing outrageously, wearing badges and living in communal households brought the promise of change to everyday life. Coming out put the world on notice that we weren't going to cop what had been thrown at us anymore. As the badges said: gay was good; better blatant than latent.

The story of the struggle for equality begins, therefore, not in 1978, but with the first people who organised themselves to speak openly for homosexual rights – the Australian Capital Territory (ACT) Homosexual Law Reform Society in 1969, the lesbian group Daughters of Bilitis (Melbourne 1969–70) and the Campaign Against Moral Persecution (Sydney 1970). For all their differences, these groups united women and men, homosexuals and heterosexuals, into a campaign for change – for equality, acceptance and rights.

And it was successful. It is no exaggeration to say that the work done in the 1970s saved lives. Those who might have internalised society's loathing found their way to community, friendship, love. More importantly still, we were able to slow and eventually stop the spread of HIV/AIDS after 1981 because of what we had learnt in our resistance to the Christian right's late 1970s attempt to roll back the gains of the previous years.

Overwhelmingly, these pioneers found that standing against hate, especially alongside others, was invigorating. There was a real joy in struggle. Of course, it was not always a cosy affair. Politics is hard. Furious arguments, sexism, political differences, accusations of extremism and moderation, agonies over whether to demand reform or revolution, organisation versus structurelessness, working at the grassroots versus meetings in the increasingly smoke-free backrooms of power – all these debates tried the patience of even the most dedicated campaigners.

What we have here in this book is the world of the movement in the 1970s. If I were to write it now, there would be some changes – but, on balance, not massive ones. I am interested in the political history of that time, of the social movement; as I said in the original introduction:

> My attention remains fairly firmly fixed upon the public rather than the private, the visible rather than the subterranean, the political rather than the cultural. As a result, much of what was going on, and much that mattered greatly, has been treated cursorily or not at all.

Now, more than ever, the value of political struggle, of activist campaigning, of direct action, needs to be recognised. We face challenges – as we always have; and an explanation of what worked in the past is vital.

I did consider updating *Living Out Loud* to deal with the years since 2000, but that would be a daunting task. The 1980s and 1990s (which I do cover in *LOL*) were marked by the emergence of something entirely new – a community. In the decades after, that community deepened and assimilated itself into the new national ideology of diversity, inclusion and equality. The job of reporting on this I am content to leave to others.

THE INEVITABLE NOTE ON LANGUAGE: FROM KAMP TO QUEER AND BEYOND

Inevitably, when it comes to discussing same-sexuality, we confront the question of language. How do we and others describe us? Usage – especially acceptable usage – has varied greatly over time. In the 20th century, the word 'homosexual' came to be used more and more, drifting across from the world of European sexology (the scientific study of sex and sexuality). It was a perfectly respectable word, even if the phenomenon which it described was not. In the vernacular, a plethora of words – to a greater or lesser extent abusive – coexisted. In Australia, 'poofter' and 'lezzo' were the most common. Homosexual people in Australia, from at least the 1940s, mostly described themselves as 'kamp' (sometimes 'camp'). This odd spelling was said to have crossed over from police language: 'Known Associate of Male Prostitutes'. This is unlikely to be true, and we are left to wonder how it came to be universally adopted by queer people. In any case, the word was a simple synonym for homosexual in Australia, lacking the connotations of flamboyance and theatricality that it had in the United States and Britain (or at least extending well beyond these). 'Homosexual' and 'kamp' remained the dominant terms until the early 1970s, although 'kamp' became 'camp' as it started to appear in print.

In 1972, 'gay' was imported from the USA, and 'lesbian' was taken up by feminist lesbians keen to establish their visibility within the new gay movement and in the broader society. The movement soon adopted the usage 'gay and lesbian' – or, for extra visibility for women, 'lesbian and gay' – which prevailed for many years. In the 1990s, bisexual people, seeking to challenge their invisibility, started to insist on their being included. This adoption of sexual identities and the assertion of their centrality to the struggle for equality generated a proliferation of labels, which shows no sign of abating. I tend to use 'gay' in the early sense to include lesbian and gay people.

Today, the most common term in Australian public life is LGBTIQ+ (lesbian, gay, bisexual, trans, intersex and queer).

Where the language question becomes difficult is in the insistence by some that there is a correct usage and that those who do not use it are causing offence. The problem is that 'correct usage' changes – often rapidly. The use of 'tranny' by, and about, trans people was very common in the 1990s; now, it is generally thought to be beyond the pale. If there were an agency in a position to make definitive rulings on language, we would all be better off. In the meantime, my own preference is to use the terms that were generally used at the time about which I am writing, varied for readability. For most of the period after 1970 – the period covered by this book– the terms are 'gay' and 'lesbian'.

THE LESS INEVITABLE NOTE ON 'SEX', 'GENDER' AND 'SEXUALITY'

One of the earliest achievements of the women's liberation movement, which erupted in the USA in the late 1960s and flowed through the rest of the Western world in the years immediately after, was to identify a distinction between 'sex' and 'gender'. It is a distinction that has almost disappeared now in public life, when every form, official or otherwise, will ask for name, date of birth and gender. When they say 'gender', they are actually asking about 'sex'.

The distinction was a rather simple one. *Sex* is a universal biological fact among humans, an expression of our X and Y chromosomes and visible in what used to be called the secondary sex characteristics – the ways in which we would recognise a naked person as male or female (genitalia, breast or chest, Adam's apple or not, extent and location of body hair, general body shape). For the liberationists (and for those on whose work they drew), there were two sexes, male and female. Today, we acknowledge the existence of a variety of intersex conditions, where this simple dichotomy is challenged by a small proportion of the population whose chromosomes express themselves in the characteristics of both sexes.

Gender, on the other hand, is a social phenomenon, a set of rules as to how men and women should express themselves in their behaviour: as either masculine or feminine. Gendered characteristics include a plethora of behaviours determined by social expectations (and sometimes enforced by laws) to be appropriate to each sex. Masculine and feminine clothing, hairstyles, given names, occupations, hobbies and interests, emotional expression, tone of voice and bodily carriage vary greatly between societies, within them, and over time. And, while any given individual will be definitively male or female or intersex, few individuals will be definitively masculine or feminine. Sex is a matter of ticking a box; an individual's gender is more of a sliding scale – more masculine or more feminine or, more accurately, a series of sliding scales. An individual's hairstyle might be rather masculine, their clothing rather feminine; their name might be sex-neutral. Conceivably, one could construct an index of all an individual's gendered features and declare them to be X-percent masculine and Y-percent feminine – but who would decide? And what would be the point?

The women's liberation movement set out to challenge and overthrow the gender norms. Women should be able to dress, walk and talk however they liked. They should be allowed to be ambitious and aggressive and to take on men's jobs, from driving trams to running companies. Men should be doing child care and housework. It was a revolution whose ramifications were to spread into every nook and cranny of public and private life. People's sex would remain unaltered; the gender order was to be eradicated, leaving everyone free to be, and to behave, as they liked.

A third term enters the discussion here: sexuality. *Sexuality* – sexual desire and the objects to which it is directed – is partly biological. The wish for sexual contact is generally triggered at puberty and involves several physiological reactions: some shared, some specific to men and to women. The direction of the desire may be biological ('born that way' or produced by hormones released at puberty). It might be a product of upbringing and family relations, as psychoanalyst Sigmund Freud thought. Other experiences (childhood seduction has commonly been identified) might influence it. It could be a choice; there are women who, having decided to withdraw their emotional energies from men and redirect them towards women, found that their sexual desires followed. It might be any of these or something else entirely. There is not one reason causing people to desire sexual contact of a particular type. A further complication is that sexuality may be expressed as an inner desire, as behaviour or as a publicly available identity. This distinction became especially important during the AIDS years: it became necessary to be able to reach out to men who had sex with men (behaviour) but who would never have thought of themselves as homosexual or even bisexual (identity). The history of sexuality is mightily entangled – in its concepts, its geographies, its social and political and lived experiences. The history of same-sexuality in Australia in the 1970s is no less complex than anywhere or anywhen else.

THANKS

I would like to thank all those who contributed to this book. Especially the gang at Queer Oz Folk and at the Australian Queer Archives. And to the photographers who have generously made their works available, including Ponch Hawkes, Phillip Potter, Barb Creed, the Rennie Ellis Foundation, Phyllis Papps and Geoff Friend. Where copyright owners are known, they are credited alongside their photos. Despite efforts, it has not always been possible to identify copyright holders. Where there are omissions, please let us know so as to allow amendments to later printings.

INTRODUCTION (2000)

In the original text of this Introduction, I usually spelled kamp with a 'c' (camp'). My more recent research has established that 'kamp' was the usual spelling until the very late 1960s; I have adjusted this text accordingly. GW 2024.

It is not so very long ago that to be a homosexual in Australia was to be feared, hated and persecuted. Lesbians and homosexual men were widely believed to be evil, psychologically disordered or, at best, pathetically unhappy people. Religion called it a sin; psychology, a mental illness. The law made male homosexual acts, even between consenting adults, illegal and prescribed harsh terms of imprisonment. Discrimination was actively pursued by state institutions such as the courts, the schools and the public service. Newspapers in the 1950s and 1960s, when they mentioned the subject at all, confined their coverage to transvestites and child molesters, soliciting in public toilets and gruesome murders. From Hollywood, the centre of the world's film industry during this period and a cultural touchstone for the whole Western world, came silence or, at best, the carefully unacknowledged presence of the homosexual as something sinister and alien.

The homosexual subculture, though growing, kept itself well away from the public gaze, and most homosexuals never came out except to others of their kind and perhaps to a few carefully chosen and sympathetic friends. The virus of hate had infected even homosexuals themselves. Many were, or believed that they were, in fact, what society said: mad or bad or sad. Others had resisted or thrown off the self-hate but lived with the fear that, if they revealed themselves, they would lose their family, their friends and their jobs.

How very different are attitudes today. In Australia, laws against homosexual sex have been reformed in every state and territory. In most states, and in the federal sphere, discrimination on the basis of sexuality is illegal. The federal government now recognises gay de facto relationships as a legitimate basis for immigration rights and allows open homosexuals to serve in the armed forces. The Family Court no longer treats homosexuality as an automatic bar to the custody of children. In most states, official liaison committees have been set up to foster better relations between the police and homosexuals, representing a remarkable break with the official practices and attitudes of the past. Meanwhile, the gay and lesbian subculture, with its bars and sex clubs, its bookshops and media, its lobbyists and spokespeople, activists and bureaucrats, is stronger than ever; and, while often professing to be apolitical, it is capable of mobilising thousands of people for Sydney's Gay and Lesbian Mardi Gras and similar festivals in all other capital cities. It provides, too, an infrastructure within which more radical and, indeed, more conservative visions can still be argued out. Gay pride is a powerful fact in the lives of hundreds of thousands of homosexual people.

Anti-gay ideas still exist in society, of course, but a basic liberal tolerance is the dominant mood. Organised homophobia has proved incapable of mobilising any real support, either in the streets or in the corridors of power. What is most noticeable about 'moral crusaders' such as Fred Nile is how cranky and extreme their ideas look. Yet what they were saying in the late 1990s was simply what most people had believed 30 years before. It is a startling indication of just how far we have come that the moral crusaders' demands are widely regarded as silly and unfair.

Living Out Loud explores and explains this remarkable transformation – both of gay and lesbian lives and of the society within which these lives are lived. It focuses especially upon the role played by political activism, upon the political movement which brought homosexuals onto the streets and the TV screens, into parliaments and cathedrals and doctors' rooms; the movement that brought people out to their families, their workmates and to the world at large. It was the gay and lesbian movement, beginning in the 1970s, that allowed homosexuals to become gay, to be proud of their sexuality, their courage and their capacity for love and lust. It allowed gay people to be visible and articulate, reasonable and angry, demanding and celebratory. It found ways to explain social hatred and ways to confront it. It offered gay people both a history and a future and a means of moving from the darkness of the one to the brightness of the other.

The story begins with the kamp scene of the 1950s, which – although a source of much greater pleasure than has often been assumed – was one in which fear played a great part and in which the idea of political action seems never to have been seriously considered. There was, as we shall see, one attempt to organise a law reform group, but it failed to get off the ground. And yet, by the late 1960s, decriminalisation was on the minds of many people – politicians, clergy, newspaper editors and liberal reformers. Everyone, it sometimes seems, was talking about the issue except those in the kamp scene. The question of how this shift came about is the concern of the early chapters of this book.

In 1970, the first gay rights organisations – the Daughters of Bilitis and the Campaign Against Moral Persecution – were established, and from that point on, political activism has been a permanent part of Australian homosexual life. The existence of these organisations transformed the terms of the debate entirely and, if they did not manage to contain the plethora of demands that they unleashed, they were nonetheless responsible for demonstrating what was possible in the climate of the time and for inspiring thousands of people – gay and straight – into action. Gay Liberation and Radicalesbians, along with myriad single-issue action groups, toiled away in the 1970s, raising issues, debating strategies, demanding change and achieving it. By the end of the decade, public opinion had shifted dramatically, and gay issues were firmly on the public agenda.

The 1980s saw a further and equally surprising shift in gay politics. While struggles around law reform continued, and made progress, the decade saw, too, the emergence of a disease that threatened both the lives of thousands and all the political gains that had been made. But the eighties were not just about AIDS. It was during this time that the gay community started to become something more than a rhetorical flourish, with the emergence of media, festivals and service organisations of its own. These developments owed much to both business's quest for the gay dollar and to activists, who set out to make the emerging gay subculture into a community, with real political and social clout.

Efforts for law reform continued through the 1980s and 1990s, and the radical potential of gay politics was nowhere more visible than in the eruption of the Tasmanian law reform campaign, which rebounded ever more strongly from each setback and ultimately entrenched the issue of gay and lesbian rights firmly within the human rights framework. If, in so doing, the Tasmanian campaign completed the long-drawn-out demise of the radical and liberationist vision of the 1970s, it nonetheless served to bring real legal equality ever closer to fulfilment. Whether legal equality will mark the end of gay politics is yet to be seen.

Lesbian and gay experience in Australia is a complex story, and a book as short as this cannot hope to do justice to its richness and detail. In particular, my concern is with activism, rather than gay and lesbian life as such. Even the account of the kamp scene of the 1950s mainly draws attention to the absence of political activity (one of the ways in which Australia was different from the USA and Britain). Activism can be – indeed, needs to be – understood fairly broadly, but again I have narrowed my focus here in the interests of clarity and the inevitable constraints of space. My attention remains fairly firmly fixed upon the public rather than the private, the visible rather than the subterranean, the political rather than the cultural. As a result, much of what was going on, and much that mattered greatly, has been treated cursorily or not at all. If people object to this (and I hope they do), I would merely urge them to get to work on memoirs and histories of their own. And if they can find a solution to the problem of terminology, we will all be in their debt. I have preferred to use the terms most commonly in use in the times about which I am writing: 'kamp' and 'homosexual' before 1970; 'gay' in the early 1970s, 'gay and lesbian' thereafter, with occasional lapses in the interests of variety.

Living Out Loud is intended as an overview, a mapping of the territory, a description of a too-empty landscape that will soon, I hope, be populated by historians and storytellers falling over each other in the rush to stake their claim. If this book inspires people to want to know more and to set about finding out, it will have done its task.

1.

The Scene and the Unseen: Kamp Life in the 1950s

The prevailing image of homosexual life in Australia in the 1950s is one of lonely, fearful lives, persecution, vilification, hatred and self-hatred. And not without reason. Yet many who remember those years have fond memories of them and will, if asked, vigorously defend the fifties. John Michael Howsen dismisses the negative picture as 'crap', as a myth, and recalls his life in Melbourne as 'not all that bad', denying that he was ever persecuted or victimised. He lived a 'don't ask, don't tell' sort of life, to be sure, and wonders whether, had he not been gay, his career might have been more successful. But his strongest memories are of 'brilliant' dinner parties, 'smashing good-looking guys' and balls at which 99 percent of those present were queens in drag.[1]

More and more, memoirs and oral histories are revealing that the 1950s were very much richer than most had thought. Certainly, this life lacked the high-profile visibility of the 1990s queer experience. No Oxford Street. No Mardi Gras. No press. No market niche. But there were cafés and parties, love and hate, sleazy sex and picnics in the park. People of all sexual orientations lived very different lives in many ways and suffered pressures of all kinds. Whether homosexuals were worse off or not – a question that would have been unimaginable even a decade ago – is now starting to be discussed.

Homosexual desire is too much a part of the human condition to have ever been absent from society, and homosexual subcultures have been identified in the major cities of Europe as early as the 1720s. In London, self-styled 'mollys' gathered together in pubs and brothels, spoke their own argot and sympathised with each other over their plight as outsiders.[2] In Australia, too, there are signs of molly-like lives, which is hardly surprising. Among the convicts and their guards and among the free settlers, there must have been more than a few who intimately knew the molly pubs and parks of Britain and brought their habits with them to the Antipodes. There are hints of this in evidence given to the inquiry into convict transportation in the 1830s, where the habit among some men of giving female names to each other – Polly, Sally, Bet, Kitty and Nancy – is attested.[3] As cities grew, so did the opportunities for sexual dalliance. No sooner had Melbourne become a major city with the onset of the Gold Rush in 1850, it seems, than Carlton Gardens became the scene of regular assignations between men. In Brisbane in the 1860s, the banks of the river served the same purpose: shocking goings-on that occasionally, at least, came to the attention of the authorities and were sternly punished.

Men certainly had sex with each other; women did too. What cannot be known with any certainty is what they made of these experiences. Did they give their sexual preference great weight in their lives? How many of them had any preference for one sex over the other? Did they socialise as much as possible with their own kind or did they think of themselves primarily in terms of their class, religion or neighbourhood?

Garry Wotherspoon has argued that, by the 1930s, some men in Sydney certainly had a sense of themselves as different. They described themselves as 'kamp' and 'queens' and were actively participating in a milieu of their own. It was a scene that was 'secret, fragmented and tainted by its illegality', but it was there.[4] It could be intensely private – networks of friends meeting in each

The Pleasures of Kamp I: In this 1930s photograph of a kamp wedding, the bride and groom are both male, and all the guests are cross-dressed. (History Inverted collection, AQuA)

other's houses for dinner – or cautiously public. Restaurants, cafés and, above all, hotels, ranging from the respectably middle class to the bohemian to the downright dangerous, offered places for kamps to gather. In Sydney during the inter-war period, kamps gathered at the Australia Hotel, the Carlton, Ushers and Pfahlerts, all in the city centre, or in any one of a number of nearby restaurants where patrons could retire after the 6 o'clock closing of the pubs. As long as they were discreet, they were welcomed.

In Melbourne, 'Bill' remembers a club in the city which, in the 1930s, was run by two kamp men, Cyril and Alfie. The premises operated as a bridge club by day, but on Saturday night there was a cabaret. On Sunday night, informal gatherings were reserved for kamps who would pay to enter, either bringing their own grog or buying it on the sly onsite. This club had an annual debutante ball; here, as a young man, Bill made his debut, all in white satin, with an ostrich feather fan and a four-foot-long train to his gown. There were also cafés and restaurants, each with its own pattern of operation. Tait's Tea House, downstairs in the Manchester Unity Building, was 'more or less the meeting place for all the gays in Melbourne then' and, although a degree of discretion was expected, the tables of up to 20 people singing along to the chorus of 'Of all the queens that ever lived, I'd choose you' must have made interesting viewing for any straights who might have wandered in.[5]

Bill also remembers a café in Acland Street, St Kilda, which held some 200–300 people, furnished with an organ and a four or five-piece orchestra. It was always a mixed but mainly kamp crowd and, as long as you bought coffee, you could sit there until it closed at five in the morning. Another coffee lounge at St Kilda Junction catered for the after-theatre crowd; when the theatre-goers arrived, the kamp boys and lesbians would go upstairs till they had left. It was not that the owner or the straight crowd were hostile to the kamp clientele; it was just that the after-theatre crowd bought meals, while the kamps nursed coffees.

Even smaller cities started to develop such scenes. By the late 1930s, the Exchange in Adelaide's Hindley Street and the South Australian in North Terrace were starting to attract homosexual people. In Brisbane, the Long Bar at the Criterion, Lennons, Her Majesty's and the Grand Central all played host, however discreetly, to kamps. After World War II, the development of this milieu accelerated and, by the early 1950s, Castlereagh Street in Sydney had a small cluster of such venues, permitting kamps to wander from one to the next as the mood took them. In Melbourne, a thriving scene developed. Half a dozen pubs and cafés in and around Collins Street harboured kamp spaces, including the Australia Hotel, the Manchester Unity Building and Embank Arcade.[6]

None of these bars were homosexual bars in any recognisably modern sense. At best, they were places where kamp men – and sometimes women – could discreetly meet with their friends and the occasional newcomer for a drink and a quiet chat. In the less reputable hotels, trade (men who were prepared to be sexually serviced by kamps) could be found, but the modern gay bar, where homosexuals were encouraged to gather openly, was almost inconceivable before the 1960s.

Making a homosexual life in the 1950s was by no means as easy as it has become. In the first place, you had to find a name for your desires. Today, the average nine year old will know what 'gay' is and what it means, drawing their knowledge from television, from magazines, from out relatives and family friends. Accepting one's sexuality may still be a trial, but knowing what it is, is much less difficult. Nonetheless, even in the 1950s, at some point in their lives, some people would, by tortuous paths or by a sudden simple act of recognition, realise they were not like other people, but were *like that*. They themselves, they realised, were one of the perverts, sodomites, poofters, lezzies or homosexuals about which they had heard. Many believed, initially at least, that they were the only one of their kind. In the late 1930s, Jeffrey Smart, at the age of 17, was one such.[7]

Even when it dawned on some that, if a name existed, there must be others, the problem remained: how to find them? Compared to today's gay community, the kamp scene was both very small and almost invisible to the world at large. There were no street parties, no newspapers or magazines. The scene operated almost entirely by word of mouth. Clues could, however, be found. In the 1950s, the press would, from time to time, report some new scandal involving prominent figures, public toilets and the police. A paper such as the *Adelaide Advertiser* might note a police raid on a café – the Quality Inn in 1949, for example – and give an address. These stories soon died away but, for some readers, the details of time, place and location could be garnered and followed up.

People met each other at work and in social settings, as well. There were, as popular mythology asserted, homosexual

The Pleasures of Kamp 2: Jan Hillier and her girlfriend at Luna Park, Melbourne, 1950s (Hillier Collection, AQuA).

occupations. In Melbourne, the Myer window dressers were notorious. And women who wanted to meet women joined sporting clubs or the army or mingled in the bohemian circles of artists and actors and writers.[8] There were even churches where kamp women and men could find each other: Christ Church St Laurence and St James' in Sydney, St Mary Magdalene's in Adelaide and St Peter's Eastern Hill in Melbourne were well known among kamps for sheltering congregations of like-minded people.[9]

This is not to say that meeting others was easy. Even where they congregated, very few homosexuals were out to anyone other than a few close friends. But there were signs, ways of asking, or saying, without it being too obvious. Any hint of effeminacy in men or masculinity in women was likely to catch the eye of those on the lookout. In Newcastle in the 1950s, it was widely believed that yellow socks and ties were a sign. After a certain amount of time, a fellow soldier, workmate or hockey team-mate might ever so carefully edge the conversation into that area. Eventually, you knew one other kamp person. And he or she almost certainly knew others.

For men, there were the beats. Parks and public toilets, beaches and changing sheds, community baths and roadside rest stops – all these were places where men could linger inconspicuously, waiting until another came along to linger with them. Finding these was not too hard. Scandalous stories or dire warnings might circulate among family, friends or schoolmates. Or one might simply stumble across them. 'Bill', for instance, discovered the existence of beats at the age of 14 when a slightly older mate went into a public toilet and someone made a pass at him. Having found a beat, the delicate task of meeting began, with the prospect of sex or, less commonly, an invitation home for sex. Not all of those who frequented the beats were tortured married men, out for nothing more than quick, guilty relief. Some men enjoyed beat sex for its own sake, and when 'Ken' found himself with a sudden lottery win that provided him with the means to buy a motorbike, he set out to experience all the beats of Melbourne.[10] The beats offered opportunities not just for the pleasures of sex, but for the thrill of the chase and, perhaps most importantly of all, to meet people.

Men who did the beats ('beat-bashers', in the parlance of the day) were not necessarily averse to conversation, and sexual encounters could well provide an opening for a long-term relationship or an entrée to a whole new circle of friends. These circles of friends were the backbone of kamp life, and finding one's way into them was essential. With hotels closing at 6 pm, beats so dependent upon the weather, balls infrequent, it was friends and private parties that provided a social life for most homosexuals who had one. The 6 o'clock swill, that great Australian custom of downing as much alcohol as possible between the end of the workday and the closing of the pubs at 6 pm (which persisted in Melbourne until the 1960s), was marked in the kamp sections of bars in the 1950s with a furious search for the party after – the address of the house or flat at which those who were invited to continue on could gather. These parties could be riotous affairs, although the spectre of the neighbours must have exercised a restraining influence on hosts and guests alike. At such parties, friends could gather, and new faces could be introduced. Liaisons could be made and broken with all the intensity or lightheartedness that one wished. Cyril Howe (Duchess Hilda, to those in the know) hosted a party every Saturday night in his converted coach-house at the rear of what is now the Scientology centre in Melbourne. These were invitation-only affairs, and your chance of being invited improved remarkably if you had some special talent, were good at drag or were humorous or attractive. Even then, some malicious 'number' might spread a story that you had a sexually transmitted disease, leading to banishment, as happened to 'Bill' on one occasion.

It was not always about racing off the 'tastiest piece' one could find, of course. Kamp relationships were common enough and could embody all the romantic paraphernalia of mainstream relationships. Paddy Byrnes describes her relationship with Robbie, a fellow nurse whom she met at work in the 1950s. They travelled as sisters, telling those who asked why they were single that in their day nurses were not allowed to marry. But in fact, they had married, as Paddy tells:

> We vowed we would never part. I had changed my name to Robbie's. On 17 March 1956 we became as one in a wee church, after lighting two candles and exchanging wedding-rings inscribed 'Keep Faith'. [11]

The kamp scene of the 1950s differed most strongly from the later gay community in its nocturnal nature. It was a scene of the night and was very largely invisible to the rest of society. It was also, and most obviously, a radically apolitical scene. Its members hoped for nothing more than to be left alone. It eschewed – indeed, never seriously imagined – political action. And what underpinned its apolitical stance was fear, a deep and abiding fear of mainstream society.

The strongest literary representation of this fear is to be found in Neville Jackson's novel, *No End to the Way*.[12] Set in Perth in the 1960s, the novel depicts a 'homosexual marriage' between two men, Ray and Cor. The characters, who are, in Ray's pithy phrase, perfectly well-adjusted to their maladjustment, nonetheless live with a series of debilitating day-today fears – of being beaten up by the men they meet in bars; of blackmail; of police entrapment; of arrest, exposure, infamy and disgrace. To avoid all this, they live lives that are intolerably constrained. They kiss goodnight only if the street is sufficiently dark, they hold hands in the cinema and the car only if their touching is kept well out of the line of sight of others. They search for a flat in which to live where onlookers cannot look through the windows and see Ray and Cor if they forget themselves for a moment and kiss. As the novel makes clear, the disapproval of family and friends constrained homosexuals from revealing themselves to the world at large:

> Is there ever a second – just a single second – when, no matter what you're doing or saying, or supposed to be keeping your mind on, that you're not also thinking to yourself: you mustn't let it show. Whatever you do, or say, or whatever gesture you make, even in a casual or off-hand moment, you must never let it show. There's not only a law against it; people will leer at you. Ordinary people. Which is even worse... Watch your step in front of your clients. Watch your step in front of your family, ordinary normal friends. Watch your step when you're on the street. Watch your very step itself, the way you walk.[13]

The consequences of error and misfortune (the question of defiance never arises) are little short of catastrophic in *No End to the Way*: Ray's business is destroyed as word of his homosexuality is spread by an enemy; Ray is unable to seek psychiatric help for stress because of his fear of 'treatment' for his homosexuality; their friend Andy is arrested and imprisoned for responding to a policeman's advances in a public toilet; finally, Ray and Cor's relationship succumbs to all of these pressures, and Cor descends into violence, madness and heterosexual marriage.

If *No End to the Way* concentrates on the anxieties of homosexuals, to the exclusion of the pleasures that other more recent accounts of the 1950s have emphasised, its depiction of a dangerous world is not unreasonable. In Australia in the 1950s, homosexuals were, indeed, persecuted. Take policing, for example. Homosexual acts between men were illegal. Statutes governing the abominable crimes of buggery and homosexual soliciting, as well as more vaguely worded offences such as indecency, gross indecency and offensive behaviour, provided the police with the incentive and the means by which to target kamp men. There were few prosecutions for acts committed in private, but homosexual life was not, as we have seen, entirely private, even during these years.

The 1950s saw a sharp increase in the number of people charged and convicted for what were officially labelled unnatural offences. In 1938, total convictions in the superior courts (excluding magistrates' courts) Australia wide numbered 50. This number had doubled by 1941 and continued to rise in all states, virtually without interruption until it peaked at 350 convictions in 1958. The total number of convictions between 1945 and 1960 was over 3,000. However, these figures are not the whole picture. They record the number of people convicted, not charged, in the superior courts only. In New South Wales (NSW), for example, charges heard in the lower courts increased from about 100 in 1946 to over 500 in 1958. And even the figures for those charged understate the extent of police activity, omitting inquiries that did not result in charges being laid but which were, no doubt, frightening enough for those being investigated.[14]

The increase in convictions was a direct result of an increase in the intensity of policing. This, in turn, was the result of policy decisions at the highest levels of the police forces. The superintendent of police in NSW, Colin Delaney, was an active campaigner against the homosexual threat, calling it in 1958 'the greatest social menace' facing Australia, and he played an important part in persuading the state government to strengthen the laws against homosexual soliciting.[15] In Victoria, *Truth* newspaper reported in August 1957: 'alarmed by a startling increase in homosexuality in Victoria in recent years, the police have formed a special squad to deal with it'.[16] The squad, established within the Vice Squad and including one-third of its personnel 'chosen for [their] looks and tailoring as well as toughness', began with a sweep of parks and lavatories frequented by 'perverts' and prowlers, making a dozen arrests in a few weeks of operation. The squad's goal ('We know there are hundreds of perverts in Melbourne and we plan to get them all') seems to have been actively pursued, if the statistics are any indication. Convictions rose from 65 in 1956 to 103 in 1957, to 166 in 1958, and remained above 100 per year until 1960.

Even more sinister was the work of the Australian Security and Intelligence Organisation (ASIO). In 1953, 1957 and again in 1964, ASIO had argued to the federal Cabinet that homosexuals ought not to be employed in public service positions where they might have had access to sensitive national security-related material. The 1964 documents, in particular, were very explicit. In them, the director-general argued that there was a:

> close relation...between serious character
> defects (such as homosexuality, drug addiction,
> drunkenness etc.) and vulnerability of persons
> possessing those attributes to pressure by foreign
> intelligence services.

That homosexuals were allegedly open to influence or coercion was not the only concern. Homosexuality was a character defect that, in and of itself, provided a chink in the armour of the state. The 'characteristics found in many homosexuals – instability, willing self-deceit, defiance towards society' – gave them a special propensity for treacherous behaviour. The 'tendency to surround himself with other homosexuals', 'to gravitate into a select clique which extends internationally' (which applied 'equally to women who are addicted to such similar practices') meant that those who had proved adept at detecting homosexual tendencies, such as the Russians, would always be able to find their way into the innermost reaches of the state once a single homosexual had been caught up in their net. In the end, while the Cabinet drew the line at a total ban on the employment of homosexuals (a ban that the US government was then enforcing vigorously), it decided that practising homosexuals ought not be employed where they could have access to highly classified information; heads of departments were requested to

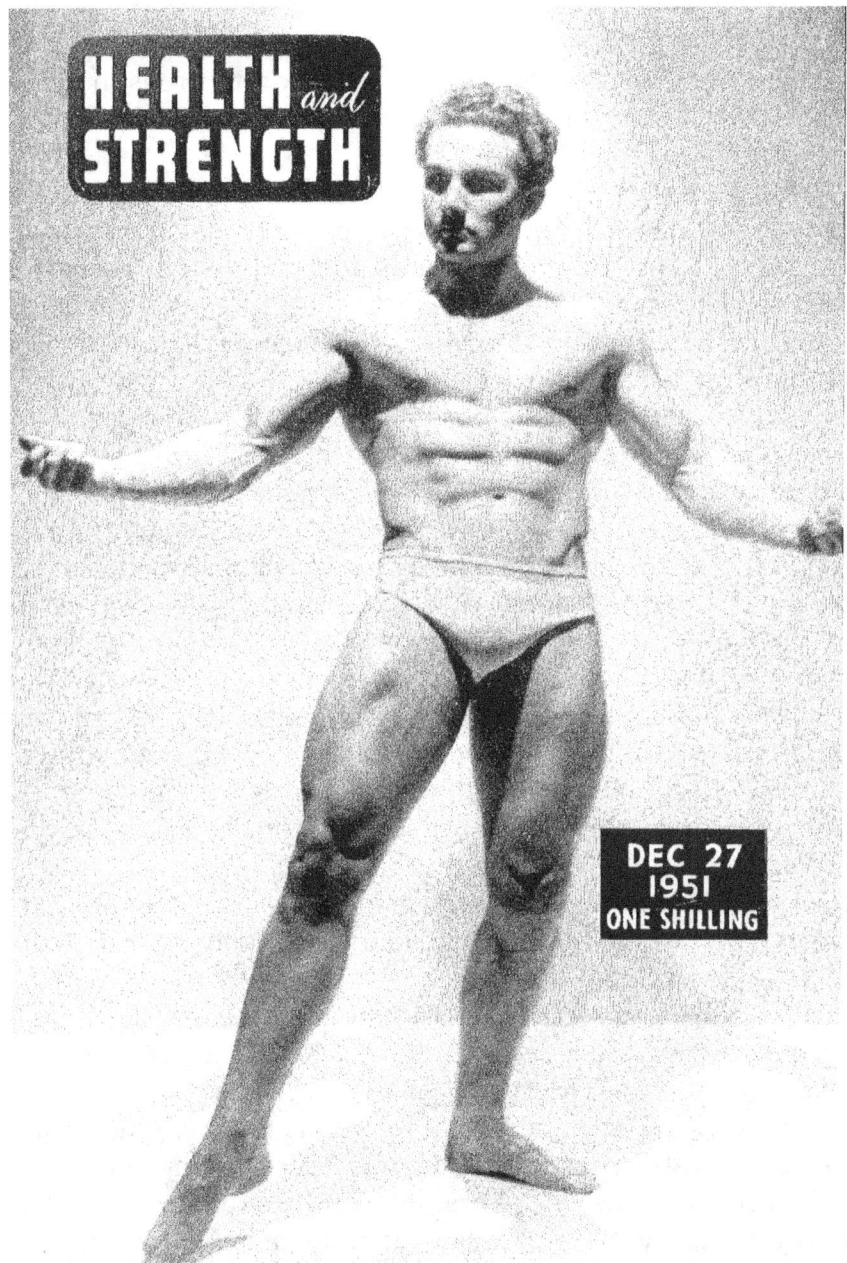

Muscle magazines provided visual stimulation for kamp men in the 1950s, but they could be damning evidence of homosexuality, as this one proved to be for officers in the Department of External Affairs. (National Archives of Australia)

watch for signs of 'homosexuality, addiction to drugs, habitual drunkenness or serious financial irresponsibility' and to advise ASIO of their presence.[17]

These were no mere paper policies. Although the evidence is scanty (questions of national security and personal privacy loom large here), there is some indication that individuals employed in the public service were in fact victimised for their sexuality. Clyde Cameron reports that, when the Liberal government took control of the federal parliament in 1949, it was enough that the new Speaker suspected some of the staff of being homosexual for them to lose their positions.[18] A Department of External Affairs file from the 1950s contains 'photographs...in connection with a report on some officers...who were engaged in some homosexuality'.[19] Most of the photographs are not available for perusal but they are described in detail. The file includes a copy of *Health and Strength*, a muscle magazine, dated 27 December 1951, and a copy of *A Camera Life Class*, which presents itself as a life-drawing course but consists primarily of photos of naked men and women whose genitals are covered only by inked-in jock straps.[20] The role of health magazines, in particular, as sources of homo-erotic imagery in a period of censorship and repression is now well-attested;[21] and, whatever the officers involved had done to attract attention to themselves, these publications seem to have been part of the case against them (as, presumably, were the still-sealed photographs).

Truth newspaper reports, in more detail, a nasty case of summary justice in an article from 1956. 'VICE SHOCK IN ARMY CAMP' reveals that an 'unsavoury cell of homosexuals' had been uncovered at Puckapunyal army camp. Acting with 'commendable speed and ruthlessness to strike at this canker', army authorities had, within two days of the first hint of the situation, identified five regular army men, paraded them at their Albert Park barracks and discharged them with loss of all service privileges. Wide-ranging investigations were reported to be continuing.[22]

The illegality of male homosexuality was not the issue here. As Ruth Ford has demonstrated, lesbians in the military were as much at risk as male homosexuals. Surveillance, silencing, fear and victimisation were all deployed with a view to suppressing lesbian activity in the forces.[23]

And yet, while there were certainly attempts to warn Australians of the danger posed by homosexuality, the overwhelming impression is of an intense desire on the part of the authorities not to have the subject discussed in public. State and federal governments actively censored books, films and plays with homosexual themes or characters well into the 1960s. Even as they amended their laws to tighten up on homosexual practices, legislators in NSW and Victoria often included these changes in larger amendments and avoided all discussion of the issue, presumably because the topic was not one for polite parliamentary chambers.[24] Indeed, during the 1961 Victorian debate that tightened and extended laws regarding prostitution and sexual soliciting (introducing in the process the new and original offence of homosexual soliciting), the MPs worried very much more about the moral dangers posed by espresso bars than they did about homosexuality![25] Even the Victorian state government's 1950 Royal Commission into the Communist Party, when it turned its attention to the communists' efforts to undermine the moral fibre of the nation, concerned itself with the party's attitude to religion and entirely ignored the issue of sexual morality.[26]

This discretion was shared by the press. While it is true that the racier sections of the press, such as *Truth*, were not averse to the odd homosexual scandal, and even the reputable newspapers such as the *Sydney Morning Herald* might report a court case if the defendant was famous enough, by and large the issue was barely aired at all. Robert French has compiled a listing of mainstream media references to homosexuality showing that, in the 1950s, the maximum number of references for any one year is 37 (in 1953), with 36 the following year, and generally there are considerably fewer than this (down as low as 12 for 1951 and nine for 1959).[27] In the context of the mass of material published by the scores of daily newspapers and weekly magazines during this period, attention to homosexuality is so slight as to be virtually invisible to the average reader. Of course, kamp people were more likely to note and to remember what reporting there was; but, given how dangerous the reports made homosexual life seem (the stories were virtually all about arrests and scandals), the media coverage can only have contributed to their fear.

The contradictory experience of kamp people in Australia during this period is captured perfectly in the life and work of Laurence Collinson.[28] Collinson was a Jew, a communist, a homosexual and a poet – any one of which would have been sufficient to raise eyebrows in Australia in the 1950s. In his papers, we see traces of how difficult it was for him during this decade. Perhaps the most poignant moment comes in his letters to friends in which he discusses his break-up with his lover, Rod. The pain that he felt seeps from the page, but what is most striking is the way he consistently referred to Rod only as 'R', and always with the pronoun 'she'. The reason, as Collinson makes clear in a very much later note attached to the papers, was a deep fear that even his private letters could fall into the wrong hands and be used against him. His friends, writing to him, maintained the charade.

While he was open about his sexuality with some few friends and family members, he did not openly declare his sexual preferences. He had, of course, the usual reasons for this and one major additional one. As a communist, Collinson could expect to attract the attention of ASIO (and did so – his file runs to over 100 pages), and homosexuality was too easy for the security police to use against him, especially as he was a school teacher. As it happens, there is nothing to indicate that ASIO was aware of his sexuality and, ironically, when he was victimised, it was not by the state but by the Communist Party. His application to renew his membership in about 1958 was blocked by a local party official who had become aware of his homosexuality.

Despite all this, Collinson made what is almost certainly the only attempt to raise the issue of homosexual law reform in Australia in the 1950s. There is very little information available about this effort, but it is clear that, in late 1958, he contacted the Homosexual Law Reform Society (HLRS) in Britain. On 3 November 1958, Andrew Hallidie-Smith, the society's secretary, wrote in response to a letter from Collinson, wondering whether 'there is any possibility of founding a society with similar aims to ours in Australia?' He apparently received a positive response because, three weeks later, Hallidie-Smith wrote: 'It is heartening to know that you think it is possible that a similar movement may be started in Australia'.[29] As late as November 1959, a full year after the first correspondence, the project seems still to have been active. HallidieSmith wrote again:

> I realise that any movement parallel to ours in Australia will have inevitably to move slowly; but if only we can succeed in our object here, and provided that some groundwork has been put in there, I think that in time your law will follow suit.

At some point during 1959, Collinson began to take steps to establish a society. His papers contain a typed sheet headed 'Suggestions for an agenda', which includes items relating to the value of such an organisation in Australia, the possibility of setting up executive and general committees, the need for an honorary lawyer and methods of raising finance. A handwritten list of 22 names is perhaps a brainstorming of possible committee members (about half of them are listed in the 1960 *Who's Who in Australia*). It is not certain that any meeting ever took place or that potential committee members were ever contacted. Zelman Cowan, one of those on the list, has no recollection of ever having been approached on the issue of homosexual law reform.[30] In

November 1959, HallidieSmith advised that he had sent 50 copies of the HLRS pamphlet *Questions and Answers* as well as 'some other literature', but the Collinson papers do not reveal whether these were received and, if so, whether they were distributed.

The failure of Collinson's effort is not surprising. While the idea of a mass political campaign was available (the Campaign for Nuclear Disarmament was a very visible part of British life at this time), the idea of such a campaign by homosexuals was probably unimaginable. Certainly, the homosexual subculture provided no basis for any mobilisation or activism. Repression by the police and the state and the public opprobrium that kamps experienced had created a climate of fear among them. Few were willing or able to do anything constructive. The realistic option was the creation of a lobby group and, certainly, this is what Hallidie-Smith recommended. But Australia had not experienced a public debate about homosexuality in the way that Britain had during the scandals of the early 1950s; nor was there any visible pool of liberal supporters such as had been generated in the UK.

In 1959, the first faint portent of change appeared. On 6 June of that year, an executive member of the Father and Son Welfare Movement of Australia published an article in the *Sydney Morning Herald* entitled 'Modern Society and the Homosexual'.[31] In what is almost certainly the first serious, substantial discussion of homosexuality ever published in an Australian daily newspaper, the unnamed author argued against ignorance and intolerance and anti-homosexual laws, urging that 'the problem...be viewed in its context with a calm objectivity'. This was something of a false dawn – there was nothing like it published again for several years – but its appearance draws attention to the kind of debate that was absent in Australia in the 1950s. It was only in the mid-1960s, with the rise of a new liberalism, that all of this was to start to change.

2.
Liberalism and its Limits

If discussion of homosexuality was carefully excluded from 1950s public life and expressed itself only within a small, timid and largely underground kamp scene, how did it come to be that, by the late 1960s, homosexuality was not only being talked about in public, but was widely seen as an issue that needed to be dealt with? And, more remarkably still, to be dealt with not by more vigorous repression, but by the repeal of anti-homosexual laws and the mitigation of anti-homosexual attitudes?

There were several factors at work. In the first place, homosexuality had become the centre of a major debate in Britain in the 1950s in a series of highly publicised sex scandals and through the establishment of a government inquiry into prostitution and homosexuality. This inquiry, led by the Wolfenden Committee, called for wide-ranging reforms to the law in its final report of 1957 and included a recommendation for the decriminalisation of homosexual acts between adult men in private. It was to be 10 years before this recommendation was carried into law (and then only in England and Wales), but the 1950s and 1960s was a time during which the issue of homosexuality was rarely far from the front pages of the British press. Much of this discussion was kept from the Australian public or presented in the most tendentious manner imaginable. The *Sydney Morning Herald*, for example, when it felt impelled to mention the Wolfenden Committee at all, habitually referred to it as the 'Inquiry into Prostitution and Perversion'. Australian intellectuals, still at this time besotted with things British, followed the debate with interest, and the Wolfenden report was to become a touchstone for liberal thinking on the question of homosexuality: a source of information, argument and even terminology. The slogan 'consenting adults in private', which was to gain currency during the 1960s, was lifted directly from Wolfenden, as were many of the arguments about the role of the state in enforcing morality.[1] The British press and law were not the only influences on Australia.

Parallel to these was a new strain of thinking among medical and legal practitioners, an evolving medico-legal model of sex offences. By the 1940s, a long-running debate regarding the respective roles of the law and medicine in handling psychiatrically disturbed sex offenders had been more or less resolved. A system was developed whereby offenders were processed through the legal system before they were handed over to doctors for treatment under the general supervision of the courts.[2] One of the issues that arose in this debate was whether or not offences such as homosexuality ought to be treated in the same way as rape or sexual acts between adults and children. A distinction between serious sex offenders, public nuisances (such as exhibitionists or voyeurs) and 'consensual homosexuals [who] do not present a serious danger to the peace and welfare of the community'[3] came into being, and, increasingly, it was argued that systems developed to deal with the former, more serious, category of offences were inappropriate for dealing with the latter, more minor ones. It followed, logically, that homosexual conduct ought not to be criminal; and various commentators explicitly argued along these lines.

These arguments and shifts in thinking were taking place within a much broader process of rethinking, marked most notably by the emergence of a new, liberal current in Australian political life which argued for wide-ranging reform of society. This new liberalism had its roots in the emergence of a new middle class as a major social force – which, in turn, had its roots in the industrialisation and internationalisation of Australia after World War II. Many members of this class, as Donald Horne (who was one of them) has noted, were revolted by the Australia in which they lived. They were gripped by 'doubt, anger and disgust' at the 'racist, anglocentric-imperialist, puritan, sexist, politically genteel-acquiescent, capitalist, bureaucratic and developmentalist' society that they saw. They were enraged by the way in which these values were buttressed by powerful social forces 'in official symbolism and rhetoric, in elite-forming institutions, in most of the mass media and in the way things were done in most of the bureaucracies'.[4]

Frozen out of the mainstream media, these new middle-class critics moved to establish their own press. In quick succession came *Overland* (1954), *Quadrant* (1956), the *Australian Book Review* (1958), *Nation* (1958) and *Dissent* (1961). Here, they developed and argued for an alternative vision of Australia. Rejecting the stultifying consensus of Liberal and Labor party politics, this new liberalism questioned White Australia and policies of restricted immigration, paternalism and racism in Aboriginal affairs, censorship, capital punishment, urban ugliness, the ban on abortion and, among this host of issues, anti-homosexual laws and attitudes. Prevailing social attitudes towards homosexuals seemed to liberal critics to be yet another symptom of a stuffy, backward-looking and conservative society.

The new liberal press provided an outlet for the discussion of homosexuality that had not hitherto existed except in the scandalmongering pages of the *Truth*. In 1962, for example, *Nation* reviewed *The Homosexual Society*, the work of an Australian sociologist based in London, and the journal's letters column saw a debate in which three homosexuals discussed the book and the review: two declared their sexual orientation but not their names, one (Laurie Collinson) signed his letter without being entirely open about his sexuality.⁵ *Nation* also reported and followed up a police raid on a private party in Kings Cross in which officers had accused some of the guests of being 'a bunch of filthy homosexuals'.⁶ The *Australian Book Review* reviewed, defended and debated books with homosexual themes (such as James Baldwin's *Another Country*) and gave space for commentators such as Beatrice Faust to discuss homosexuality in general terms.⁷ The Humanist Society, in particular, discussed the issue frequently at meetings and conferences, in newsletters and its journal.

Out of all this debate and discussion was forged a new understanding of homosexuality as an issue. The notion that homosexuals and homosexuality were threats to society was increasingly questioned. In an article in the *Bulletin* in May 1965, Gordon Hawkins raised NSW Police Superintendent Colin Delaney's 'greatest menace' remarks and immediately set about demolishing much of the underlying argument. Hawkins railed against the 'prudery, obscurantism and ignorance' that marked attitudes to homosexuality in many English-speaking countries and set out systematically to address what he described as the myths surrounding the issue. Homosexuals were not, he asserted, the depraved, degenerate types of popular mythology, nor were they any more likely to attack, assault, molest or seduce children than heterosexuals. Legalisation was unlikely to result in proselytism on the part of homosexuals for the rather simple reason that the 'vast majority [of homosexuals] regard their homosexuality as an affliction'. Indeed, all in all, it was difficult, according to Hawkins, to say anything significant about homosexuals at all: 'the principal distinguishing feature is simply that they prefer their own to the opposite sex'.⁸

A year or so later, Beatrice Faust took up these themes in the first issue of the *Australian Humanist*. If there was a threat to society, she suggested, it came not from homosexuality, but from the laws against homosexuality. The existing law was 'damaging to the social order that it claims to protect'. It was impossible

Laurie Collinson. Jewish, communist, homosexual and – perhaps most damning of all in 1950s' Australia – a poet, Laurie Collinson nonetheless attempted to establish a homosexual law reform group in Melbourne in the late 1950s. (Elaine Bryant)

to administer fairly and so encouraged corruption of the entire legal system. Ian Davidson, also writing in the *Australian Humanist*, argued: 'Anyone who wanted to commit murder with impunity need only claim, as three NSW cases prove, that his victim propositioned him'.[9]

Concern about police techniques was widespread by the middle of the 1960s. Allegations of entrapment, police spying and the informal granting of pardons to some homosexual men in order to entice them to testify against others became common. Craig McGregor, another liberal commentator, suggested in his *Profile of Australia*:

> it is now commonly regarded as unsafe to visit certain public lavatories [in Sydney], not because they are used as a pick-up centre by homosexuals, but because of the danger of being picked up by the police and charged with indecent behaviour.[10]

The new liberal attitude did not confine itself to a critique of existing viewpoints but, rather, set out to construct an alternative basis for social policy. This new policy revolved around the notion that sexual behaviour was a matter of individual, not social, concern; that where no one was hurt or coerced, and the acts took place in private, sex ought to be of no concern to the state. The notion of the 'consenting adult in private' is crucial here. In part, to be sure, this embodies a defensive posture: 'consenting' stands against the notion of homosexual-as-predator, 'adult' against the homosexual-as-child-seducer, 'private' against the homosexualas-public-nuisance. But it also contains within it a decisive shift in the way in which homosexuality should be seen – as a matter for individual conscience rather than public policy. There is, of course, an irony in all of this: in order to win the argument that homosexuality is properly of no concern to anyone other than those who engage in it, the liberals had to break the prevailing wall of silence, bring the issue into the public realm and persuade opinion-makers to take a stand.

As part of this debate, a new attitude towards homosexuals themselves started to emerge. Far from the shadowy, dangerous and repulsive figure of the 1950s, the homosexual was coming to be seen, by some at least, as someone to be pitied: 'Homosexuality, like blindness and congenital heart disease is an abnormality which must be treated accordingly' said one sympathiser.[11] Many of the liberal commentators retained very negative attitudes towards homosexuals and homosexuality even while they were arguing for law reform. These attitudes were a problem, but, by the mid-1960s, homosexuality could at least be spoken about and spoken about as a public issue upon which lawmakers and opinion leaders ought to have a view. Homosexuality, in short, had moved onto the public agenda.

Over the course of the 1960s, it became clear that the arguments of the new liberals were finding an audience, or rather, a number of audiences. Among the earliest of these were university students and especially the student press. The new liberals spoke highly of the university newspapers, praising their outspokenness and their willingness to tackle subjects that could not be raised in the mainstream media.[12] Certainly, the student press seemed comfortable including homosexuality as one of its issues. There were reviews aplenty of books, films and plays with homosexual themes, and these reviews almost always reflected a sympathetic outlook. But *Lot's Wife* (Monash University) and *On Dit* (Adelaide University) also published in 1964 what may well be the first article by a self-proclaimed (albeit anonymous) homosexual. A few years later, *On Dit* published a series of four articles, again by anonymous homosexuals. The student press was also one of the few places where the extent of homosexual activity among Australians was discussed, with the results of student questionnaires being reported in *On Dit* in 1963 and *Semper Floreat* (University of Queensland) in 1965.[13]

The tolerance expressed by the student press was not entirely out of touch with its readership. In late July 1964, students at a Debating Union meeting at Melbourne University, after hearing the case for and against law reform, voted 281 to 98 in favour of the legalisation of homosexuality.[14] The three to one majority in favour may well have been unrepresentative at the time; but, a few years later, this majority had indeed been established in student thought. A survey of 638 Melbourne University students in 1968 revealed that 67 percent were in favour of legalisation of homosexuality between consenting adult males, while only 30 percent were opposed, and three percent had no opinion.[15]

In the legal profession, too, there was a reflection of the new thinking, especially in the academic realm. In May 1962, Rupert Cross, fellow and tutor at Magdalen College in the UK, delivered the Allen Hope Southey Memorial Lecture at Melbourne University. In it, he discussed the problem of unmaking existing laws, including those relating to suicide, euthanasia, abortion, prostitution and homosexuality. On 'private homosexuality between consenting male adults', he argued that removal of criminal sanctions would be unlikely to lead to an increase in homosexuality, undermine the moral condemnation on the part of society or demoralise society. In the light of all this, he concluded that 'the prohibition on this practice among the criminal laws...ought to be unmade'. Some years later, Terry Carney, a fourth-year law and criminology student at Melbourne University, published a paper, 'Homosexuality: A Case for Reform', arguing a very similar case and coming to very similar conclusions.[16]

By the 1960s, this reasoning was being reflected in comments from the bench. In February 1965, Judge Hidden of the Darlinghurst Quarter Sessions found himself sentencing two 20-year-old men who had pleaded guilty to having indecently assaulted each other. Homosexuality, opined the judge, was 'as much a disease as a crime' and he declared: 'I am convinced, after many years in this court, that putting these people in gaol is no remedy'. His preference was that the legislature should provide him with an institution to which he could send offenders. In the absence of such an institution, he released the men on good behaviour bonds.[17]

Just how far this new thinking on homosexuality had gone is indicated in the response of the NSW magistrates to a sharp increase in prosecutions for homosexual offences, which they noticed in the late 1960s.[18] In 1967, 388 people had been charged with unnatural offences in the NSW magistrates courts; in 1968, 511; in 1969, 510.[19] The magistrates discovered that, sometime in 1967, a special team had been set up within the NSW Vice Squad (known, informally, as the Indecency Squad) to patrol public lavatories in Sydney in order to detect homosexual behaviour by men.[20] In response to this revelation, the magistrates organised a seminar under the auspices of the Institute of Criminology to discuss the question of male sex offences in public places. The seminar was attended by 'a large crowd' of judges, magistrates, lawyers, police officers, social workers and psychiatrists. It was opened and chaired by no less a figure than the Chief Justice of NSW.

According to the official summary of the discussion:

> There was a consensus of opinion at the seminar that there was no possibility of preventing all such behaviour in public places, and that in view of the triviality of the offence and the difficulty of policing it the situation might be better dealt with other than as a police matter.[21]

What is striking about this conclusion is that a gathering of those most intimately involved in the legal process should have found themselves reasonably united in their belief that even public homosexual acts ought not necessarily be the subject of legal sanctions. There was no question of the seminar endorsing the legitimacy of homosexual acts, but the tolerance of them, the sense of them as 'trivial' and the search for medical solutions represented a substantial shift in opinion from the 1950s blanket disapproval.

The only strong opposition to this ever-widening consensus came from the police. At the NSW magistrates' seminar, Sergeant V. Green of the Vice Squad had stood out from the general view, asserting:

> the role the Police are fulfilling in the community today in the detection and determent of homosexual activity can only be regarded by every decent citizen as an important one.[22]

While there was a decline in convictions for homosexual offences over the course of the 1960s, this was not due to less vigorous policing. From a peak of 343 convictions in the higher courts in 1958, there was a stabilisation and decline over the next decade. But, as an examination of the NSW Court of Petty Sessions figures shows, the decline in the numbers charged was less dramatic than the increase in the number of cases where no conviction was recorded (that is, where the cases were either withdrawn or discharged), indicating that it was among the magistrates, rather than among the police, that the shift in attitudes and practices towards a greater tolerance was taking place. This is confirmed by the available material where police reflect upon this issue: although there are doubts expressed as to the role of the law in enforcing morality, there is little question that, while such laws existed, the police had a duty to enforce them.[23]

The process of liberalisation that was making itself felt in other opinion-making circles was also at work in the churches in Australia, in particular among Methodists and Presbyterians in the second half of the 1960s, although the Anglican archbishop of Melbourne had endorsed homosexual law reform as early as 1964.[24] The role of the British churches in the Wolfenden debate is especially important here. The Church of England issued two major statements in support of homosexual law reform, and the UK Methodist Church's Department of Church Citizenship endorsed Wolfenden's recommendations in 1958.[25] These documents, as well as the final Wolfenden report itself, loomed large in the thinking of Australian churches of various denominations when they finally turned their attention to the question of homosexuality in the second half of the 1960s. But so, too, did a sharply drawn distinction between the church's role as defender of Christian moral standards (which homosexuality offended against) and the state's responsibility to respect all private behaviour that was not socially damaging – a distinction between private morality and state regulation precisely in line with that which had been advanced by the new liberalism over the previous decade.

This shift by the churches alerts us to the way in which homosexual law reform and tolerance had moved from the margins of political culture towards the mainstream. This shift was reflected, too, in the Australian media, which set out to capture the new middle class and to deliver it into the hands of the advertisers. The first indication of this shift came with the establishment of the *Australian* in 1964, a paper whose liberal line on the issues of the day reflected, spoke to and, indeed, reinforced and deepened the liberalism of its readership. It was the *Australian*, alone of all the press, that reported the debate at which Melbourne University students had voted in 1964 for homosexual law reform. The next day, it reported comments endorsing the vote from various public figures, including the Anglican archbishop of Melbourne. In the subsequent letters column debate, one homosexual reader pointed to the importance of the paper's role in raising the issue, noting that, less than a month previously, there was no newspaper that would have allowed such a discussion.[26] By the late 1960s, other media enterprises were competing for the same ground. The *Age*, the *Canberra Times* and the *Bulletin* were all revamped for this market, adopting as part of their shift liberal views on a number of issues, including homosexual law reform. Coverage of homosexual issues, as measured by Robert French, actually decreased in quantity in the early 1960s, with no more than 12 items in any year (1964) and as few as three in 1963. But then, in 1966, the number of items jumped to 32, rising in subsequent years to 53 and 50 and then, in 1969, virtually doubling to 99 items. While crime and scandal remained staples, letters and comments from experts of various sorts and advice columnists increased markedly.[27]

But if there is a decisive moment in the rise of the new liberalism to dominance in Australian politics and society, it came with the victory of Gough Whitlam and his program within the Australian Labor Party. The ALP's stubborn adherence in the 1950s to the very values that the new liberals despised had repelled reformers from any serious engagement with it. Their revulsion was reinforced by the ALP's consistent electoral failure during the 1950s and 1960s, which confirmed the liberals' view that independent organising was the most useful way to defend and advance their ideas. It was only when pressures for reform within the ALP – expressed in the rise of Whitlam – started to build that the liberal intellectuals and reformers were prepared to look anew. The major breakthrough came at the 1969 Federal Conference, where progressive policies were adopted on a whole raft of social issues.[28]

Homosexuality was not directly addressed in the reform of the ALP's program. But the success of the new liberals' project for the reform, renewal and renovation of Australian society advanced the cause of homosexual law reform anyway. By its association with the whole cluster of themes related to modernising Australia – throwing off old prejudices, deepening personal responsibility, enhancing personal privacy, building a tolerant society, dismantling the influence of religious attitudes and so on – the decriminalisation and toleration of homosexuality rode into the mainstream on the coat-tails of a broader movement. As early as 1967, Bill Hayden had raised the issue in parliament; in 1971, he proposed a law reform motion to the Queensland ALP conference. In both cases, he was abused for his pains. In order to shore up his position, he undertook some research and circulated a paper through the Fabian Society.[29]

In September 1970, Gough Whitlam expressed his own support for homosexual law reform, declaring that private moral decisions should be separated from public political attitudes and calling for a conscience vote in the parliament.[30] Some elements within the ALP remained as hostile to homosexuality as they had always been,[31] but the tide of change was running fast – and not just within the ALP. As one commentator noted at the time of the 1969 Federal Conference, the ALP had 'set the lead for Australian politics in small "l" liberal questions'.[32]

Observing the success of Whitlam's programmatic reforms, some members of the Liberal Party started to speak up. When Tom Hughes, the federal Coalition government's attorney-general, raised the possibility of homosexual law reform in 1970, no one was deeply shocked.[33] The issue provoked some interest and debate, and although Hughes' idea ('proposal' would be too strong a word) was quashed within the party, the issue was by now firmly on the mainstream political agenda. The *Canberra Times*, for example, took the opportunity to call for the decriminalisation of homosexual acts.[34] And, in any case, the Liberals' long reign was drawing to a close, and it was ALP opinion that mattered most at the time. Gough Whitlam, Bill Hayden and Moss Cass had spoken up for homosexual rights and they came to represent the mainstream and the wave of the future.

If the foregoing developments leave an impression that there was an easy progress at work in Australia in the 1960s, a look at the attempt to achieve homosexual law reform in the Australian Capital Territory (ACT) in the late 1960s shows not only the strengths of liberalism, but also its limitations. The ACT HLRS was the earliest, largest and most public attempt by liberals to decriminalise male homosexual acts. It was not a gay group, nor was it particularly concerned with issues other than decriminalisation. Both of these factors mark it off from the soon-to-appear gay movement, and it makes sense to think of the HLRS as being part of (indeed, marking the end of) the phase of reform politics that centred on a notion of civil liberties and the activism of civil

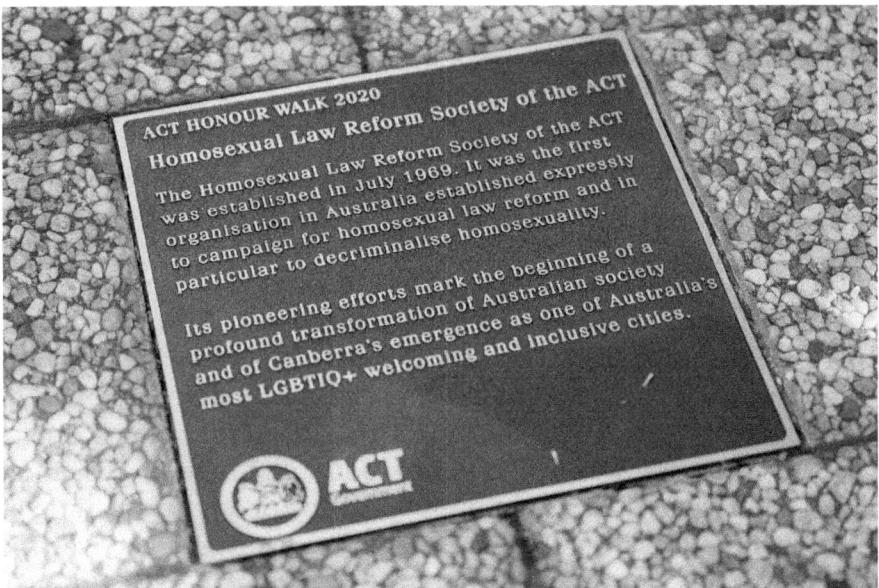

Remembering the HLRS on the Canberra Honour Walk (Graham Willett)

libertarians.[35] This is especially clear when we look at the group's origins, which lay in a discussion between Thomas Mautner and Dennis Rose in Canberra in 1969 on the subject of abortion law reform.[36] Mautner was a lecturer in philosophy at the Australian National University and a supporter of liberal humanist issues. He had been urged by Beatrice Faust to involve himself in the establishment of an abortion law reform group in Canberra. In the course of a conversation with Rose, discussion turned to a recent newspaper article in the *Canberra Times* concerning two men who had been arrested in a car in the bush and charged with indecent assault upon one another. A few days later, Mautner, Michael Landale (the men's solicitor) and a journalist, Peter Sekuless, met to discuss the idea of forming a homosexual law reform society; and, on 27 July 1969, a public meeting was held, attended by about 30 people, at which the Homosexual Law Reform Society of the ACT was formally established.

The HLRS drew upon the well-established acceptance within liberal humanist circles of an anti-criminalisation stance and embodied this in its draft ordinance and submission. The draft law, guided by the British law reform act of 1967, relied upon the notion of the consenting adult in private, but with two important differences: the age of consent was to be 18 rather than 21; and 'private' was not to be interpreted in the narrow sense of 'in the presence of not more than two people'. Penalties for remaining offences were reduced, and the draft required that courts seek a medical opinion before passing any sentence of imprisonment upon a homosexual.[37]

The HLRS actively sought to bring its demands and arguments for reform to the attention of legislators and other opinion-makers. It commissioned an opinion poll of Canberra residents that found very high levels of support for decriminalisation; it published a newsletter; and its members participated actively in public debates. Among the targets of its lobbying were the ACT Law Society, the clergy, members of the medical profession and judges. Aside from these activities by the HLRS committee and members, the society operated as a lightning rod for all those concerned with the issue of homosexual law reform. It was assisted in this by prominent articles by Don Aitkin in the *Canberra Times*, Henry Mayer in the *Australian* and Michael Richardson in the *Age*.[38] All three writers spoke out strongly in favour of homosexual law reform, marshalling the by now familiar range of liberal arguments. All reported the work of the HLRS and (except for Richardson) provided a contact address. The result was a wave of letters to the HLRS from people praising its efforts, offering support and proposing to set up branches or similar organisations in other cities. Although the committee's view was that the state-based nature of anti-homosexual legislation made a national organisation impracticable, where a number of people had written to it from the same city, the committee was able to provide a list of names and addresses to potential convenors. In Melbourne, Sydney, Adelaide and Perth, meetings were organised to discuss the issue.

How then to explain, in view of the overwhelmingly favourable response to the demands of the HLRS, that homosexual law reform was not achieved in the ACT until 1976 – several years after the society itself had ceased to exist and several years after public opinion and professional attitudes had been reformed? There is an assumption that law reform is a simpler task than social and cultural transformation. Certainly, activists at the time thought so. In September 1970, James Grieve had written to the founders of the Campaign Against Moral Persecution (CAMP), whose goals, the founders had declared, were 'much wider than law reform' and included the changing of public opinion, professional attitudes and so on, wishing them well and declaring that their task would be 'a much harder job' and that 'no doubt we [the HLRS] shall succeed long before you do'.[39] But actually, law reform has its own peculiar constraints. Public opinion is everywhere and offers numerous targets for activists. Professional opinion (medical or religious) is held by reasonably large groups of people who can openly express their opinions and so feed into processes of change. Legislators, on the other hand, are a relatively small, tightknit and somewhat cautious group, and legislation can only pass if a majority can be induced to openly and publicly commit themselves to a particular policy. When the federal attorney-general, Tom Hughes, publicly floated the idea of decriminalisation in 1970, it did not take long for the more conservative of his colleagues in the Liberal and Country parties to bring him to a humiliating backdown. But even with the ALP government of 1972–75, no reform came, despite a solid pool of supporters. Here, the problem was that the issue did not loom large enough in the minds of party leaders, MPs or activists. In the early 1970s, the problem was not any great hostility to the demand for homosexual law reform; it was just that the issue was not a pressing one for politicians, and there was nothing the HLRS could do to make it so.

In the span of a single decade, the wall of silence isolating homosexuality from mainstream political life had been undermined and overthrown. In its place, a space was cleared within which demands for decriminalisation and a degree of tolerance could be argued. The HLRS raised the issue of law reform and lobbied successfully for support from significant numbers of influential people. But, in the end, it lacked the capacity to overcome the relative insignificance of the issue to those who alone had the power to change the law. In July 1970, the space cleared by the new liberals was to be noisily occupied by lesbians and gay men themselves, raising their voices and flinging their bodies into a movement that, in the subsequent quarter century, was to transform both homosexual life and the society of which it was a part.

3.

CAMPing Out

If the Australian lesbian and gay movement can be said to have a birthday, 19 September 1970 is it. It was on that day that the *Australian* published a full-page feature article entitled 'Couples'. In it, Janet Hawley reported on her interview with John Ware, his partner Michael and Christabel Poll. She reported, too, on the organisation they had formed – the Campaign Against Moral Persecution (CAMP). Within days, letters began to flood in, to both the newspaper and to the group directly. Within a few months, CAMP had branches in most states. Within a year, it had about 1,500 members nationwide.

This is not at all what Ware and Poll had expected. As John Ware recalled somewhat later, he and Christabel, who were friends and neighbours, decided one night in mid-1970, over a 'very large bottle of whisky', to start a homosexual rights group, with the words: 'Stuff it, let's do it'. Their intentions were remarkably modest:

> We had the notion that this would be a society of half a dozen people who would meet once a month or so and keep our presence in the public eye by publishing letters to the editor and challenging statements that came out...
> Really a sort of book club you know.[1]

The first question that Ware and Poll confronted was whether or not the formation of such a group was even legal. This was

Francesca Curtis (right) and Phyllis Papps (left), founders and early members of Daughters of Bilitis (AQuA)

not as odd as it might seem. A year or so later, no less an authority than the University of Sydney's solicitors declared that, by allowing an organisation of homosexuals to be established on campus, the university was opening itself up to charges of condoning a gathering of criminals.² Ware and Poll's decision to seek advice was a reasonable one, and finding advice was not difficult. Michael Cass, Ware's lover, knew Berenice Buckley of the NSW Council for Civil Liberties (CCL), who invited a lawyer to discuss the matter with a few of the founders. Reassured that an organisation for homosexual rights would indeed be legal and, even more importantly, that 'If anyone did try anything we'd have an awful lot of support from the legal profession', Ware and his friends decided to proceed. The decision was taken in July 1970 and involved a group of about a dozen people, including Ware, Cass and Poll, Jill Roe and Bill Lockwood – a group named (informally) for the block of flats in which many of them lived as the Delmont group.³ The advice of the lawyers did deliver one setback, however. A proposal to call the group 'Queens Dykes' was sternly rejected by those who imagined that the jokey reference to the lawyerly Queen's Counsel was quite inappropriate.[4] The more suitable Campaign Against Moral Persecution – which delivered the playful acronym CAMP – was chosen instead.

CAMP was not an exclusively homosexual organisation. Civil libertarians played a significant role in the group in the early days, reflecting their longstanding interest. Although Dorothy Simons' recollection is that she was not all that active in CAMP and that her real role was to provide a name so that the group could point to heterosexual participation, and Berenice Buckley emphasised her contribution in terms of moral and potential legal support (in the event that the police created difficulties), John Ware has praised their roles, declaring:

> the person who was doing the work before CAMP Inc came along and who was a very strong member was Dorothy Simons. Berri [Berenice Buckley] helped us with legal problems and Ken [Buckley] helped us with legal things. But Dorothy was in for quite some time.[5]

John Ware remembers this early support as 'very comforting'. It was also very practical. The NSW Humanists provided a mailing list to CAMP, and the CCL sent legal observers to the group's first demonstration. In March 1971, the Buckleys attended the first dance, in case the police appeared. These groups and individuals also provided advice and guidance drawn from their involvement in the earlier, failed, law reform groups – advice that surfaces briefly in letters that Simons and Berenice Buckley published in the first issue of the group's journal.[6]

CAMP's first action was to send a letter to the press. In it, Ware, who was the sole signatory, announced the existence of the society and outlined its aims as being 'to represent the interests [of homosexuals and] to promote homosexual law reform and greater public tolerance of homosexuality'. The letter called upon interested people to contact the organisers at a given post office box number for more information. The letter began, interestingly enough, by acknowledging the increased media interest in homosexuals over the previous few months and attributing this to the rise of militant homosexual groups in the USA. While welcoming the attention, the letter recognised that 'the public in its attitudes is grossly misinformed' and it was in response to this that the normality of homosexual people was asserted ('We are good citizens and contribute much to our society'), as was their resentment at being treated like 'freaks, mental defectives, dangerous perverts, or all three'. There were solutions posed in the letter, as well. Though the term was not yet in use, coming out was emphasised because 'We as homosexuals, feel [public ignorance] will remain...unless we offer our point of view and attack misconceptions where we see them'.[7]

Orienting to the press was not an unreasonable strategy. In the second half of the 1960s, the liberalisation of the mainstream press had contributed substantially to the propagation of liberals' views on homosexuality. The media references for early 1970 cited in Robert French's index show just how extensive, and how diverse, the coverage of homosexual issues was becoming.[8] Certainly, there were still crimes and scandals aplenty, but new issues were being raised: the ethics of police surveillance of public toilets; law reform proposals from such luminaries as the federal attorney-general, the Humanist Society and the South Australian government; gay rights marches and gay church and anti-psychiatric protests in the USA; and the appearance of controversial plays and books dealing with homosexual themes, such as *Boys in the Band* and *The Other Love*. It is hardly surprising that Ware and Poll and their friends were hopeful of being able to get a hearing in the press. And their hopes were fulfilled. Ware's letter first appeared in Brisbane's *Courier-Mail* on 9 September 1970, though without his name or the group's postal address, which rather defeated its purpose. It was first published in full in the left-liberal magazine *Nation* 10 days later.

CAMPING OUT

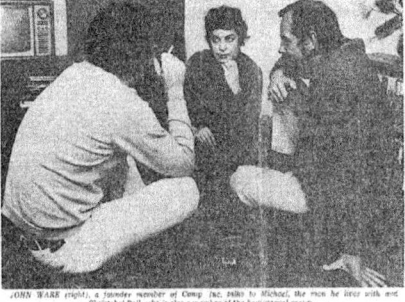

With national publicity provided by *The Australian* and by daring to come out as homosexual, John Ware, Christabel Poll and Michael Cass turned a small discussion group into the founding organisation of a movement that was to transform Australia.

But, while the founders of CAMP could be reasonably sure that they could gain some media attention for their group, they had no reason to expect that they would achieve much more than this. The lack of success by the Humanist law reform groups that had preceded CAMP was a discouraging sign.

Inspired by the example of the ACT HLRS, Humanist Societies in Sydney, Melbourne, Brisbane and Perth had attempted to set up their own law reform societies. In October 1969, at a meeting addressed by Thomas Mautner of the HLRS, some NSW Humanists decided to form a small committee to 'press for reform in NSW'.[9] Hoping to find 'ten really dedicated people' with which to work, the committee was disappointed by a number of circumstances: a fairly rapid decline in the numbers attending meetings; the lack of 'legal, political or sociological experts willing to be active'; and the fact that 'the people to whom this particular social change is of interest – ie, the homosexual community – [did] not come forward in great numbers'. This, and the result of a 1967 opinion poll that showed a mere 22 percent support for homosexual law reform among the public at large, led the Humanists reluctantly to the conclusion that 'the climate of opinion is clearly not ripe for change'.[10]

In Melbourne, the Humanists had set up a committee in late 1969 or early 1970 that included two homosexual men (Carl Reinganum and Walter Hillbrick) to 'study and recommend what action should be taken to reform the law on homosexuality'. After a few months' work, the committee produced a five-page pamphlet, *The Homosexual and the Law – A Humanist View*. In Queensland, the Humanist committee had even managed to organise a public meeting on the issue, addressed by Tony Lee of the University of Queensland's Law School.[11] But, for all their efforts, none of these groups was able to report any great success.

More telling still was the history of the lesbian group, Daughters of Bilitis (DOB). DOB – the organisation to which the description 'Australia's first openly homosexual political organisation' properly belongs – was established when two Melbourne women, Marion Paull and Claudia Pearce, independently approached the US Daughters of Bilitis as distant and isolated readers of its widely circulating magazine, *The Ladder*. The two were subsequently put in touch with each other and with other readers in Melbourne by the US group and, in January 1970, a group of about 15 women met to found the Melbourne chapter.[12]

In its activism, Melbourne's DOB very much followed the liberal model: information, education and outreach were the group's main concerns. Over the first few months, DOB found ready support from a number of sources: student union leaders, social workers, psychiatrists and prominent businesspeople. The Women's Liberation group at Melbourne University and the Humanist Society also expressed support. With their confidence bolstered, the group was ready to go public – except that none of the members was willing or able to come out. Instead, they enlisted the support of Beatrice Faust, whom we have seen already as a prominent (heterosexual) humanist and liberal, to be their spokesperson. As word of the group's existence was spread by television appearances, radio interviews and the daily and weekly press, a sympathetic curiosity grew, and new members joined.[13]

Despite these important breakthroughs, the group held an overcautious, even pessimistic, assessment of the times. One member wrote in 1970: 'it would be idealistic to think that we, in our lifetime, will see a great change in public attitudes to Lesbianism'.[14] Despite the positive reaction that the group had received from activists, professionals and the media, the group's practice remained enmeshed within a political model that no longer suited the times. When DOB spoke of education, it aimed not only to educate the public in order to 'break down erroneous taboos', it wanted also to educate the lesbian, 'enabling her to understand herself and to make her adjustment to Society'.[15] The form of the organisation, too, was very conservative. No one under the age of 21 was permitted to be a member, and heterosexually married women were required to present the written consent of their husbands to join. This, coupled with the fact that it was a woman-only organisation, certainly had an impact on its prospects for growth. Jude Munro tells how, as a young woman aware of her lesbianism and outraged by social attitudes, she wrote, produced and distributed in the streets of Melbourne a leaflet about homosexual oppression. This is precisely the kind of dynamic, creative, courageous person that would build the movement – and yet, when she applied to join DOB, she was unceremoniously rejected because of her age. Rebuffed by DOB, she ended up as a founder of Gay Liberation instead.[16]

Given this cautiousness, it is not surprising that, in July 1970, at the very time when Ware and Poll were drawing heart from the media's new interest in US homosexual activism, DOB broke with its US parent, rejecting their sisters' new, more radical practice. Tactics, Melbourne said, such as:

> 'Gay Power' demonstrations [and] the wearing of T-shirts embellished with the labels 'butch' and 'femme'...may possibly be effective in the United States, but could certainly have been nothing but deleterious to [lesbians'] image in Australia.[17]

Oddly, the organisation, to signal its break with the Americans, took as its new name the Australasian Lesbian Movement. The closet name Daughters of Bilitis was gone, lesbianism was openly proclaimed, and the word 'movement' had appeared. Even as they thought they were rejecting the new mood of assertiveness and the new wave of radical and countercultural ideas, Melbourne's lesbian activists were, in fact, adapting to them. But the process was too slow and too uneven for many. Those who were alert to the new possibilities often left to pursue different political paths. Marion Paull, for instance, departed for the women's movement.[18] At the hands of those who remained, the organisation became more and more inward looking, focusing increasingly upon its social support role. By 1972, it was presenting itself explicitly as a social, rather than activist, group; and in 1973, the group finally disappeared.

So, with their talk of a 'sort of book club', Ware and Poll and their friends were very much reflecting the modest hopes of homosexual activists in 1970 and the modest achievements of the Humanists and DOB. Nevertheless, by the time they spoke to the *Australian*'s Janet Hawley in 1970, they had expanded their ambitions somewhat. They hoped, they said, to organise 'debates, lectures, discussion groups', and to target 'social workers, hospitals, police, P and C [parents and citizens] groups, churches, trade unions, employers'.[19] These were important activities, to be sure, in a climate where accurate information about homosexuals and their lives was thin on the ground, but hardly the stuff of revolutions.

What made the difference and took CAMP from a modest little group to a national organisation was editor of the *Australian*, Adrian Deamer's decision not to publish CAMP's letter when he received it. Instead, he dispatched Janet Hawley, his human interest reporter, to check out the authors. After meeting them, Hawley decided that they were a serious group and worth writing up – a decision that was to change the nature of the existing discussion immensely.

Unquestionably, it was the willingness of CAMP's leaders to come out publicly as homosexuals that elevated CAMP from a 'sort of book club' to the founding organisation of a social movement. Never before had anyone in Australia willingly identified, indeed proclaimed, themselves as homosexual to the media, as Ware and Poll were doing. Their courage was the spark that lit a bushfire.

Looking at Hawley's article today, we might perhaps see that its most remarkable feature is its concern to present homosexuals as perfectly normal people. There are frequent references to 'straight, largely unrecognisable homosexuals and lesbians', 'completely all-male Men' and John and Michael's having 'lived together in a form of marriage' for eight years. This can be explained in many ways. Janet Hawley herself attributes it to the fact that she – young, heterosexual, newly a mother, with no exposure to homosexuals or kamp life – was struck most by precisely that 'normality'. She observes, too, that some of the odder passages in the article (for instance, a discussion of the decor of the Ware-Cass flat, of their red enamelled saucepans and their 50 different herbs and spices) emerged in response to questions from her colleagues back in the newsroom as to how 'they', homosexuals, lived.[20] But Ware and Cass and Poll themselves were a party to this, in what was almost certainly a tactical decision. In fact, as we shall see, their politics were not nearly as conventional as their remarks might have led readers to believe.

Whatever the expectations, motives and intentions of Ware and Poll and Hawley, the effect of the article was electrifying. In allowing homosexual people, for the first time ever, to speak openly, to speak on their own behalf, and to speak of the need for homosexuals to organise politically in their own interests, the article captured the attention of thousands of people. A firestorm of interest followed. In the following weeks and months, Ware and Poll wrote for, or were written about in, the *Australian*, the *Bulletin*, *Pix*, the *Newcastle Morning Herald*, the *Age* and various student, left and countercultural newspapers. They were interviewed on radio and television and appeared on such high-profile national programs as *This Day Tonight*.

Many people still remember opening the *Australian* that day in 1970 and seeing Hawley's article. Robert French, for instance, snapped the paper shut and retired, as casually as possible (so as not to alert his parents to his interest) to his room, where he read it with interest, excitement, even elation and with a strong sense of satisfaction that someone was, at last, applying the politics of liberation to gay people.[21]

Similar events must have been taking place all over Australia. Many reacted both actively and enthusiastically. Ware remembers:

'The response was absolutely amazing. Letters poured in... We were inundated with letters.' David Widdup, who had also seen the article and who had contacted the group to offer his support, remembers there being something like 400 letters. Clearly the idea of a small group of half a dozen or so had been superseded. Sorting through the letters, Ware remembers, he and Poll:

> picked out the ones from people who looked as though they had some understanding of what the whole thing was about... And we invited them to a party at Christabel Poll's place. I forget how many of us were there, maybe a couple of dozen, maybe a dozen.[22]

This gathering, part barbecue, part meeting, was held on 21 November 1970 and provided a group of activists – the 'initial nucleus', as Terry Bell put it – around which the organisation was to be built in its early years.[23] This group encompassed the Delmont group as well as new arrivals including David Widdup, Peter Bonsall-Boone, Peter de Waal and Ian Black. The barbecue/discussion agreed on the need for a public meeting, which was duly held on 6 February 1971.

Ninety-four people turned up, of a national membership reported to be 400.[24] Garry Wotherspoon, who (anonymously) reported the meeting for the *Bulletin*, describes an informal but businesslike event, chaired by Ian Black, at which John Ware and Christabel Poll talked about the issues and the group. Ware presents a somewhat different picture, with him and Christabel and a flagon of wine cultivating an atmosphere that stretched well beyond relaxed to the positively casual. Merely to be at the meeting was a daring act for many of those who went. Some of Wotherspoon's friends, whom he had arranged to meet there, simply never turned up. But those who did found it a strangely liberating experience. Wotherspoon describes entering the hall without receiving the 'cold appraisal' that he experienced in kamp bars. A young man whom he spoke to had suddenly realised what it was to be able to talk to people without the burden of fear of letting his secret slip. It was a taste of what thousands of men and women would experience over the coming months and years as they came into contact with CAMP and its offshoots.

By this stage, the organisation was starting to go national. People found their way to CAMP in a number of ways. The *Australian* article of 19 September, appearing in a national paper, reached well beyond Sydney, and the flood of letters sparked by it included many from interstate. Personal connections were important too. In Melbourne, for example, David Conolly received an excited phone call from Peter Bonsall-Boone, one of CAMP's early activist members, and immediately joined and agreed to help form a branch in Melbourne.[25]

In November 1970, David Widdup, armed with several names and addresses, arrived in Melbourne to sound people out about the possibility of a group; and in January 1971, at the Chapter House of St Paul's Cathedral (a venue organised by David Conolly, who was an Anglican priest), the group was formally established. Those present – about 40 to 50 people – were drawn primarily from the list of those who had written to Sydney in response to the *Australian* articles. A committee of about half a dozen, including two women, was elected and began to meet regularly, usually in private homes. The committee organised events for the members – a barbecue in April, a picnic in the hills and general meetings at Melbourne University. A turning point seems to have come in about May, when the group adopted a new name, Society Five, and undertook its first high-profile publicity work, with a newspaper article and a television appearance.[26]

Meanwhile, in February 1971, when John Ware and Michael Cass happened to be in Brisbane, they met with CAMP members from Brisbane as well as the chair and three executive members of Lynx, an organisation that had been set up in 1969 by some members of 'a set which frequented one of the Gay Bars'.[27] At this meeting, Lynx decided to form the Brisbane branch of CAMP. The group had something of a history. In 1970, it had worked closely with the Queensland Humanist Society, which, like its fellows in other states, had set up a law reform subcommittee and had sponsored a public meeting on the subject of law reform in October of that year, addressed by Tony Lee, a lecturer in law at the University of Queensland.[28] Lynx had met with the police commissioner in November 1970 and with the justice minister – to ensure that the group's premises could operate without police harassment and to argue for law reform. The involvement of Lynx, with its history of activism, including fundraising dances that attracted over 300 people, was a great asset to the new branch. CAMP was formally set up at a meeting of some 50 women and men held in the second week of March 1971 and, within a month, had opened its clubrooms at a gala event attended by some 100 people.[29]

In May 1971, it was Perth's turn.[30] Again, David Widdup was the key figure, arriving in Perth after having contacted a number of those who had written to CAMP NSW. He spent several days talking to journalists, the police public relations officer and the Anglican dean. He organised a post office box and a small advertisement in the press and then, on 29 May, CAMP WA was formally established at a meeting of about a dozen held at the Anglican cathedral's meeting rooms. Many of those present had a history of organising. Graham Douglas had been a Western Australian member of the ACT HLRS as early as 1969 and, with others, had been involved in an attempt to set up a similar organisation in Perth in about 1970. So when, in the first week of the group's existence, some 60 or 70 letters were received in response to Widdup's advertisement, the committee had enough organising experience to cope. The first public meeting was held on 6 June; by the end of the year, the group numbered some 300 members.[31]

Surprisingly, given the strongly liberal atmosphere that had marked South Australia in the late 1960s, Adelaide did not establish its branch of CAMP until quite late. In January 1971, Women's Liberation in Adelaide had expressed its support for gay liberation

In Brisbane, Cora Zyp and Paul Lucas were part of the process by which CAMP became a national organisation. The launch of the Brisbane clubrooms. (Cora Zyp)

and called for the establishment of a South Australian branch of CAMP, offering to distribute its literature until a local branch was set up.[32] But it was not until May that an advertisement appeared in CAMP's national journal urging interested South Australians to make contact. On 9 August, a preliminary meeting was held at the art gallery, and on 13 October, the first formal public meeting founded the branch. The leadership of the group was composed of people with a variety of connections – Roger Knight to the ALP, Warren Harrison (widely recognised as one of the most dynamic leaders) to the kamp subculture, David Hilliard to religious circles – all of which seemed to provide a basis for solid growth.[33]

In September 1971, a branch was established in Canberra by members of CAMP NSW who were living in Canberra, including Paul Foss. Early reports give details of well-attended and successful social events, including a chicken and champagne picnic and film nights. During Orientation Week at the Australian National University (ANU), the group organised a forum addressed by a number of speakers. By this time, organisers were trying to hold fortnightly meetings, although they found, as gay activists did well into the 1990s, that there was a strong resistance among Canberra public servants to any visibility.[34]

There was also a branch in Tasmania, although details are hard to ascertain. In September 1971, CAMP NSW's executive noted that an organisation called the Alpha Trust, set up to fight a court case, had decided to stay together and was considering whether to become the state branch of CAMP. From mid-1972 until March 1973, a Hobart postal address was included in branch listings in *Camp Ink* (the monthly newsmagazine of the organisation), after which a Launceston address begins to appear – initially alongside the Hobart address, then alone. During all this time, despite the regular coverage of the doings of state branches, Tasmania never appeared in any article in *Camp Ink*. In early 1974, Walter Hillbrick, secretary of Society Five, replied to an inquiry from a Tasmanian and was able to offer only a post office box as an address. Even then, he added: 'I presume they are still in action'.[35] By the end of 1971, CAMP had an undeniable claim to being a national organisation. Membership was approximately 1,500, and John Ware had given up his course at university to be a full-time, albeit unpaid, worker for the organisation.[36] There was a monthly journal, *Camp Ink*, and clubrooms were established in Brisbane (March 1971), Sydney (April 1971), Melbourne (October 1971) and Perth (December 1971) as permanent sites at which the groups could meet, hold socials and be approached by interested supporters and potential members.

But the group was more than just these branches. University sections, Campus CAMPs, followed quickly at the University of Sydney and the University of NSW, then at the Australian National University and the universities in Newcastle, Adelaide and Queensland. The campus groups were important. They had access to meeting rooms, printing and postage allowances and space in the student newspapers. They had access to audiences – students – among whom habits of political activism were very strong. They brought members together on a regular basis, which allowed strong bonds of trust to develop and political positions to be argued out and developed. All through the 1970s – and beyond – campus groups were a vital part of the activist movement.

In 1972 and 1973, as we shall see, more radical varieties of gay politics were to arise in Australia, and it has often been assumed that CAMP was simply a rather conservative group of middle-aged, closeted, acceptance-seeking males. In fact, like most political organisations of the time, CAMP embraced a broad range of political views, and the inevitable tensions added a certain spice to the life of the group, which has often been overlooked.

Certainly, liberal ideas had a strong presence, which is hardly surprising given the role of liberalism in making homosexual politics possible and the involvement of liberals (especially Humanists) in early gay rights organising. Decriminalisation was explicitly stated to be one of the movement's goals, and the

In Perth, as in many other states, establishing and maintaining clubrooms provided a focus for activism and a point of contact for homosexual men and women (Camp Ink).

notion of the 'consenting adult in private' occurs frequently in early writings. But law reform was not, as it had been for the ACT HLRS and for the Humanist law reform groups, the primary aim of the group. In an information brochure of late 1970, law reform ranks third on the group's list of four principal aims.[37] The first aim (providing a 'forum for the exchange of ideas relating to homosexuality') and the second (to 'work towards a better understanding of homosexuality') reflected the liberal belief that correct ideas, among both kamp people and society at large, were a key element in changing the status of homosexuals. In particular, CAMP's spokespeople were keen to emphasise the fact that homosexuals came from all walks of life and did not necessarily conform to common stereotypes. The idea that 'we are just like everybody else' is strongly present in the September 1970 Australian article and was a common theme, expressed nowhere more starkly than in Christabel Poll's statement: 'simply we wish to arrive at a situation where people's sexual and emotional preferences are no more relevant than the colour of their eyes'.[38] In May 1971, in Newcastle to address the Hunter Valley Women Graduates' Association, John Ware assured the *Newcastle Morning Herald*: 'Our members form a cross-section of society, from ditchdiggers to university professors...They are just ordinary people'. He added:

> I must emphasise that homosexuals are not half men, half women. It might seem a paradox but I see no reason why homosexuality means reduced masculinity. You can be a man and a homosexual at the same time.[39]

Christabel Poll made the same point in relation to lesbians:

> The ladies who go stomping around in tweed suits and dressed up like female truck drivers are just as limited as the screaming homosexual drag queens. Another misconception is that all lesbian unions consist of a rampaging butch lady and a clinging fem.[40]

Given this normality, it was argued, the social prejudice and legal victimisation directed against homosexuals was both unfair and unreasonable, and gay activists were not above appealing for sympathy for the 'law-abiding criminal'[41] or for those like 'Dave', arrested twice and facing up to 14 years' jail 'for committing a crime which to him is a perfectly natural act'.[42]

But holders of liberal ideas did not have it all their own way. In Sydney, particularly, the countercultural politics of Ware and Poll played an important part in the organisation's life in its first two years. In John Ware's vision, the organisation was far from a formal one. Indeed, despite the founders' preference for referring to the group as CAMP Inc, the organisation was not incorporated under state law until very much later. CAMP NSW was initially composed of a number of small groups that would operate around their own concerns and issues, with monthly general meetings, open to all members, at which all the money raised (and pooled) would be distributed by vote.[43] Groups were set up as a need was identified. The Church Group first met in November 1970, followed by a Law Reform Group in February 1971 and a Women's Group, a House Committee Group and a Married Members Group in May 1971. Although the organisation operated along these lines for some time, some members began to believe that Ware (even if against his will) had become 'de facto leader surrounded by an informal clique of activist friends'.[44] This was not an entirely unreasonable view. There was, at the heart of the organisation, an Advisory Committee, appointed by Ware (according to Bell) which, until August 1971 at least, was in the habit of meeting privately rather than at the clubrooms and did not advertise or open its meetings to members.[45] But, by August–September 1971, the distinction between those who, like Ware and Poll, were hostile to 'the whole idea of structure, of the need for leaders and led' and those who, like Dennis Altman, were arguing for the need for a more formal organisation, was becoming more acute.[46] The question was resolved in April 1972 when CAMP's first constitution was adopted, creating elected office-bearer positions, including male and female co-presidents (filled by Lex Watson and Sue Wills). Although the organisation announced the changes in terms of the 'resignation from active involvement in the running of the branch of John Ware and Chris Poll',[47] in fact, Ware maintained some level of activity until at least February 1974, and Poll seems to have actually withdrawn somewhat earlier.[48]

In the meantime, Ware and his supporters were keen that CAMP should look beyond its own immediate concerns to identify itself with other causes that they saw as part of the same broad struggle for change.[49] The most notable of these was the campaign around obscenity charges laid against countercultural activist Wendy Bacon. In March 1971, Ware had enclosed a leaflet in *Camp Ink* that reprinted the poem (entitled 'Cunt is a Christian Word') for which Bacon was being prosecuted and urged members to support her.[50] At the most basic level, this could be seen as a reflection of the civil liberties roots of the Ware group. The nature and content of Bacon's poem, however, meant that this was a case that took the organisation outside of the respectable paradigm of freedom of speech and into the realm of countercultural shock tactics. Twenty letters were received from members protesting against the poem itself, the cause that Bacon represented or the tactical wisdom of associating CAMP with this particular example of free speech. Those that Ware and Poll selected for publication complained of 'vile and disgusting things thrust upon us', depravity and 'corruption of the young' – the very complaints, the editors noted pointedly, that were hurled against homosexuals by moral conservatives.

If CAMP had seemed, early on, to be critical of the radicalism of the US gay movement, this was due less to any real hostility than to a lack of confidence that such techniques could be applied to Australian conditions. Introducing a report about the 1970 gay pride march in New York (which marked the first anniversary of the Stonewall riot), the *Camp Ink* editors observed:

> We do not advocate that homosexuals should immediately march down the street carrying Gay Liberation placards but we do feel that it should be recognised by homosexuals that this is a necessary step to be taken eventually – maybe not for twenty years.[51]

In fact, it was only a few months later that the group began its active participation in the radical life of demonstrations. Ware attributes much of what he called the 'politicisation' of the group to Lex Watson; it was, he says, Watson who had initiated, argued for and done much to organise what is now recognised as the first gay rights demonstration in Australia.[52]

This demonstration took place outside Liberal Party headquarters in October 1971. It was not, however, a protest against the Liberals, but a demonstration of support for the sitting member for Berowra, Tom Hughes, against his preselection challenger, the prominent conservative morals campaigner Jim Cameron.[53] Hughes was the federal attorney-general who had raised the issue of homosexual law reform in 1970 and, although he had retreated, a CAMP spokesperson summed up the group's reasoning as follows: 'We have no great love for either Hughes or Cameron, but we have some hopes for Hughes.' So a demonstration in support of Hughes seemed to be the best option; and on 6 October 1971, 70 or 80 lesbians, gay men and their straight supporters gathered outside the Liberal Party's main office in Sydney.

It had not been easy to organise such an event. Fear of anti-gay violence meant that the time and place could be advised only by word of mouth. Despite this, the demo itself seems to have been a rather jolly affair, with balloons and streamers complementing the more traditional placards and banners. Even the placards were not above a little humour, with comments such as: 'Don't let the wowser spoil the party' and 'Cameron hates homos, but he'll sure b-g-r the Liberal Party'. A leaflet explaining CAMP's position and demands was handed to delegates as they entered the building.[54] In the end, Hughes won the preselection fight, although it would

By October 1971, CAMP was ready to hit the streets, or at least the laneways, of Sydney. Armed with pink helium-filled balloons, jokey placards and more than a little courage, 70 members and supporters staged the first gay rights demo in Australia (Phillip Potter)

be drawing a long bow to imagine that the picket contributed very much to the outcome. Nevertheless, CAMP had taken, if not to the streets, then to the off-street laneways of Sydney and had survived the experience.

More to the point, members had enjoyed themselves. The coverage of the demonstration in *Camp Ink* bordered on the euphoric. Noting that it had taken the US gay movement 20 years from its formation to stage its first demo, the organisers were 'understandably anxious lest no-one turned up. BUT WE DID. And we were beautiful, standing there carrying our placards and our helium-filled balloons.'[55] Participants reported upon their experiences getting to the demo – carrying banners and placards on public transport – and on the events of the night, universally describing it in enthusiastic terms.

If all of the branches of CAMP had their roots in the liberal civil liberties milieu, the strong countercultural element in Sydney and its shift towards a more public activism was less universal. Perth and Brisbane had leaderships sympathetic to the politics of the Sydney group. In Perth, Graham Douglas, the first president of CAMP WA, spoke of the need to 'change and reorganise society', calling for alliances with the women's liberation movement and anti-censorship groups.[56] His successor and partner Brian Lindberg saw the campaign as 'part of the total revolutionary movement', identified capitalism and the nuclear family as the greatest threats to gay people and extended the list of causes to which the movement needed to be committed to include Aboriginal advancement, abortion law reform and progressive education.[57] Brisbane went further still. In September 1971, the branch's Campaign Action Group published a manifesto that included the demand to 'support the struggle of exploited people throughout the world'.[58] In the August 1971 issue of *Camp Ink*, Cora Zyp and Paul Lucas, co-presidents of the Brisbane branch, urged members to take a stand against the South African rugby tour – an extremely controversial issue in Australian politics at the time – adding:

> We would argue that social issues such as racism must of necessity be discussed within the structures of CAMP... CAMP must not appear to be a social refuge but emerge as a reference point to the restructuring of society as we know it.[59]

If Brisbane and Perth were in step with Sydney's emerging commitment to radical repertoires, the same could not be said of other branches. The earliest indicator of the differences of opinion was a private debate in May 1971 over the decision by CAMP in Melbourne to change its name to Society Five. The question of the name had been an issue for some time, according to David Conolly, co-founder in Melbourne, and it was he who had come up with the new name as a solution to an increasingly bitter and distracting debate. Winsome Moore, branch secretary and a

The Homosexual Family. John Ware (standing) and David Widdup mocking the idea of the nuclear family, in one of CAMP's most popular posters (Camp Ink). (Phillip Potter)

leading member in Melbourne, wrote to John Ware defending the decision, noting that the change had been made without opposition by a general meeting.[60]

It may well be that the decision reflected, as Moore suggested:

> the conservatism down here, not only in the community, but amongst ourselves, because we have always lived in a Victorian atmosphere, and it's difficult to change your personality traits overnight.

It was precisely this conservatism that the Sydney leaders were so critical of. Within a year or two, the branches were in a state of open warfare. David Widdup published a savage article in *Camp Ink* accusing the Victorian leadership of elitism and commercialism, of heading up an organisation that was 'male dominated and male chauvinist' and discriminated against the young. The membership was hardly, in his view, better: conservative, subservient, closeted, too 'nice' for their own good, infiltrated by heterosexuals. They had, he implied, the leadership they deserved.[61]

Some months later, it was Adelaide's turn to feel Sydney's wrath. In early 1973, a brawl erupted between CAMP NSW and the South Australian branch. 'Trevor Hughes' (Lex Watson) savaged CAMP South Australia's booklet *Homosexuality in South Australia* for its inclusion of articles by non-homosexuals and anti-homosexuals (in the form of aversion therapists such as John Court and François Mai) and for ignoring the issue of lesbianism.[62] In mid-1973, John Ware attacked CAMP WA for having electing a president who could not come out because of his occupation and for adopting a minimum membership age of 18 years as a way of avoiding police harassment.[63] In all these cases, the Sydney leadership's radicalism was the source of the criticism. These were unpleasant developments, although the autonomy of the branches – there were virtually no national structures at all other than *Camp Ink* – meant that there was little damage done to the

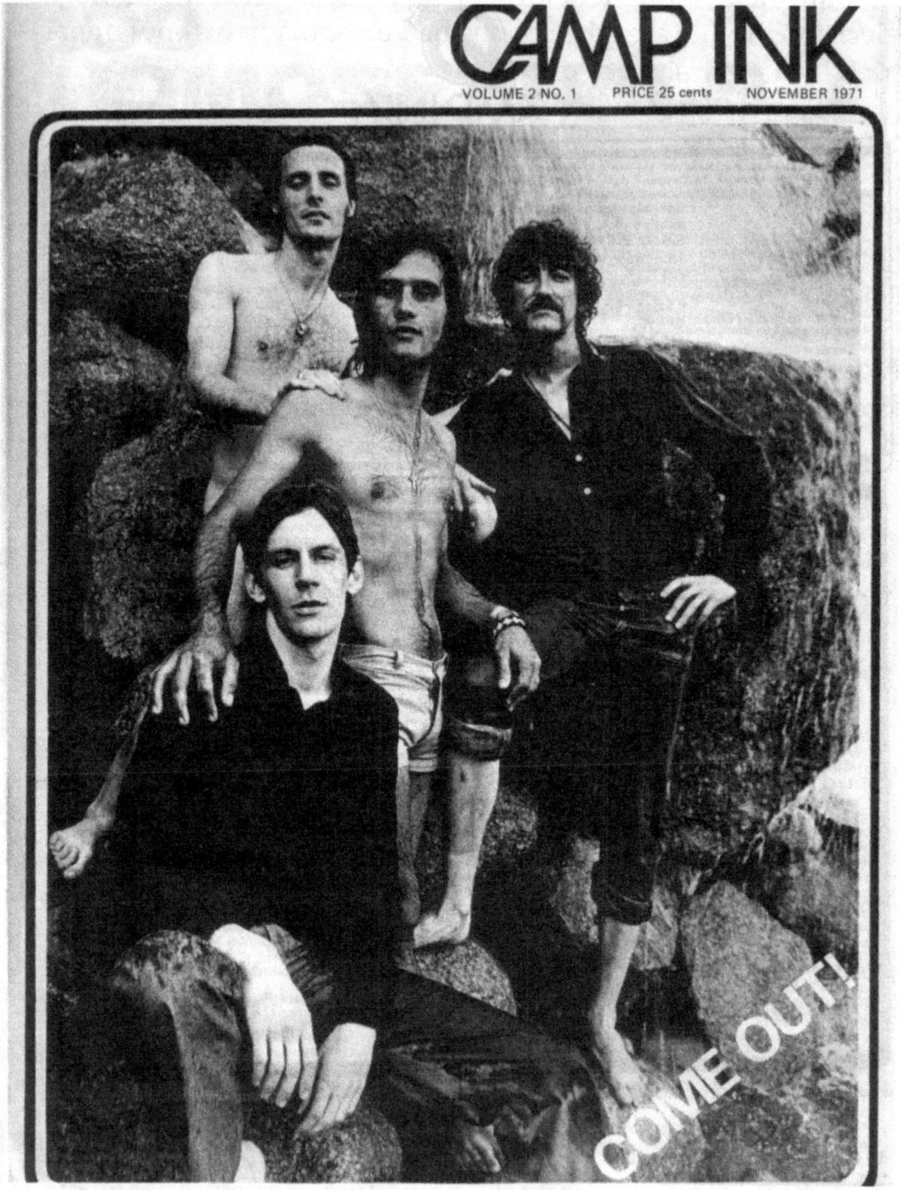
CAMP INK
VOLUME 2 NO. 1
PRICE 25 cents
NOVEMBER 1971
COME OUT!

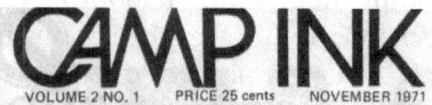

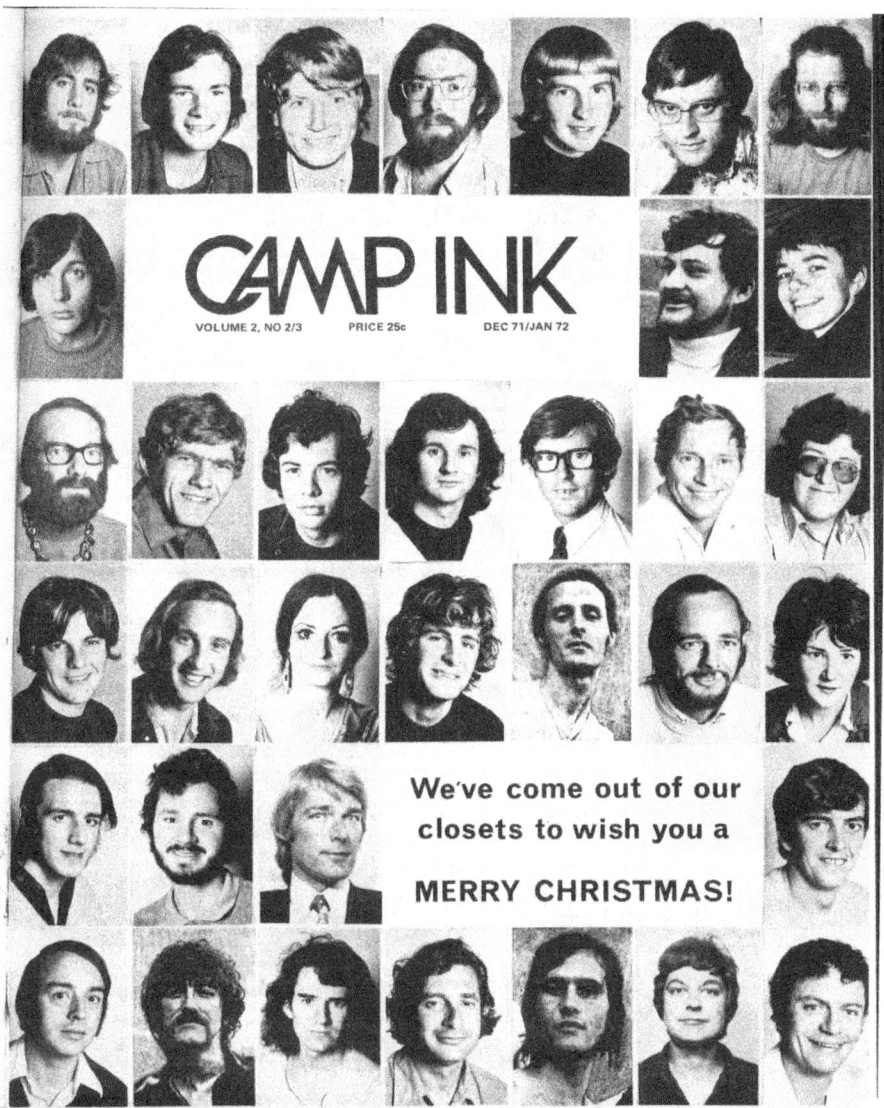

Coming out on the cover of Camp Ink. Brisbane comes first, but Sydney does it better (Camp Ink).

organisation as a whole. Branches simply continued on along their own paths.

CAMP straddled the various political positions available in Australia at the time, drawing upon a range of political viewpoints and practices to forge a politics of homosexual rights and homosexual freedom. In the end, however, it was unable to encompass all gay activists. By the end of 1971, challengers were arising, from both within and without.

4.

The Challengers

If modernising liberalism provided the nest within which gay rights thinking developed, it was not the only influence upon the fledgling movement. By the late 1960s, two challengers were presenting themselves: radicalism and the counterculture. So close have these two become that it is now difficult to separate them; even in the 1970s, there were common features: a commitment to far-reaching social change ('revolution') and a belief that ours was a society that, by its very nature, denied all that was best in human beings. But there were important differences between the way radicals and counterculturalists conceived of the world – and between their politics.

Radicalism supported grand visions of change, militant tactics, mass resistance and coalitions of all the oppressed and exploited against their common enemy, capitalism. It was a very old school of thought, although, for much of the 20th century, the Communist Party had been the main base of organised radicalism. The party remained silent on the question of homosexuality, and most of its members, if they thought about it at all, probably believed either that it was a symptom of bourgeois decadence (which was the line of the Soviet Union) or a mental disorder (which was the idea that prevailed in society more generally). As we have seen, Laurie Collinson's membership of the party was terminated in 1958 when his sexuality came to the attention of a local official.

The struggle against the Vietnam War and conscription in the 1960s expanded the appeal of radicalism spectacularly, bringing thousands of people into contact with its ideas and breaking the stranglehold of the Communist Party. Late in the decade, the party began to adapt to the changing times, but it was already being bypassed and outflanked by a swag of far Left challengers. Yet even these more radical groups initially showed little interest in homosexuality. The sole exception to this silence was a pamphlet produced by the Draft Resisters' Union and reprinted by the far Left group Resistance in about 1970 called *How Not to Join the Army*. The authors urged those trying to avoid being conscripted to:

> BE 'GAY': Play the homosexual bit... Wear white slacks, have your hair cut rather camp, wear a charm. Visit a couple of camp pubs and study homosexuals. Learn the gestures, the wrist movements. And the delicate body movements, how to touch the fellow you're talking to suggestively, how to smoke a cigarette. Be a little pathetic, talk melodically, act embarrassed in front of the other inductees when you undress. Ask your girlfriend to show how.[1]

It is a shockingly offensive passage and, even with its closing injunction ('don't overact'), there is nothing in it that suggests even the slightest awareness of its bigotry. It would not be long, however, before these attitudes changed.[2] By about 1972, gay liberation had been taken up by the Communist Party and other far Left groups as one of the causes for which they were fighting. While some of the more recalcitrant organisations, such as the pro-Chinese and pro-Soviet communist parties, remained hostile (publicly, actively and occasionally violently in the case of the Maoists), the rest of the revolutionary Left saw in gay experience the sort of oppression and resistance around which their worldview was organised and moved quickly to an active solidarity with their gay brothers and sisters.

The counterculture stood apart from radicalism in its emphasis upon the need for personal change in the here and now and its focus upon changing the self as an integral part of the broader struggle to change society. For radicalism, the structures of society (capital, patriarchy) were the chief enemy. For counterculturalism, challenging the way that these institutions had embedded themselves within individual consciousness was the first struggle. The exemplary countercultural slogan was 'the personal is political'. From this flowed a conception of politics and social change that was significantly different from radicalism's:

> revolutionary politics must permeate the very essence of one's personal life...politics [is] the total involvement of one's personal and social being as the only potentially revolutionary force...revolution is the process of life style and structural change.[3]

Given all this, sexuality was as legitimate a site for struggle as any other aspect of life. Indeed, given the extent to which sexual repression was coming to be seen as a major source of personal and social dysfunction, attention to sexuality came to be considered positively essential. In the course of the 1960s, the liberals' opposition to censorship had brought books, films and plays to a central place in the struggle to change society. Under the influence of counterculturalism, depicting that which could not be shown and saying that which could not be said were elevated to a political activity of the highest importance. The depiction of nudity (usually female), sex and sexuality was not simply profitable (though it was that); it was a political act. The notion that one could, by shocking the bourgeoisie, contribute to the transformation of society came to be widely held and underpinned a new interest in the depiction of homosexuality in particular. Perhaps the earliest manifestation of this development in Australia came in 1961 with the publication of the novel *Wake in Fright*, with its lurid representation of homosexual rape.[4] By the early 1970s, homosexual characters and references were becoming more common. Melbourne playgoers, for example, had experienced *The Boys in the Band*; *A Hard God*; *Cat on a Hot Tin Roof*; *Norman, Is That You?* and *Fortune and Men's Eyes*. Films of the time included *Sunday Bloody Sunday, Deliverance, Day for Night, Satyricon, Beckett, Lion in Winter, Mary Queen of Scots, The Music Lovers, Little Big Man, If, Cabaret, Something for Everyone, Performance, The Fox, Therese and Isabelle, Secret Ceremony, Bazza, The Killing of Sister George, Les Biches* and *Threesome*.[5]

The most substantial example of this trend towards the use of homosexual themes for their shock value came in 1972 with the Australian television program *Number 96*. The lawyer Don Finlayson (played by Joe Hasham) was a remarkably conventional character – except for his homosexuality. Don experienced all the trials of the average soap opera character:

> He fell in and out of love, he had relationships, long relationships, he even went off the rails and had a series of one night stands when he was really very low, he was blackmailed, he had his job threatened.[6]

But Don's real impact came from the fact that the writers steered clear of the 'screaming queen' stereotype, presenting him as 'a nice guy, an ordinary bloke' who just happened to be homosexual. The program's effect on public attitudes is widely acknowledged, with Dennis Altman suggesting that it was 'just as important as all of us activists'.[7] If this seems to be an overstatement, it is worth remembering that *Number 96* was one of the most watched programs of its time, and it brought issues into Australian lounge rooms that had hitherto been confined largely to *Truth* or, more recently, to the theatre-going and literature-buying publics. By stretching the boundaries of what could be portrayed on television, it allowed other programs to follow suit.[8]

The relationship between radicalism and the counterculture on the one hand and between both of these strands of thought and gay politics on the other, was strengthened by the fact that it was not a one-way interaction. Large numbers of gay activists drew upon these ideas, finding in them inspiration and direction for their work. Nowhere is this clearer than in Dennis Altman's *Homosexual: Oppression and Liberation*, the definitive statement of gay liberation ideas. This was a book that captured widespread international attention when it was published in New York in 1971, being reviewed even in *Time* magazine. The fact that Altman was Australian and that he returned in 1972 after some time abroad to a national tour for the Australian edition served to amplify the effect of the book in this country. Altman's ideas, a fusion of acute observation with extensive reading and thought, provided the basic thinking on most questions related to homosexual politics for the whole of the liberationist period. His use of Marx and Freud (especially as reworked by New Left Marxist Herbert Marcuse), his attention to both personal change and social transformation and his vision of a radical liberation of the truly human was what those involved in the movement needed. They snapped up the book, facing down their own fears to do so. Michael Hurley tells, for example, of the anxiety attendant upon buying a bank cheque made out to Gay Sunshine Press to import a copy of the book.[9] Gay activists read, absorbed, argued with, applied and reworked its ideas. They compared them to what was coming in from overseas in journals and newsletters and bounced the ideas off their own experiences in an attempt to make sense of the world and to find ways to change it.

Most gay activists shared radicalism's view that society was the problem. Individual prejudice and discriminatory acts had to be understood as the products of a twisted society, as symptoms not of prejudice, ill-informed opinion or ignorance, but of oppression, the systematic denial of civil rights and social legitimacy by powerful forces. The aspects of society that made it so anti-gay were

Number 96, Australia's premier soap. If Bev was about to discover that Don (played by Joe Hasham) was a 'filthy, dirty little queer', millions of viewers were to discover that he was also a decent, ordinary sort of bloke.

named with a variety of adjectives: capitalist, hierarchic, Judeo-Christian, straight, patriarchal, sexist. But the interconnectedness of the institutions of oppression was taken for granted. In one leaflet, the Melbourne University Gay Liberation Front identified education, big business, the public service and government as the sites of oppression. In another leaflet, the 'legal system, the police, the church, the nuclear family, the mass media, the psychiatric establishment' were highlighted.

If oppression was to be eradicated, society had to be transformed – replaced by 'a new society, open and [sex] role-free', as the Melbourne University Gay Liberation group wrote. The struggle for gay liberation was therefore a broad one, fought on many fronts and alongside many allies:

> Gay Liberation has a perspective for revolution based on the UNITY OF ALL OPPRESSED PEOPLE. There can be no freedom for gays in a society that enslaves others through male supremacy, racism and economic exploitation (capitalism).[10]

The goal was freedom: freedom from personal oppression and sex roles; freedom for all, gay and straight, women and men – a recognition of the natural right to diversity that all human beings had. These are very much more ambitious demands than anything ever imagined by the liberals of the 1960s.

From these demands flowed a commitment to, and enthusiasm for, militancy. Demonstrations, occupations, defiance, abuse and the silencing of enemies were essential tools in the struggle (although deployed perhaps more in rhetoric than in reality). If powerful social forces benefited from, and worked actively to maintain, the structures of oppression, it followed that the most vigorous and combative tactics were both needed and justified in the struggle for justice. Confrontation, rather than mere education and debate, was the order of the day. In an address to members of Society Five in Melbourne in 1972, Dennis Altman described militancy as not being about 'throwing rocks through newspaper windows or having sex in Collins Street', but rather as being 'a willingness to directly confront the institutions and individuals who are repressing homosexuals'.[11] Not that he was opposed to throwing things; in an interview with Sue Wills, he explained his reaction to a demonstration against aversion therapy:

> You see, I'm always divided... One sort of argument is the rational argument thing and the other is that if you really confront people it forces them to take note of what you're saying, even if their immediate reaction is anger, they can't forget about it.[12]

From the Left repertoire, the movement drew its deep suspicion of the commercial scene and commercialism in general. When radical gays denounced the 'parasites [who] run oppressive bars and dances for their profit' and 'the greedy gay capitalists and greedier criminal syndicates',[13] they were voicing a widely held suspicion of capitalist and commercial enterprises and a refusal to believe that these forces were anything other than enemies of gay people.

This revolutionary perspective made many deeply hostile to any complacency about apparent improvements in the public status of homosexuality. If anti-gay laws and attitudes were so deeply embedded in society and if they served the interests of powerful social forces, even progress had to be viewed with suspicion. In 1972, CAMP noted an opinion poll showing majority support for the decriminalisation of homosexuality, commenting:

> This is very encouraging, even though we are aware that most of this 52 per cent is in fact supporting the concept of homosexual law reform and not the concept of the complete restructuring of society which would be needed before the aims of CAMP were realised.[14]

Tess Lee Ack, a member of the Socialist Workers' Action Group, reviewing media images of homosexuals, noted:

> Poofters are no longer invariably evil pederasts lurking in the doorways of public toilets. Rather they can be entertaining, witty, sparkling, artistic, successful, TRENDY people.

But she warned against accepting this as the breakthrough that gays had been working for. Tolerance and trendy stereotypes were not enough; gays needed to create their own images, not rely upon those created for them.[15]

Countercultural politics enabled activists to identify the problem of self-oppression, which Campus CAMP in Brisbane described as the 'ultimate success of all forms of oppression'.[16] 'All of us realise', said Sydney Gay Liberation in June 1972, 'that we can be our own worst enemies: for we too have internalised this society's sexual norms and values which are anti-homosexual'.

They argued:

> The starting point of our liberation must be to rid ourselves of the oppression which lies in the head of every one of us. This means freeing our heads from self oppression and male chauvinism, and no longer organising our lives according to the patterns with which we are indoctrinated... It means we must root out the idea that homosexuality is bad, sick or immoral, and develop a gay pride.[17]

Gay pride was rather more about what one did, and how one lived, than what one was. Asking what gays had to be proud of, Jon Ruwoldt of Adelaide's Gay Activists Alliance suggested that gay people could be proud of having overcome the pressures and temptations to exercise power and to treat each other as sexual objects, of having stepped out of straight roles in order to be more truly human, of having built a community and of their support for transvestites and transsexuals – all summed up as 'Proud of our unity, our lifestyle, our community and our struggle'.[18]

The counterculture provided the gay movement with the notion that gay liberation was not about rights for homosexuals, but about changing the very nature of sexuality and gender. It was not the disadvantage of gays relative to straights, but the common experience of all humans trapped within restricting roles that was the real problem. In this line of argument, 'gay' did not always operate as a simple synonym for 'homosexual'. The Melbourne University Gay Liberation Front, for example, argued:

> Gay, in its most far-reaching sense, means not only homosexual, but sexually free... Gay is good for all of us. The artificial categories 'heterosexual' and 'homosexual' have been laid on us by sexist society.[19]

The task of abolishing gender was expressed by Jon Ruwoldt, among others, in his assertion that 'we recognise that androgyny is the ultimate, the biological revolution'.[20] As time passed, and

more limited goals became the order of the day, counterculturalism provided much of the intellectual underpinning for the idea that homosexuality was, and ought to be treated as, a 'valid alternative lifestyle'. Although radical and liberal elements of the movement soon took up this demand, the notion of a 'lifestyle' as being an important and legitimate political demand has its roots in the counterculture's interest in just these sorts of issues.

It is important to recognise that, far from being monolithic, these competing sets of ideas – liberalism, radicalism and counterculturalism – each encompassed a wide range of assumptions, theories and rhetorics about the world, how it worked and how it should work. Surrounding the core ideas of these currents of thought swirled a variety of concepts, beliefs, goals

Dennis Altman (far right) at the January 1972 Sexual Liberation Forum where he would announce, to a background of noisy cheers, the establishment of Gay Liberation in Australia.

and values that shaded into one another. Among those who held and used these ideas, it is even more difficult to distinguish neat boundaries. While social movement theory relies upon a notion of 'repertoires', it is just as useful to think about these sets of ideas as 'currents' which mingled and eddied together within a pool from which those in the movement drew, in often quite indiscriminate ways.

The range of political ideas available – liberal, radical and countercultural – was a source of considerable conflict. As activists found themselves drawing quite different conclusions about what it meant to be homosexual and what was needed to redress disadvantage, CAMP came under increasing pressure. The first serious rupture came with the rise of Gay Liberation, which emerged in Sydney in January 1972 and spread, in one form or another, around the country.

Although Gay Liberation was to define itself in opposition to CAMP primarily in terms of its greater radicalism, its origins owed a great deal to countercultural goals and, particularly, to the need for greater consciousnessraising among CAMP members. This need was originally identified by John Ware,[21] but it was taken up most seriously by a group of people who came to be known as the 'gay liberation cell'. This cell, as Dennis Altman (one of its leading members) emphasises, should not be understood in any conspiratorial way. It was not a secret group; it did not have any sort of decision making or disciplinary functions; and it was not aiming at either a takeover of CAMP or at splitting it.[22] But it did create tensions within CAMP, with John Ware, in particular, being increasingly critical of what he saw as the cell's 'navel gazing' and its reliance upon overseas models.

The final rupture came with CAMP's reluctance to let the gay liberation members hold a fundraising dance at the clubrooms, because gay liberation wanted to keep the money for its own activities, in clear violation of the policy that all money was pooled before being redistributed by a vote at the monthly general meetings.[23] Finally, in January 1972, at a Sex Lib Forum at the University of Sydney, Altman announced to a noisily excited response the 'first appearance...in Australia of a Gay Liberation group'. Sue Wills suggests that about 10 or a dozen people, including John Lee, Robert Tucker, John Storey, Pam Stein and Tony Crewes, left CAMP to form Gay Liberation. By June, gay liberation groups existed at the University of Sydney, the University of New South Wales and at 67 Glebe Point Road, which had been a centre for radical and countercultural activity for a couple of years.

Given the extent to which society's authorities – the law, the church and the medical profession – contributed to the oppression of homosexuality, it was hardly surprising that the counterculture's hostility to experts and leadership was taken up by gays.

At the very time that CAMP was moving towards a more formal structure with its first constitution and the election of co-presidents, Gay Liberation was keen to emphasise its non-hierarchic structures. The small group was declared as the preferred form of organisation, loosely tied together by monthly general meetings and a monthly newsletter.[24] Not only were formal office-bearer positions disavowed; informal leadership was considered, if anything, even worse. In an effort to combat it, Sydney Gay Liberation (SGL) employed a variety of forms – caucuses, appeals for participation and consciousness-raising. There was also the tactic of leaders withdrawing: Pam Stein and Tony Crewes, the first leaders, were the first to do so. In mid-1972, John Lee and Robert Tucker followed suit. The effect of all this, according to Sue Wills, was not the abolition of leadership, but its rotation.[25]

Melbourne Gay Liberation was set up shortly after Sydney, although there was no split from Society Five – the group emerged quite independently. Society Five had proved too conservative to attract students, and the decision to set up a different group was taken in early 1972 when Dennis Altman (visiting from Sydney) met with a number of people, including Jude Munro, Rodney Thorpe, Jeffrey Hill, Tony Crewes, Julian Desailley and Rex Rohmer.[26] Shortly after that, the first meeting of the group was held at Melbourne University. Attended by about 30 people and chaired by Jude Munro, the group decided to establish itself as a university club (which would give it access to meeting rooms and a small amount of money for printing and other activities). Regular Friday night meetings were held in the Union building and became very large indeed. The meetings were often split into small groups, usually concerned with consciousness-raising, to keep them manageable. In April, a meeting was called at Monash University to form a local group.[27] Within a few months, Gay Liberation organised Melbourne's first gay rights demo when, in May 1972, ABC management refused to screen a current affairs segment on Altman's *Homosexual: Oppression and Liberation*.

Social events, like CAMP and Gay Lib dances, brought together kamp and gay, women and men, the closeted and the out (AQuA)

Adelaide's gay liberation group was first set up in August 1972 when Altman and Lex Watson, co-president of CAMP NSW, addressed a meeting of some 350 people at Adelaide University. After they had spoken and answered questions, Jill Matthews (from a table top, as she recalls) asked those present who were not interested in forming a gay liberation group to leave. One hundred or so people remained, and the meeting broke up into small groups for brainstorming and consciousness-raising.[28] Weekly meetings at Women's House began immediately, as did a newsletter, *Gay Times*. But by late 1972, the newsletter was warning that the Friday night meetings would collapse, and the group seems to have become moribund shortly thereafter.

In May 1973, CAMP held its first (and only) national conference in Adelaide. Inspired by the presence of so many activists, and especially by the Melbourne women, a number of Adelaide people immediately formed a consciousness-raising group. Within a short time, several groups were in existence, and out of these a new organisation, Gay Activists Alliance, was formed.[29]

In Perth, the intention to establish a Campus CAMP was overtaken by the arrival of gay liberation ideas, and in January 1973, a group called CAMP University Society (CAMPUS) was formed. It attracted about 30 members who organised speakers, street theatre and dances. CAMPUS saw itself as aligned to gay liberationist ideas rather than to CAMP, which it suggested was more top-down in its structure and more social than political in its orientation.[30]

Gay Liberation soon found itself under pressure from internal divisions, especially over the position of women within the gay movement. This is one of the few aspects of the Australian movement that has attracted scholarship, and what these accounts in effect say is that, after trying to find ways to work with men, lesbians simply withdrew from the gay movement, leaving it male-run until 1978, when the national mobilisation around the Festival of Light (FOL) and the Mardi Gras arrests in Sydney brought men and women together for the first time in many years.³¹ Craig Johnston commented in 1976: 'After September [1973], the involvement of women in Gay Liberation virtually ended.'³² The 'virtually' is significant. So, too, is the focus on Gay Liberation and Sydney.

The problem with these accounts is that they create too neat a picture of what was, in fact, a very complex situation. In the first place, not all women withdrew from the gay movement or from working alongside men. As late as 1975, the members of the women's group within CAMP Queensland were surprised by the level of antagonism between women and men that they saw at the National Homosexual Conference, 'never [having] been exposed to these frictions in Queensland'. Vivienne Cass, Western Australia's delegate to the conference, had the same reaction.³³

In Melbourne and Sydney, some women continued working with men. CAMP NSW, even after the resignation of Sue Wills and Lex Watson and their supporters in April 1974, included women and men, and the editorial collective of the relaunched *Camp Ink* more often than not included more women than men. Women were published consistently in *Camp Ink*. In Melbourne, the most successful organisations – Gay Liberation, the Gay Teachers' and Students' Group (GTSG), Gay Liberation Radio and the *Gay Liberation Newsletter* collective – all involved both sexes. In the Australian Union of Students (AUS), a number of prominent lesbians held office alongside homosexual men and used their positions to support activities such as the National Homosexual Conference and the Homosexual Research Project. Liz Ross's important account of her own experiences as a lesbian and women's liberationist gives further evidence of the rich history of women and men working together during the 1970s.³⁴

It is also worth noting that there were women who withdrew from active participation in the movement, not because of male sexism, but because of the opposition they faced from women to their view that lesbians and gay men ought to work together.

Helen Pausacker, for example, tells of her distress when she publicly spoke out in favour of joint work during the debate at the 1975 National Homosexual Conference, only to find herself heckled during her speech and aggressively interrogated by lesbians throughout the rest of the weekend. It was to be many years before she could bring herself to return to the movement.[35]

Especially in the first year or two, it was generally assumed that men could – and, indeed, ought to – participate in the struggle against women's oppression, just as whites, heterosexuals and Westerners were expected to take their place in the struggles against racism, homophobia and imperialism.[36] Many of the men involved in CAMP and Gay Liberation were very supportive of women's liberation theory and practice.[37] When John Ware chained himself to his chair at the opening session of the Women's Commission, a women's liberation conference in Sydney in March 1973, to protest the exclusion of men, his action reflected not so much macho arrogance as a politics of unity that has almost disappeared today. When the motion to exclude him was passed by the audience, he left, but it is notable that several women went with him in protest.[38]

There were lesbians who were hostile to women's liberation, either because it was too radical or because it was a movement for bourgeois women.[39] And it did not help that many women's liberationists were not especially sensitive to the needs of lesbians. In a famous (perhaps notorious) paper to the Women's Liberation Theory Conference at Mount Beauty, in Victoria, in January 1973, a group of Hobart women asked why it was that straight sisters often cried when they were accused of being lesbians and provided a litany of ways in which lesbians were marginalised and abused within the women's movement.[40] Ironically, while John Ware was chaining himself to his chair at the Women's Commission, CAMP women were leafleting the same event for its initial refusal, followed by a tokenistic concession, to schedule a discussion of lesbianism.[41]

In the early 1970s, membership of the women's liberation movement was more a matter of politics than of sex. As radical feminism emerged as a distinct current within the movement, however, attention shifted from the structural roots of women's oppression towards the role of men in maintaining those structures.[42] More and more, women's liberationists were inclined to see men – all men – as having a vested interest in the maintenance of women's oppression. These ideas reached the gay movement in full force in 1973, when a number of lesbians returned from London to Melbourne.[43]

It was not as if women in the gay movement were unaware of the existence of sexist behaviour, especially among the men. In Sydney, as early as May 1972, a CAMP Women's Association (a name chosen to cash in on the initials which it shared with the conservative Country Women's Association) was formed by about 20 women as a special-interest group within CAMP. Over the next few months, a women's liberation consciousness developed; and, by early 1973, the group was concerned as much with the oppression of women within CAMP as within the wider world.[44] In Melbourne in January 1973, at a meeting of women to plan their contribution to the gay liberation newspaper, a number of prominent lesbians, including Barb Creed, Jocelyn Clarke and Sue Jackson, had started sharing their experiences as women in a mixed-sex organisation. After a spontaneous discussion at the regular Friday night Gay Liberation general meeting, they and some other women began to meet separately, constituting themselves as the Gay Women's Group. The initial impetus for this group was not, as Radicalesbians' historian Chris Sitka has noted, explicitly feminist. Rather, these women were angry with the sexism of the men of Gay Liberation and wanted to meet apart from them occasionally. They still attended the regular Friday night meetings, and Gay Women's Group meetings were held at Gay Liberation's Davis Street centre.

The arrival in Melbourne of Jenny Pausacker and her friends was to rechannel this discontent markedly. They had been reading women's liberation theory in London – 'in that kind of marvellous, way-ahead ethereal state that is born of no practice whatsoever', as Jenny Pausacker later put it[45] – and their ideas and their personalities had an immediate impact upon the lesbians of Gay Liberation. Central to their thought was the radical feminist notion that men were the problem. Although the Radicalesbian Manifesto referred to 'our gay brothers', there was no question but that women had to organise separately. Radicalesbians was born. The first question was: what should politicised homosexual women call themselves?

> We made an actual decision to use the word lesbian – rather than camp, gay, woman-identified-woman – to describe ourselves at that point. We also chose Radicalesbian as distinct from Radical feminist because we wanted to identify ourselves positively as lesbians... Coming out was also a strong imperative in those days. Radicalesbian was about the most 'out' and outrageous name we could confront our various oppressors with.[46]

The Radicalesbian Conference, held in Sorrento over the weekend of 6–8 July 1973, attracted some 60 women from around Australia who discussed a wide range of topics.[47] The conference papers addressed the problems of living as a lesbian, and the questions and answers reflected the powerful hold of counter-cultural thought. Jenny Pausacker and Sue Jackson tackled the problems of monogamy, loyalty and hierarchy in relationships. Barb Creed presented a paper written by two other women on bisexuality and her own piece on lesbian identity. Issues such as dependency in relationships were tackled in print and in debate. Basic problems were addressed, too: coming out to parents; whether you were a lesbian if you hadn't had sex with a woman yet; the church and abortion.

A meeting of Radicalesbians at Barb Creed's house (Barb Creed)

From Sorrento emerged the 'Radicalesbian Manifesto', which captured the ideas of the lesbian feminist current better than anything produced in Australia at the time. The manifesto identified the word 'lesbian' as a label that worked to keep women in line but declared that women would no longer accept this. By taking the term up, using it defiantly and combining this use with a vigorous coming out, lesbians could confront the world with their existence and pride and start to face down prejudice and fear. The manifesto did not promise an easy time, however. The struggle was for a genderless society, which did not differentiate on the basis of sex but allowed people to relate to each other as people, rather than through their roles. The threat that this posed to the patriarchy and its institutions promised a long hard struggle, but it was one that could begin in the here and now: 'We will not set up copies of marriage, of role-playing, of power dominance', the manifesto declared.[48]

The group, which at one point numbered about 60 in Melbourne and had a mailing list of about 200, operated a number of small consciousnessraising groups 'where we learn to trust each other and extend our analysis of a society based on the division of sex roles' and was active in writing leaflets, protesting against pornography, beauty contests and sexist advertising (often responding with graffiti) and in speaking to women's groups, schools and universities. The *Melbourne Feminist Collection*, a booklet of political and creative writings, was published in 1973.[49]

Through the first few months of 1974, the group seemed healthy enough, meeting, acting and socialising. But, in the April–May issue of the *Gay Liberation Newsletter*, a 'death notice' appeared: 'RIP Radicalesbians, 1973–1974. Due to lack of interest, lack of trust, acute factionalism, chronic gossip.' Chris Sitka sees the demise of the group as the result of several pressures. As the most visible lesbian group in Melbourne (DOB had transformed itself into the hard-to-locate Claudia's Group),[50] Radicalesbians attracted many women who were not particularly interested in, or sympathetic to, its politics, and this created tensions. The intensity of beliefs and the levels of activity among the radical core led to 'burn out' or exhaustion for many; and, in such a small group, the break-up of even one or two relationships could be profoundly disruptive. There was also, increasingly, an alternative. The women's liberation movement had thrown off its unease about lesbianism and, as a rapidly growing and enormously effective movement, it seemed a better option to many lesbian activists.[51]

But, if the organisation ceased to exist, the politics that underlay it did not. There is a rich history of lesbian feminist attempts to construct a women-centred culture as part of an effort to change the world.[52] It was a culture that would be constructed in the living of it, in the withdrawal of sexual and social engagement with men and in the creation of new ways of living and loving and working together that would eschew masculine and patriarchal values and practices. In this model, lesbianism itself was seen as a political

Why? Because homosexuals were everywhere. (AQuA)

choice rather than as a simple sexual desire. Lesbianism was the decision to devote one's emotional energy to women rather than to men, and there was a clear distinction between:

> lesbians with no political consciousness and those who are politically active. Lesbians without political consciousness believe that all they do that is different is fuck a woman... whereas politically conscious lesbians want radical change.[53]

The centrality of male power and the need to combat it was strong in lesbian feminist thinking, and the critique of male sexuality and the attempt to develop a genuinely female sexuality was important. Opposition to pornography, prostitution, sadomasochistic or fetishistic sexual practices and butch–femme role-playing was a given. A women's sexuality that did not rely upon penetration as the main source of pleasure, or which rejected it entirely, was developed. Even dress was politicised: lesbians 'dressed for comfort and freedom of movement, forgoing constricting clothing and time-consuming makeup, in line with feminist ideas'.[54]

Taking it to the walls (AQuA)

Some women believed that a complete physical withdrawal from men was required. This culminated, most famously, in the foundation of Amazon Acres in 1974 as:

> a spiritual community free from men and male values; a space where women could work towards gaining control of their lives; where they could interact with one another, help each other, be alone but safe; where they could live a self-sustained country life as part of a lesbian community.[55]

Others remained in the cities but lived in households that were off limits to men or allowed only limited access to particular men or boys.

Most lesbian feminists dedicated their political work to strengthening women's consciousness. Lesbian newsletters came and went during the 1970s and 1980s, and lesbian action groups were commonplace, especially around lesbian custody rights. There were frequent conferences, national and regional. Lesbian theatre was a popular activity. After the demise of Radicalesbians, Jenny Pausacker and a number of other women were involved in a flourishing women's theatre movement in Adelaide. Jai Greenaway's history of lesbian theatre in Sydney from the mid-1970s offers an insight into the pitfalls and pleasures of acting-as-activism.[56]

Lesbian feminism was very much a minority affair, as indeed all gay and lesbian activism was. Most lesbians, like most gay men of the 1970s, spent their time at home with their lovers or among friends or in bars and were inclined to be critical of, or indifferent to, politics of any sort. But among lesbian activists, even those who chose to work with men rather than apart from them, lesbian feminist ideas exercised an influence that was to last at least until the late 1980s.

The influence of these ideas was not confined to women. In late 1973 and early 1974, their echoes started to be heard among radical gay men as well. The February 1974 'Draft Manifesto of the Revolutionary Homosexuals of the GLF' is the earliest and, as Angelo Rosas says, 'the most important, comprehensive and detailed critique of Gay Liberation in Australia to have appeared till then'.[57] Signed by Craig Johnston and Brian McGahen, both members of the Communist Party and active within the gay movement since at least the year before, the paper criticised Gay Liberation for its individualism (for having a conception of liberation that boiled down to 'sort yourself out mentally – screw without guilt feelings – get more fucks'), for its sexism ('orienting itself to men and mimicking male politics') and for its reformist lack of theory and program.[58] Although the 'Draft Manifesto' exhibited (as might have been expected given the party affiliation of its authors) the influence of socialist ideas, it showed a great deal more of the counterculture. The appearance of this document marks the beginning of the brief flowering of effeminism in Australian gay circles.

Effeminism argued that 'the oppression of women is basic to all other oppression', including that of homosexuals, and that, in order to contribute to the struggle, men (gay and straight) had to work to become 'unmanly', to oppose hierarchies, to share, to be sensitive to the feelings of others, to raise children – in short, to live out alternative, non-masculine values and lifestyles.[59] The goal was a world 'where there are no fixed sex roles, where people's sexuality and personality is developed and expressed freely'.[60]

Effeminism offered men a way of attaching themselves to what seemed at the time the most dynamic and exciting part of the social movements: radical feminism. In Melbourne, effeminist men formed themselves into a group in about September 1973.[61] They were probably responsible for reprinting Tony Crewe's 1972 leaflet 'On Maleness' in the October 1973 edition of the Melbourne *Gay Liberation Newsletter*, and members Steve Oram and Ken Howard distributed a leaflet of their own called 'Why We Are Not Marching' at the 1975 May Day parade, arguing that the event was 'a show of male supremacy'.

By September 1975, Craig Johnston had become much more critical of his earlier position. In a paper co-authored with Michael Hurley he criticised effeminism as 'an inadequate response with 'a defective analysis'.[62] Although other speakers at the conference were still operating within the effeminist paradigm,[63] and Johnston acknowledged how important it was 'to insist on the primacy of the woman question and to relate the feminist analysis to our own lives', effeminism's moment was passing rapidly. Again, as with radicalesbianism, its after-effects lingered on. In 1976 and 1977, a group called Males Against Sexism was meeting in Melbourne, organising annual conferences and producing a newsletter.[64] Even in the early 1980s, feminist ideas would present resistance to the advance of a new homosexual masculinity among gay male activists.

In a few short years, homosexual politics had moved from liberal heterosexuals interested in law reform into the hands of lesbians and gay men. The aim now was, at minimum, to shift public attitudes and, at maximum, nothing less than a total transformation of society, its institutions and structures. A range of groups embodied a variety of goals and strategies and analyses. And yet, these groups and ideas could not, on their own, deliver social change. It was their activism that was to change the world, and it is to this that we now turn.

5.

Lobbying Eggs and Lobbying

We have seen that the rise of modernising liberalism, radicalism and the counterculture had provided new ways of thinking about homosexuality and about the place of homosexuals in society. But, on its own, new thinking was not enough. It was the coalescence of people in organisations committed to action – the emergence of DOB, CAMP, Gay Liberation, Radicalesbians and the Effeminists – that was important, marking as it did the emergence of something new: a movement dedicated to advancing the interests of homosexual people. The theorising of, and talking about, homosexuality was all very well, but it was the ways in which those ideas were put into action that changed society.

By the early 1970s, social movements were becoming an increasingly common part of Australian political life. The campaign against the Vietnam War and military conscription provided a model that was quickly adopted by women, Aboriginal and Torres Strait Islander Australians, gays and, in later years, many other social groups. Social movements are not lobby groups or political parties; indeed, they are not organisations at all. Rather, they are processes of activity and networks of those who undertake that activity. The plurals here (networks, processes) are important: social movements are irreducibly composed of a multitude of networks, groups and organisations, a diversity of ideas, strategies and beliefs and a variety of forms of action.

Already by 1973, the gay movement in Australia was developing a range of organisations. Some, such as CAMP in most states, were formally organised groupings, legally constituted associations with broad programs of aims and activities. Others, such as Gay Liberation and Radicalesbians, were groups that avoided the formalities of constitutions and struggled to eradicate all signs of such hierarchic thinking and practice from their work. After 1973, as we shall see, small-scale single-issue action groups emerged as the key form of organisation within the movement; but, even before that time, such groups were foreshadowed in the various task groups within the established organisations – for example, subgroups that concentrated on law reform, the churches, the medical profession, managing the clubrooms, producing the newsletter, organising a demo or running a candidate in a state or federal election.

As a form of political activism, a social movement has options not available to other forms. The variety of demands and goals encompassed in the gay movement produced an extraordinary range of targets: politicians and opinion-makers, the professions, members of other social movements and other oppressed and exploited groups, ordinary people in the streets and, of course, all lesbians and gay men themselves. The movement also produced a range of strategies: lobbying, public speaking, demos and pickets, direct action, street theatre, boycotts, publishing, consciousness-raising, counselling and standing candidates in election campaigns. And, on days when nothing else was happening, being openly gay – wearing gay lib badges, makeup, radical drag – could become a political action. Different groups within the movement could target different groups within society in various ways. A lobby group could hardly throw eggs at its opponents, dump buckets of brains in their offices or even dress to shock. Sections of the gay movement, however, were able to engage in exactly this sort of behaviour, while others donned their suits and frocks and politely debated the pros and cons of particular reforms with the powerful. The purposes of all this activity were equally broad: to elicit a statement of support or a favourable vote from public figures; to get publicity for a cause or grievance; to protest against the existence of an oppressive system; or to disrupt that system's operation, either temporarily or permanently. Other activities were used to express solidarity with friends and allies, both actual and potential.

This activity worked upon those involved in the movement themselves, generating enthusiasm, commitment and a sense of achievement. This is important, because central to the gay movement, as to any movement, was the activist – 'constructor, organiser, "permanent persuader;"',[1] leader, articulator of demands and developer of strategies. At the heart of the activism, both the thinking and the organising, were those who did it all – those who convened and attended the meetings and argued into the night, organised the dances, called the demos, lobbied and occupied and picketed and threw eggs. It was the activists who wrote leaflets and letters, produced newspapers and submissions and published critiques and programs and proposals for action. Without them, there was no movement.

We cannot know with any certainty who they were, however. The very diversity of movement work means that the idea of membership must be used cautiously; indeed, the idea was firmly rejected by the radical and countercultural organisations. People flowed in and out of activism as the mood took them. Numbers, therefore, are entirely speculative. In the 1970s, the national membership of CAMP as well as the smaller action groups, including turnover, was perhaps as low as 2,000–3,000. CAMP's membership probably peaked within a year of its formation at about 1,700, and the extent to which these people were activists varied. CAMP's AGMs in the various states usually attracted fewer than 50 people. The radical groups often attracted scores to their meetings in their early days. Demonstrations of several hundred were held in Melbourne and Sydney. National homosexual conferences, which were important events on the movement calendar, attracted between 300 and 600 participants. These figures overlap considerably, of course. In the 1980s and 1990s, the expansion of the number of groups and the armies of volunteers doing AIDS care and other work lifted the figures dramatically. Perhaps 20,000 people, the members of numerous community groups, marched in Mardi Gras and the Pride marches.

If numbers are doubtful, we do at least have some idea of the social composition. A survey of 84 members of CAMP NSW in 1972 found that 80 percent were men. Nearly half were under 30 years of age; 80 percent were under 40. The men were, by occupation, mostly clerks, accountants, public servants and teachers.[2] A more extensive survey of the participants at the 1980 National Homosexual Conference in Sydney showed that two-thirds were male, two-thirds had a degree or diploma, three-quarters were under the age of 30, half had attended previous conferences and two-thirds described their politics as radical or very radical.[3] Young, educated and politically committed – it is hardly surprising that their efforts were to have such an impact on society. They had the confidence, the skills and the networks to speak, to write, to persuade and to agitate. As they moved into the workforce, they often rose rapidly up the career ladders and, even when they did not, or chose not to, their activity as workplace union representatives or solid, reliable workers often gave them the respect of, and an influence over, those around them. Not all activists fitted these generalisations, of course, but enough did for their social composition to play a part in explaining the movement's impact.

We do know one other thing about the activists: overwhelmingly, they were homosexual. Even after the withdrawal of heterosexuals from organisations such as CAMP, straights continued to play a role in other parts of the movement well into 1972 and often did very good work, especially in smaller communities where it was harder for gays to come out. A Miss Lovejoy in Armidale found herself writing on gay rights for the student handbook and planning the University of New England orientation week stall because many of those in the gay group seemed content with its operation as 'a secret society cum refugee camp'.[4] But, more and more, this was seen as undesirable. David Widdup, looking for people to appear on an ABC television program, pointed out:

> there are any amount of heteros, and some time ago that would have done. Now I am convinced it must be all camp even if all alone.[5]

It was a view shared by many straight supporters of the gay movement; and, for the most part, heterosexuals simply passed the reins to gay people, retiring to other causes or doing their bit in other ways.

In Melbourne, however, there was something of a struggle. In 1972, the Gay Liberation Publications Group produced a document entitled 'Queens and Dykes Want Gay Lib Back'. The authors argued that the continuing presence of heterosexuals within the group was a problem. Surely, they thought (although they admitted to being unsure of this), gay liberation was a movement for gay people only, 'that is, homosexuals and bisexuals'. The presence of heterosexuals, non-sexuals or sexually confused people was hindering the subtle and intangible processes by which 'gay self-understanding, group identity and solidarity' were being developed. In the end, after a series of bitter arguments, the group's homogeneity was settled by the withdrawal of the 'non-gays'.[6]

The movement's most dramatic and original contribution to the repertoire of political activity was the tactic of coming out – of publicly declaring one's homosexuality. This could be done in a number of ways: by telling people, most obviously, but also by wearing badges and T-shirts, or by simply living openly in a day-to-day sense, practising the behaviours that heterosexuals took for granted but which so many homosexuals were afraid to display, such as holding hands in the street. There were, of course, rather practical reasons for coming out. Homosexuals speaking for themselves were much more likely to attract attention than were experts and liberals. Certainly, media attention on homosexual spokespeople was widespread during the early months of the movement, delivering invaluable publicity.[7] Rod Thorpe reports from his own experience that one ABC radio program was so keen that he appear that they sent a car to collect him and that, after he had finished his interview with them, he was then whisked upstairs for a television program.[8]

Also, coming out was seen as having important political effects, especially for homosexuals themselves – for those coming out and for those just watching. Melbourne Gay Liberation argued:

> We believe that it is important to remind everyone that you are homosexual – COMING OUT – for yourself so that you won't be subjected to anti-homosexual acts against yourself, and so other homosexuals who haven't come out can realise that other people are homosexuals and they enjoy it'.[9]

Or, more succinctly: 'One hour on the streets screaming and proclaiming your homosexuality is worth six hundred hours in a consciousness raising group'.[10] Or, more succinctly still, 'I like this coming out. Such a sense of freedom.'[11]

Mim and Sue, for instance, wrote of the pleasures and politics of 'kissing in the park, arabesques in the art gallery, pirouettes on the pavement, holding hands in the street'. Reactions ranged from verbal abuse, giggling and whispering, to an embarrassed averting of the eyes, but they found that verbal attackers were often nonplussed by a simple, open acknowledgement of their lesbianism. Their conclusion was that 'it's not an entirely unfriendly universe'. The exhilarating effect of coming out is emphasised here, but so, too, is its political importance:

> Holding hands in public is a step towards educating the public, towards having lesbianism recognised as something that exists. After people realise that it exists, perhaps next generation, they will accept it.[12]

There is some evidence that it did, indeed, work like this. In March 1971, for example, at a forum organised at Melbourne University, one of the speakers, Alan Begg of CAMP, identified himself as gay and spoke very simply: 'I'm a homosexual. I prefer to go to bed with boys. That's all there is to it.'[13] According to one observer, he 'thus won the immediate support of the audience for his audacity, if not his disposition'.[14] When members of Society Five addressed a Church of Christ meeting in early 1972, one doctor announced that his views had been favourably revised, and one woman declared: 'If I ever have a Camp grandson, I hope that he will be just like you'.[15] One woman wrote that hearing Peter Bonsall-Boone – one of CAMP NSW's earliest members – lecture at Monash University on religion and homosexuality 'really shook me', so much so that she immediately wrote to her church paper asking them to share her change of heart.[16]

The willingness of gay people to come out both to themselves and to the world at large was of fundamental importance, but it was not an easy choice. Consciousness-raising helped. Gathering on a regular basis, small groups of lesbians and gay men could 'explore with others one's personal feelings as a homosexual, and relate it to the feelings and experiences of others'.[17] The diversity of the homosexual experience between different individuals and within one person was revealed, providing a solid basis for tolerance of difference and solidarity. Over time, details of what worked in a group and what didn't became clear; for example, no couples, not more than eight and not fewer than four, and a commitment to participate for a given period. The intensity of the experience can be gauged from the fact that, even today, many circles of friends have their origins in such groups, and people still speak highly of their time in consciousness-raising.

When there were no conventional forms of activity taking place – demos to attend, articles to write and leaflets to distribute – it was possible to be politically active simply by living openly as gay. Radical drag was one of the movement's most notorious

'Everyone can be beautiful in make-up' declared Robert Tucker of Sydney Gay Liberation. Radical gay men all over Australia took to radical drag, or genderfuck, challenging sex role norms and male privilege. Melbourne 1973 (Rennie Ellis)

activities. Unlike kamp drag, which aspired either to allow men to pass as women or operated as a highly theatrical parody of femininity, radical drag or genderfuck aimed to offer a direct challenge to gender as such. The broader radical rejection of gendered hair length was supplemented by a defiant this-goes-with-that mélange of styles. Lesbians, reflecting feminist norms, refused to wear dresses and makeup or remove body hair and often went further. Helen Pausacker, around but not part of Radicalesbians, watched with interest as lesbians came out, acquired politics and, often within weeks, cut their hair. (The style was not as short as we have come to take for granted, but it was shocking enough at the time.) Gay men wore beards, dresses and workboots with makeup in an effort to explore their masculinity and to challenge both social norms and their own access to masculine privilege. It wasn't always easy and didn't always work. Bill Morley reports his frustration that, while sitting in tutorials wearing 'a Gay Liberation badge virtually everyday, and makeup quite frequently...green eye shadow and red nail polish', people preferred to discuss the Russian Revolution rather than the revolution he was endeavouring to bring about there and then.[18] Living a different kind of life involved one's residence, as well. The communal household became an important part of the effort to remake the world. Among women, in particular, the radicalesbian household became a feature of many lives, enabling lesbians to direct their energies towards each other rather than towards men. The women of Canterbury Castle in Sydney talked of an intention to live differently, to help 'lesbians to get to know, help and understand themselves'.[19] Such living was, in part, 'a bit of an escape' from the harsh realities of everyday working life and a way to support and bolster each other. But it was a place, too, where political action could begin. The household did graffiti runs together and some street theatre and protested in gay bars to challenge the sexism they found there. Such households existed in all major cities during the 1970s and 1980s (there were a few concentrated in Lake

Street in Northbridge, Perth, in the mid to late-1970s)[20] and they remain an important, although often unnoticed, part of lesbian lifestyles today. Many gay men, too, tried to live this way, but with rather less success, and there were mixed-sex households.

Even without the efforts to remake personalities, the gay and lesbian households were politically important. In most cities during this time, the core activists lived together in a small number of households, in relationships that were simultaneously political, sexual and social, in which the social and the political, free time and meetings, alliances and love and lust were inextricably intertwined. The disintegration of such households and of the relationships that evolved within them could be important, too. The attempt to found a national radical gay paper in 1973 failed precisely because of a complex falling out among those who were planning it.[21]

There was still the hard work of more traditional forms of political activity. CAMP produced a monthly magazine during this period – *Camp Ink* – which published news, features and opinion pieces. The journal served two functions. It was widely circulated to opinion-makers in the community (journalists, MPs and so on) and served to bring the movement to the attention of influential people. But it was also directed at the membership of the organisation and was intended to press upon them the idea that homosexuals needed to be politically active. A movement-based press enabled the detailed discussion of issues that the mainstream media, with its focus on news, would not have considered publishing, including issues that may have been deemed too controversial. Promiscuity, homosexual prostitution, debates about the sinfulness of homosexuality and the role of beats, sat alongside reports on the victimisation of naval personnel, law reform, separatism and book reviews. *Camp Ink* was published from 1971 to 1977 – an achievement other gay newspapers could not match. The one and only issue of Melbourne Gay Liberation's *Gay Rays* appeared in December 1972. *Radical Homosexual* – organised by SGL – never got off the ground at all. Even *William and John* (1971–72) and *Gayzette/Stallion* (1973–74), although backed by commercial organisations, lasted barely a year.

Alongside these were the newsletters, such as those produced by Gay Liberation in both Melbourne and Sydney, as well as CAMP SA's *Canary*, Gay Activists Alliance's *Boiled Sweets* and CAMP WA's *West Campaigner*. These were very much more modest affairs – line art roneoed and stapled, rather than printed and bound – and of variable editorial quality. They nonetheless served the same useful function, circulating information and debate to those on the mailing lists.[22]

The roneo machine – cheap to operate and widely available at universities – also provided the means for the production of leaflets, of which the movement produced scores during this period, in print runs of hundreds or, occasionally, thousands. Because they could be produced at short notice, leaflets were ideal for emergency actions. Because they were cheap to produce (especially when the university-based gay groups had a monetary allowance for publicity activities), they could be freely handed out.[23] Minutes, position papers and interventions into meetings could also be churned out quickly, easily and inexpensively.

The movement's capacity to produce its own printed material became increasingly important as the mainstream media lost interest. It was widely believed that, after the initial flurry of interest, a blackout on gay issues had been imposed by some media outlets. This was first noted in 1971 when the press failed to use material provided by CAMP NSW about the dismissal of a number of sailors from the navy on charges of homosexuality. Increasingly convincing evidence of a deliberate suppression of reporting accumulated. This culminated in reports of a memorandum circulating within the *Sydney Morning Herald* to the effect that the paper was a Christian paper and that homosexuality was not to be reported. In response, in late 1972, David Widdup, assisted by an influential and well-connected friend who supported the movement, went to see Warwick Fairfax, the owner of the newspaper. As a result of their representations, editorial policy shifted, and reporting on gay events and issues was allowed.[24] In the meantime, the movement's own media had allowed it to continue to communicate effectively despite the blackout.

Public speaking remained one of the movement's stock-in-trade activities and was something that members of CAMP branches, and later Gay Liberation, were frequently called upon to do. Sue Wills joked: 'we were cheap after-dinner entertainment for Rotary, Lions and Apex Clubs'.[25] To select a single and not unrepresentative example, Society Five's secretary listed the following among the groups addressed in his annual report: Cheltenham Church of Christ, La Trobe University Forum, Burwood Teachers' College, Williamstown JayCees, Monash medical students, Epping Rotary, Kew ALP, Toorak Young Liberals, Doncaster Young Wives, various tertiary institutions, Malvern Rororact, Footscray Lions, Merlmaz Jewish Youth, Upwey Humanist Society, Knox JayCees, Ringwood JayCee-ettes, sociology students, Wills Young Liberals, Lifeline, Moorabbin Technical College, Essendon Young Liberals and Ballarat Teachers College.[26] It is a list that could easily be reproduced for any of the branches of CAMP for any of these early years.[27]

These appearances allowed lesbians and gay men (and members of the movement were always keen to ensure that both participated where at all possible) to explain themselves, to address issues of concern to the audiences (Why coming out? Why make a fuss about it at all?), to refute common myths (the homosexual as child molester or as predator upon unsuspecting heterosexuals), to explain the ways in which homosexuals were victimised and disadvantaged and to elicit support from the audience who, as parents of gay people, friends of parents, newspaper editors, doctors, teachers, library workers and churchgoers, could all help to bring homosexuality into the open.[28] Sue Wills draws a distinction between audiences – between community groups, on the one hand, and professional bodies (including university medical, sociology and psychology students and the professional associations of such groups) on the other, arguing that the latter were 'of considerably more value'.[29] But it is important that literally thousands of people were directly exposed to the ideas of homosexual rights and/or gay liberation and to real, live homosexuals – many of them for the first time in their lives (as far as they knew). Activists argued at the time that, by overcoming their fear and speaking out, homosexuals were achieving tangible results:

> Once the opponents of law reform in morning tea discussions, in synods, at trade union meetings, in the suburban discussion groups, find themselves on the defensive, and the experience of those who have taken part in such discussions shows that little more than breaking the wall of silence is necessary to achieve this, then the battle for homosexual law reform will have been won.[30]

Television and radio provided access to hundreds of thousands more people. Homosexuality was a topic that was controversial and interesting enough to justify reasonably frequent coverage by midday talk shows, evening current affairs programs and talk-back radio. Very shortly after the foundation of CAMP in Sydney, Ian Black appeared on a radio program hosted by the prominent journalist and social commentator Anne Deveson. Several callers rang in; all were sympathetic (which must have strengthened the view among listeners that many people were tolerant), and two asked for CAMP's postal address, which was broadcast.[31] A well-known speaker – and the movement started to generate stars, however much some wanted it not to – could provide a focus for attention. Lex Watson's visit to Adelaide in August 1972 created a great deal of media interest in CAMP, including two extended interviews on church-run radio programs (which itself was controversial enough to attract further comment on radio and television news).[32] In May 1972, Society Five reported media appearances which effectively launched the organisation onto the public stage, and there was more media coverage in December 1972, which resulted in many inquiries and 100 new members.[33]

There were risks, of course. When Lesley Rogers was invited to speak on television for Society Five, she was prepared to do so only if filmed from behind. Two of the men who appeared with her lost their jobs; one was bashed at work and then fired. Rogers herself believed that her career suffered as a result of her appearance.[34] But the rewards for the movement could be enormous. Dennis Altman's appearance on Monday Conference, a highly regarded and high-rating current affairs program, in July 1972 indicates the impact such appearances had.[35] Altman was on a panel alongside two critics. Although the program was ignored by virtually the entire print press, Altman's own papers provide an insight into the impact of television upon its audiences. The papers contain scores of letters and telegrams from people in every capital city and from places as far-flung as South Tamworth, Coogee and Fairy Meadow. In Perth, Altman was told CAMP's coffee-room 'was crowded and you were cheered to the rafters'. Ian Black wrote to suggest that 'the programme might loosen things up quite a lot'. The secretary-director of the Australian Council of Churches wrote to 'apologise for the Church'. A. G. W. Keys, national secretary of the Returned Services League, described Altman's appearance as 'articulate and thoughtful [and] courageous'. Watching the program with some conservative friends, Keys said, 'we all agreed that you made your interrogators look like amateurs'. A member of the ALP branch in Fairy Meadow described the interviewers as 'prejudice-clogged, slug-witted' and wrote to offer to move a few resolutions at her party branch, to speak to her MP and to send the odd letter or two. The program's call log (a listing of telephone calls maintained by the station's switchboard) was favourable to Altman, hostile to the presenter, Bob Moore, and critical of Altman's opponents. One of those opponents, Peter Coleman, did a tour of Liberal Party branches in his electorate in the week after the program and found a high level of support for Altman and much criticism of his own position. Hostile interviewers and unwise tactics by opponents also helped Sue Wills when she appeared on *Monday Conference* in November 1972 to debate the use of aversion therapy to treat homosexuality, giving her a sympathetic audience that she might not otherwise have had.[36]

Members of the movement also attended public meetings and other forums where they could argue their ideas. In March 1971, the Debating Union at Melbourne University arranged a forum at which Richard Ball, a psychiatrist, and Julian Phillips, a lawyer from the university's Law School, spoke on medical and legal aspects of homosexuality.[37] The psychiatrist, in particular, according to a report published in the Monash University student paper, was subjected to a great deal of hostile questioning (presumably from gays in the audience). Then two members of CAMP spoke – Winsome Moore, the secretary, and Alan Begg, whose impact (with his simple statement 'I'm a homosexual. I prefer to go to bed with boys') has been mentioned earlier. In June 1972, Gay Liberation and Women's Liberation at Melbourne University jointly organised a day of activities, including a public meeting (with views on sexual liberation from the sponsoring groups), discussion groups and a dinner dance. At Sydney University in late 1971, 400 people heard a number of (heterosexual) speakers on the subject of legalising homosexuality, organised by Campus CAMP.[38]

Behind the scenes, too, gay voices were being heard increasingly often. Talking to MPs, clergy, newspaper editors, professionals and academics was a central part of the movement's work – especially CAMP's. And gay voices were not only being heard, they were also being taken more and more seriously. In 1973, Dennis Altman received a letter from a man who was concerned that his homosexuality would be an obstacle to obtaining a social security benefit. (This is a nice example of the importance of the movement's capacity to generate high-profile figures who could

CAMP Women's Association (the other CWA) at a Sydney Women's Liberation march, 1973

be identified, located and approached.) Altman wrote to the minister for social welfare, Bill Hayden (who, as we have seen, was an early liberal supporter of homosexual law reform), noting the man's case as an example of the sort of discrimination that would not be addressed by any law reform confining itself to decriminalisation.[39] In response, Hayden wrote: 'I know of no case where this [discrimination] had happened', but still instructed his department that 'homosexuality should in no way interfere with a person's right to receive benefits from the Department'. Within a month, the head of the department had issued a formal memorandum to all state directors making the same point.

Appearing on television and radio and lobbying ministers and members of parliament and other prominent people were firmly entrenched liberal political tactics by the 1960s. The members of the ACT HLRS and DOB had regularly used such means to get

Street protests were the natural habitat for early activism

their message across. Demonstrations and protest actions were more recent features of political life (or rather had been revived during the 1960s after a long period of disuse). The gay movement employed such forms of action cautiously at first, but with greater and greater confidence over time.

Some branches of CAMP, such as Melbourne, Adelaide, Brisbane and Perth, never organised demonstrations during the earliest years. As we have seen, however, in October 1971, Sydney CAMP organised its first public protest outside the Liberal Party headquarters. In March 1972, Gay Liberation and CAMP NSW formed a joint contingent at the Women's Liberation march; and, in June, the two groups staged a march through the streets during late-night shopping to mark Sex Lib Week and the fifth anniversary of homosexual law reform in Britain.[40] The mood of these events was always rather jolly. There were pink helium-filled balloons,

Among the first to declare that homosexuality was starting to dominate the TV screens was the ABC management, which then banned a segment on Dennis Altman's book *Homosexual: Oppression and Liberation*, a step which provoked demos in Melbourne and Sydney. (John Storey collection, AQuA)

brightly dressed crowds of people, amusing banners and slogans, boiled lollies and 'gay apples' for passers-by. Melbourne's Gay Liberation demo on 1 December 1972 was very much in the same mode: a breakaway group of demonstrators darted into Myer, and same-sex couples noisily tested the beds and the makeup.[41] Demonstrations in these cases were essentially celebratory – big, splashy, visible expressions of gay pride.

The decision by CAMP to run a candidate in the 1972 federal election had the same exuberant quality. David Widdup, one of CAMP's earliest members, stood for the seat of Lowe (then held by Billy McMahon) under the punning and very camp slogan, 'I've Got My Eye on Billy's Seat'. The fact that McMahon was prime minister at the time guaranteed press coverage. The fact that he was widely rumoured to be homosexual added a frisson of naughtiness to the whole event, which Widdup (describing himself as the 'acknowledged homosexual candidate') was more than prepared to play to. The publicity garnered was, of course, of immeasurably greater significance than the 218 votes Widdup received.

More serious in style and purpose were the pickets and protests against discrimination and the victimisation of homosexuals. When ABC management suddenly quashed a segment prepared for a current affairs program on the launch of Altman's book, *Homosexual: Oppression and Liberation*, gay liberationists in Sydney and Melbourne gathered outside the ABC buildings to protest. Such protests were usually peaceful, although it was at this event in Sydney that the first arrest for gay political work took place.[42] In the case of the picket outside St Clement's Church in Mosman, Sydney, to denounce the sacking of Peter Bonsall-Boone for coming out on television (see Chapter 8 for more detail), the leaflet calling the protest emphasised the intention to be 'quiet, orderly and dignified' and urged demonstrators to attend the church service when it began. Melbourne staged two protests over this episode, the one in Geelong being one of the first to be held outside a capital city.[43]

Showing our pride

Protesting the Anglican Church's victimisation of one of its gay members in Sydney, November 1972. Oddly enough, the dancing man in the frock (centre) was not one of the demonstrators. (Phillip Potter)

To be successful, demonstrations need a reasonable number of demonstrators – as much for the morale of those involved as to impress those observing. Because numbers were not always available, activists (especially those coming out of Gay Liberation, who employed radical methods more readily) adopted the zap, a small-scale, confrontational action that allowed small numbers of people to protest on short notice with a minimum of organising. In early 1973, SGL threw itself into a burst of activity, relying almost entirely upon the zap.[44] Members spent a Saturday afternoon on Circular Quay trains holding hands. Armed with leaflets, they went to a Bondi Junction pub that was rumoured to be refusing to serve homosexuals. On a sunny Sunday in June, a group descended upon the happy families in Sydney's Domain, handing out a leaflet entitled 'Homosexuality Is a Valid Alternative'.

Gay Activists Alliance (GAA) in Adelaide, too, used the zap.[45] In June 1973, in the very first issue of its newsletter, *Boiled Sweets* (the title itself was a defiant and provocative reference to the supposed means by which homosexuals/pedophiles lured little boys into their clutches), GAA listed a number of zaps in which it had already engaged. There were actions against a gynaecologist who had displayed arrogance and ignorance about lesbianism; a religious conference at Parkin-Wesley College; and John Court's speech to the Liberal Studies group at the art school. In later months, the group zapped Steele Hall, prominent Liberal Party dissident; Ernie Sigley, a television performer; and a meeting at which John Court and Mary Whitehouse of the FOL were speaking.

What is remarkable about all this work is how localised it was. Even CAMP, which was a national organisation, left the state organisations to themselves, by and large. Although there was a national conference in Adelaide in May 1973, it did little to bring the branches together. (Given the acrimony of the debates, it did much to drive them apart.) This fragmentation of the movement was largely inevitable. Law reform was a state matter, of course, and even large national organisations such as the churches and the professional associations tended to be centred in the various state capitals.

Two factors overcame parochialism. Firstly, those involved adhered to the idea of a gay movement and drew upon ideas that were national – indeed, international – in orientation. They were, wherever they lived and whatever their differences, part of one movement. Secondly, and more practically, although travel between cities was time consuming, it was not particularly expensive. Students and the unemployed, in particular, moved freely between Melbourne, Sydney and Adelaide. By about 1973, as SGL disintegrated, Melbourne, conveniently located halfway between Sydney and Adelaide (the centre of a flourishing lesbian community), became the national capital for radical gay activism. It was to Melbourne that John Lee and his friends came when

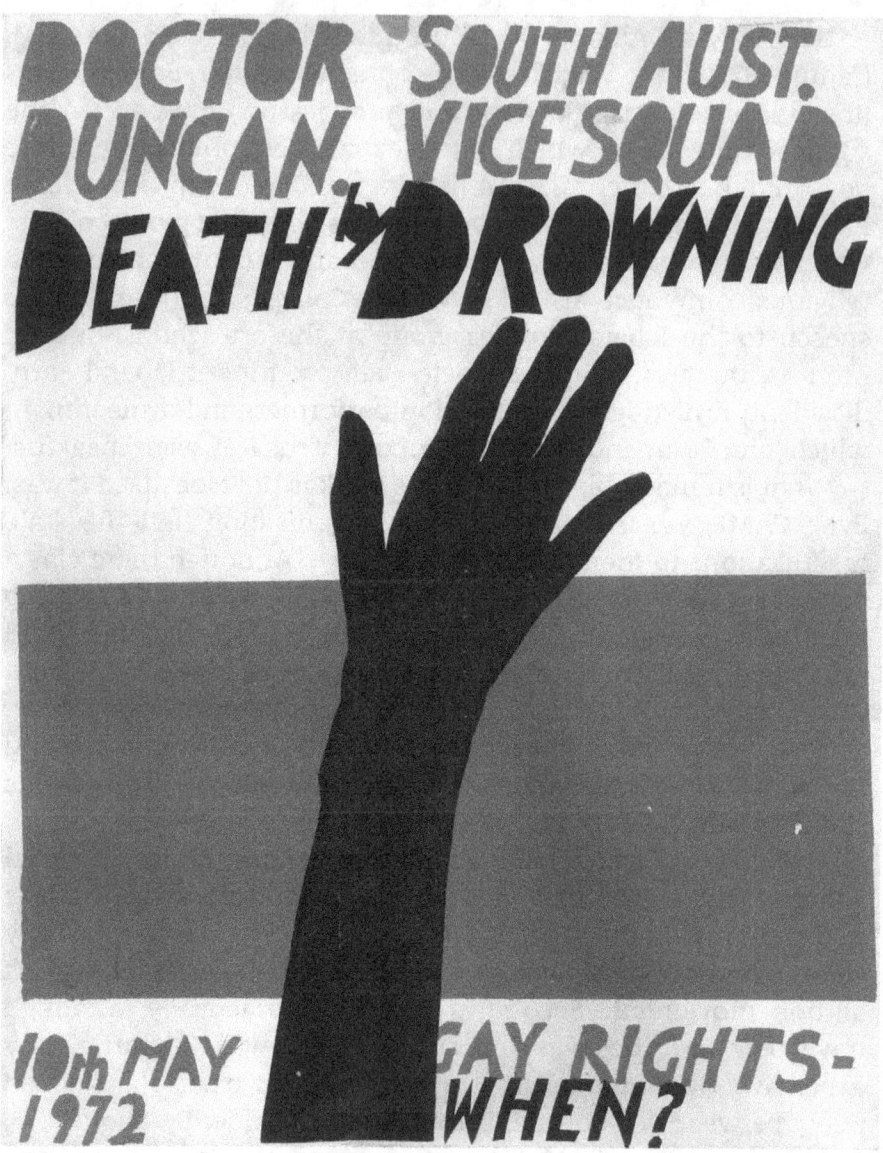

The murder of Dr George Duncan had it all – seedy sex, police corruption, violent death. Gay activists were not alone in drawing from this episode the need for homosexual law reform (AQuA).

they wanted to set up a national homosexual paper (although the fundraiser was held in Sydney). It was in Melbourne that Radicalesbians was born.

When the opportunity presented itself, the movement's activists showed that they were able to take up issues and make them national. The most dramatic example of this in the early 1970s was the campaign around the murder of Dr George Duncan. From the moment Duncan's body was dragged from the Torrens River on 11 May 1972, his death captured the imagination of the media, the public and the gay movement. Over the next few weeks, it became clear that Duncan was one of three men thrown into the river during the night of 10 May, at Adelaide's best-known beat. Gay murders were not exactly commonplace, and interest in this case was further boosted by the heady mix of respectability (Duncan was a law lecturer at Adelaide University), sex in public, violent death and police involvement. The presence of three police officers at the scene at the time of Duncan's murder, their refusal to cooperate with the investigation, the decision by the police command to call in Scotland Yard to undertake an inquiry and the South Australian government offer of a $5,000 reward and a free pardon to anyone helping the inquiry all kept the issue in the press for months (and years, on and off, given that two police officers were finally charged in 1988 and the final report was issued in 1990). Members of the gay movement took up the issue with alacrity. For many, Duncan's murder was simply the natural end point of anti-gay prejudice, and the involvement of the police was further evidence of the way in which all society's institutions were implicated in the oppression of homosexuals. Investigative journalism by Paul Foss, by this time editor of the ANU student paper; badges; and annual commemorations in many cities around Australia served to harness Duncan's death to the broader campaign for gay rights and against gay oppression, having a lasting impact on social thinking. Twenty-five years later, prominent public figures such as Bill Hayden and Moss

Cass (a sponsor of homosexual law reform in Canberra) would refer to Duncan's murder in order to illustrate the way in which society treated homosexuals in earlier days. Observing the South Australian contingent in the Mardi Gras parade in 1998, Toni Lamond remarked: 'I'm just glad they're not throwing them in the Torrens any more', a remark that a substantial proportion of her audience would have found quite incomprehensible, but which reflects the grip of Duncan's murder upon the imaginations of a generation of Australians, gay and straight.[46]

The diversity of the gay movement – its organisations, its ideas and its actions – was an important part of its effectiveness. In the first place, there was a level of activity and a type of activity for everyone. For those who were intimidated by the formality of the committee and the annual general meeting, there were dances, picnics (public and private) and consciousness-raising sessions to organise and attend. For those who couldn't afford to risk being seen on the streets or arrested, there were newsletters to produce, banners to paint and Lions Clubs to talk to. For those who wanted the intellectual stimulation and could bear the heat, Gay Liberation offered sometimes furious debates. And there was also the exhilaration of the zap and the graffiti-run. People found the work they wanted to do and settled into it. But, in doing this, they could develop the skills and confidence to go very much further than they had imagined.

Between the members and activists on the one hand, and society on the other, there was a periphery of supporters or broader layers of sympathisers, some gay, some straight, who backed (some of) the goals of the movement and who participated in (some of) its activities: attending demonstrations and pickets and other public protest actions, writing letters and lobbying opinion-makers, buying and selling the gay newspapers, wearing the badges and supporting the fundraising events. Many people became involved at some point, and they were an important pool of new participants for the movement. (Lack of new recruits was a problem that the HLRS, for example, with its more limited repertoire, had been unable to solve).[47] But even if those on the periphery didn't join up, they provided a point of contact between the movement and society more broadly. On the one hand, they took the arguments that had been made to them by gay activists into their lives – their workplaces, their families and their dinner parties – debating, persuading and testing. On the other hand, their experiences were fed back to the activists, providing a reality check on the movement's actions and ideas.

The miscellany of activities and ideas that made up the movement provided scope not merely for a very wide appeal, but for an appeal to quite contrary groups of people. It was possible for politically aware people of all persuasions (other than moral conservatives) to find a point of contact with the movement and to find a way, if they had any goodwill at all, to support the demands of lesbians and gay men. If counterculturalists were offended by the revolutionary rhetoric of the radical elements of the movement, they could nonetheless identify with the gay communal households and the talk of changing relationships. If liberals were appalled by the heckling and abuse of a prominent scientist at an academic conference, they could read with greater approval the journal distributed at the same event, which put the arguments in a calm and rational manner. Revolutionaries could simply focus on the militancy.

A good example of the way this worked was the support given to the movement by the Builders Labourers' Federation (BLF) in NSW. A union of blue-collar workers whose militancy verged on the macho, the BLF nonetheless played an important role in the early 1970s in defending victimised gay people. In June 1973, when Jeremy Fisher was expelled from his college at Macquarie University, and in March 1974, when Penny Short's teaching scholarship was revoked by the Education Department (both were discriminated against because their homosexuality came to the attention of officials), BLF members placed bans on building works on campus in support of the victimised. The role of the union's Communist Party officials was important in these instances, but they did not simply order their members into action. They appealed, successfully, to their union members' commitment to the struggle against oppression and to their traditions of solidarity.[48]

Among other social movements, too, the gay movement loomed large. Women's liberationists were often quick to support the gay movement. In Adelaide, Women's Liberation had called for the formation of a branch of CAMP some months before gays moved on the issue. Prominent Aboriginal activists such as Cheryl Buchanan acknowledged that many in the Aboriginal community were intolerant of homosexuality, and Lionel Lacey openly discussed his own homophobic past, but both were quick to draw links between the various movements for liberation. Gary Foley, then publicity officer for the Aboriginal Medical Service, wrote to CAMP in 1975 noting: 'We, as an oppressed minority group would like to express our solidarity with your group in our mutual struggle for recognition and fundamental freedom'. While Foley did not pretend that all medical service members would agree with his view, he assured CAMP that an educative process was being undertaken to 'make our people aware of the fundamentally similar aims of both organisations'.[49]

Inspired by their own courage, reassured by the extent of support that they elicited and driven by the size of the task that confronted them, members of the gay movement of the early 1970s threw themselves into their effort to change Australia. It was an effort that was to prove successful in an astonishingly short period of time.

6.

The Three Pillars of Ignorance

If members of the gay movement in the early years were committed to transforming all aspects of society, they believed very strongly that some aspects were more urgently in need of attention than others. Three areas in particular were given special attention: law, medicine and religion. It was widely assumed among liberationists that, either by design or by ignorance, legal, medical and religious institutions were the keystones of homosexual oppression. Gays were not alone in their challenge: liberalism's progress in the 1960s meant that there were many within these sectors who also hoped to bring about change. Gay activists found themselves working in conjunction with these people, sometimes in tandem, sometimes in parallel and sometimes at odds with them, in struggles that generated – despite false starts, hiccups and sudden lurches forward – clear progress.

LAW

Homosexual law reform did not always have a high priority in the 1970s. Unlike the liberals of the 1960s, who had seen their task as being primarily the decriminalisation of male sex acts in private, gay activists emphasised their wider goals and tended to think of law reform as not very important or as something that would sort itself out when public opinion had been transformed.

From its first issue and for many years after, CAMP campaigned against psychiatric abuse and pseudo-science

THE THREE PILLARS OF IGNORANCE

CAMP INK
VOLUME 2. NUMBER 11.   PRICE 30CENTS

AVERSION THERAPY
HOMOSEXUAL GUINEA PIGS
THE FORGOTTEN INDIVIDUAL

When people did turn their minds to the question of law reform, there were a number of jurisdictions that seemed likely to decriminalise. The ACT, where the issue was first raised in 1969 and where no less a figure than the federal attorney-general had expressed interest, was one. So, too, was Western Australia, where the ALP had adopted reform as party policy in 1970. But South Australia, where Don Dunstan was leading the ALP firmly in a liberal direction, claimed the prize – twice, as it happened.[1]

As early as the mid-1960s, according to his own account, Don Dunstan, attorney-general and de facto leader of the ALP in South Australia, had been pushing for homosexual law reform as part of a broader program of change and modernisation. He found himself consistently blocked by caucus; and it was only when he was elected premier in 1970 that he was able to put the wheels of change in motion.[2] They were, however, wheels that would move very slowly if Dunstan had his way. During the 1970 election campaign, Dunstan had declared the need for a complete review of the state's criminal code, including the 'spheres of private morality'. In December 1971, his government announced the establishment of an inquiry under Justice Roma Mitchell. Homosexual and drug law reform were within the terms of reference but, quite deliberately, there was no timeframe for their consideration.

This did not perturb members of the local branch of CAMP. For CAMP, law reform was very much a long-term project to which its contribution would be, initially at least, largely educative. To this end, CAMP produced an information pamphlet, and members set about meeting with opinion-makers such as clergy and medical professionals. George Duncan's murder on 10 May 1972 and the subsequent furore threw CAMP's careful plans into disarray. Suddenly, the oppression of homosexuals was big news, and the law reform genie was out of the bottle. Members of CAMP, civil libertarians, such as the Moral Freedom Group, and the *Advertiser* all drew from the murder arguments for law reform. As late as 6 July 1972, the ALP's attorney-general refused to refer the issue of law reform to the Mitchell inquiry; but, as his views were being reported, Murray Hill, a little-known Liberal Country League (LCL) member of the upper house, was announcing that he intended to introduce a private member's bill to decriminalise homosexuality. Forced to respond, both major parties declared that they would allow their members a free vote, although it seems clear that the ALP had decided to seize the moment and to ensure that the bill was passed. In a meeting with the executive of CAMP, Dunstan's press secretary indicated that the ALP would deliver a majority in the lower house. It was CAMP's task to win over the upper house, by far the harder job. In a chamber heavily weighted to rural and conservative interests, the ALP had four seats out of 20; while some of the LCL members shared Hill's liberal outlook, no one estimated the number of supporters to be more than six or seven.

The sudden eruption of this debate at a time when CAMP was too new and small to manage all the issues was a serious burden. Nonetheless, the group took up its task as best it could. The executive produced a circular for MPs that presented the case for reform and posted it off, along with copies of two eminently liberal books – Brian Magee's *One in Twenty* and D. J. West's *Homosexuality*. The executive also wrote to all members of CAMP urging them to lobby their MPs, providing a list of 15 points to be made, and produced 1,000 badges ('How Many More Duncans? Legalise Homosexuality Now') for public distribution. But important areas of activity were overlooked: in the *Advertiser*'s letters column over this period, only four of 15 letters supported law reform.

Hill's bill was far from ideal. CAMP objected to the age of consent being set at 21, to the very narrow definition of 'in private' (in the presence of not more than two people, a law that did not apply, for example, to heterosexual sexual encounters) and to provisions on procuring that made it impossible for one man to proposition another under virtually any circumstances. CAMP argued with Hill on these points to no avail and, as it happened, the final outcome was even worse than Hill intended. In the upper house, the bill was amended beyond recognition. No longer did it decriminalise homosexual acts between consenting adults in private. All it did was to make the conditions under which sex took place – two men aged over 21, in a consensual act, in the presence of no other person – a defence in court. That is, homosexual acts were still illegal, and arrests could still be made, but where the conditions were met and were proved in court, no conviction would be recorded. Attempts in the lower house to reverse these changes failed and, after consultation with CAMP negotiators, ALP members in the upper house allowed the bill to pass into law. On 18 October 1972, South Australia became the first place in Australia where homosexual acts were, if not exactly legal, no longer entirely illegal.

A further attempt at reform was on the cards even before the ink was dry on this first effort. CAMP declared immediately that it saw this as merely a staging post, and Murray Hill himself was soon discussing the best means to effect changes. Central to these hopes was the fact that, of the 10 members of the upper house who had voted against decriminalisation, seven were up for re-election in March 1973. If enough of these were replaced by ALP members, there might be the numbers to pass a better bill. Although these hopes were to be disappointed when the ALP won only eight of the 20 seats, the newly elected ALP member Peter Duncan (no relation to George) immediately flagged his intention to introduce a radical reform of the South Australian criminal code's sex laws that would include, among other things, the complete decriminalisation of homosexual acts and the introduction of an equal age of consent.

CAMP did what it could during this round of reform, but the organisation had been seriously strained by its efforts in 1972, and there was a nagging sense that perhaps its visibility had been counterproductive. For the most part, in 1973, CAMP chose to remain in the background, concealed behind an organisation called CHARLES (the Committee for Homosexual Law Reform in South Australia).

CHARLES was established as the respectable face of law reform and composed of (heterosexual) luminaries, and it was felt that it offered a better conduit for pro-reform argument and lobbying.

But the shape of gay politics had been shifting during this period. In mid-1973, CAMP's most active member, Jon Ruwoldt, frustrated by what he saw as the conservatism of the organisation, broke away to form the more militant GAA. Although GAA was initially committed to supporting the campaign for reform, it was soon advised that, because of the cautiousness and conservatism of many MPs, including many of those prepared to support homosexual law reform, it should 'tread carefully to ensure [the law's] safe passage'. It can hardly have been a coincidence that, at this moment, GAA suddenly rediscovered the radical, abstentionist position on law reform, declaring in September:

> In effect, we have changed our heads so much that thoughts of law reform have long been left behind. Gay activists are generally far removed from the conventional power struggle that decides which laws are enacted and which repealed.[3]

Abstention was not as easy as it seemed, however. In late October 1973, a debate erupted in Melbourne about the presence of gay speakers in high schools, where, at the invitation of teachers, they had been addressing classes on the issue of gay rights. To give the debate a local flavour, a journalist with Adelaide's *Advertiser* approached Jon Ruwoldt for his views. Not surprisingly, he indicated his support for such initiatives and suggested that GAA would be seeking to emulate the Melburnians in the new year. The *Advertiser* was a keen supporter of decriminalisation, so it is unlikely that the article was a setup – and it is hard to see how any radical could have said anything else – but the timing could not have been worse. Duncan's bill was before the parliament, and the issue of homosexuals and school children was seized upon by his opponents to argue that reform was opening the way for proselytising among impressionable young people.

The bill failed again in the upper house, though only by a single vote – that of a supporter of reform who claimed he failed to hear the call to vote. Members of GAA, among others, were furious at this further setback and declared: 'We must actively resist the demands of the Institution and Government on us, defy and even destroy them'. Such statements did not help when the bill was, extraordinarily, reintroduced under an obscure regulation. This time the vote against was stronger, with at least one member blaming the media fuss and the alleged threats of violence from GAA for his change of mind. However, Duncan's fight was not over. Two years and another election later, with the numbers now decisively in favour of reform and the press, the archbishop of Adelaide, the Council of Civil Liberties and the Australian Psychological Association all publicly voicing their support, the bill finally breezed through parliament. It received Royal Assent on 18 September 1975 and took effect one week later. Despite all the to-ing and fro-ing, failures, setbacks and delays of one sort or another, South Australia was still the first jurisdiction in Australia to enact real homosexual law reform.

Next cab off the rank was the ACT. Here, too, the reform process was a long one; but rather than coming out of the blue, as had been the case in South Australia, it was preceded by years of agitation, during which hopes were repeatedly raised only to be dashed again. The story begins with the publication in 1969 of a draft criminal code for the ACT that proposed to leave unchanged the criminal status of homosexual acts. It was a proposal that the ACT HLRS and other organisations strongly opposed; and when Tom Hughes, the federal Liberal government's attorney-general, suggested publicly in May 1970 that homosexual acts ought not necessarily to fall within the ambit of the criminal law, expectations for reform were high. James Grieve of the HLRS sent Thomas Mautner a copy of Hughes' speech with a scribbled note that declared: 'Mon cher Thomas: Salut! As you see, we blew our trumpets and the walls of Jericho came tumbling down.'[4]

Confidence in Hughes was, however, misplaced; under pressure from his conservative colleagues, he soon retreated. But grounds for optimism remained. The *Canberra Times* had responded to Hughes' initial comments with an editorial calling for reform, and key members of the ALP were also starting to voice support. The election of a federal Labor government in December 1972 was taken to be a good sign.

Measured against the early storm of reforms in other areas, the decriminalisation of male homosexuality did not loom large for the Whitlam government, but it is surprising that – in its entire three years in power – the ALP failed to carry through any kind of homosexual law reform at all. Again, there had been early positive signs. On 18 October 1973, the House of Representatives endorsed by 60 votes to 40 a motion that read: 'That in the opinion of this House homosexual acts between consenting adults in private should not be subject to the criminal law'. The motion was a private member's bill moved by the former Liberal prime minister, John Gorton, although it had been initiated (and was seconded) by the ALP's Moss Cass.[5] Cass was a longstanding supporter of liberal causes, including homosexual law reform, who decided, at the suggestion of staff member Peter Blazey (gay, but not yet out), to act on the issue. The motion did not create much public interest. Cass remembers little in the way of lobbying, for example, and has suggested that, after the crushing defeat of an earlier abortion law reform bill, it was assumed that this motion would fail too. Gorton expected no more than eight or nine votes from Liberals and none at all from the Country Party. Cass thought that a majority of ALP members would vote against.[6]

The debate was brief. A mere hour was allowed, because the house was scheduled to attend an official luncheon with, by a happy chance, the Queen. Gorton and Cass spoke, and there was time for only two other speakers. John Cramer's speech against the motion was not unexpected; he was known to be a conservative on such matters. Bert James, on the other hand, who rose to speak next, was a surprise. He was a Labor man of the old school, as Cass recalls, gruff, rather unsophisticated and an ex-policeman to boot. To everyone's surprise, he spoke quietly and passionately in favour of the motion, and it is Cass's view that he swung many votes. Whatever the reasons, the vote found odd bedfellows. A significant bloc of opposition to the motion came from the right-wing faction of the ALP, reflecting the conservative Catholicism of this group. Among these was a young Paul Keating, who, as prime minister some 20 years later, was to play a very different role in relation to the gay rights agenda. From the other side of politics, a number of conservatives unexpectedly voted for the motion. Approached afterwards by Peter Blazey, who noted this, Doug Anthony, the leader of the Country Party and one of those who supported the motion, is said to have laughingly declared: 'You Labor boys think you're so trendy. But what you don't realise is that a lot of us have been to boarding school!'[7]

Even so, law reform was not in place; the motion had been an expression of opinion only. Because the ACT was shortly due to receive self-government, Cass and Gorton had agreed that they would not impose reform, but merely state the parliament's view that such reform was desirable, leaving it to the soon-to-be-elected territorial assembly to act. The ACT Legislative Assembly had its first sitting in October 1974, so, debating the issue on 2 December, it, at least, was moving promptly on the matter.[8] Unfortunately, it had only advisory powers. Its debate resulted in a motion in favour of law reform, but no actual reform. The final bill for reform was presented to the assembly in May 1975,[9] and it was finally passed on 22 July. By the time the ALP government fell in November 1975, however, the ordinance had still not been signed into law by the attorney-general. In mid-1976, the whole process began all over again under a new Liberal attorney-general, Bob Ellicott, who had not been happy with the earlier version.[10] The decriminalisation of male homosexual acts in the ACT finally took place in November 1976.

RELIGION

Many gays identified Christianity and the Christian churches as the most ancient and implacable enemies of gay people. For those influenced by the radicalism of Gay Liberation, 'Christianity [was] an agent of reactionary capitalism', the church was 'one of the greatest oppressors of homosexuals' and the idea of a gay Christian was a contradiction in terms.[11] Even more moderate gays felt compelled to note both the power and the negative role played by the churches. CAMP NSW observed: 'Most Christian theologians condemn homosexual practices; the Christian church in Australia is powerful in the maintenance and formation of public attitudes on morality.'[12] It is not surprising that much of the movement's work in the early years was directed at challenging the churches and their oppressive attitudes and behaviour.

Yet there is good reason to doubt the assumption that Christian churches have been consistently homophobic, either in their theology or in their social practice. Even in the 1950s, it is surprising how little attention they paid to the issue. David Hilliard has observed that, prior to the 1960s, this question was 'rarely mentioned, let alone discussed, in the Anglican church press'.[13] And when the Anglican archbishop of Brisbane spoke at length to his synod on the 'new morality' in 1964, he noted:

> the falling away of Christian standards of morality and sexual relationships;...the prevalence of fornication and pre-marital intercourse;... the increase of indecent and pornographic literature[14]

but made no mention of homosexuality. Until the late 1960s, homosexuality was not a topic that the clergy felt the need to address.

In the 1960s, when they did start to take up the issue, far from opposing the new, more liberal attitudes that were emerging around them, many churches actively embraced such views. At a 1967 NSW Presbyterian Church seminar on the church's responsibility towards homosexuals, Arthur North, the convener of the Church and Nation Committee, expressed this attitude clearly:

> it is not the function of law to intervene in the private morality of citizens. Nor is it the duty of the Church to try to impose Christian standards ...upon people by means of the law.[15]

These were not merely North's idiosyncratic views. The General Assembly of the church, which followed this seminar, voted to publish and circulate the seminar's papers and endorsed its call for homosexual law reform. If the letters columns of the press are any guide, this distinction between sin and crime had been taken up, too, by the congregations. In response to a *Sydney Morning Herald* report of the Presbyterians' vote, the Reverend H. A. Brown of Cootamundra wrote to protest against the 'moral landslide' towards sin that had caught up 'Church leaders, parliamentarians, newspaper editors, etc'. On 8 August, six letters in reply were published: all positioned themselves within the terms of the religious debate, and all but one disagreed with Brown, expressly drawing a distinction between sin and crime.[16]

None of this support for law reform should be taken as support for claims that homosexuality was a valid expression of sexuality. The Presbyterian Assembly pointedly amended the Church and Nation Committee's motion to note that it believed homosexuality to be 'contrary to man's ethical development [and] productive of personal moral disintegration'.[17] And even those who were prepared to go further, as the Reverend W. G. Coughlan did in his paper to the seminar, arguing: 'we are coming to see that all sexual need, attitude and expression is inseparable from the total personality, and reflects that personality with remarkable faithfulness',[18] were forced to admit under questioning that homosexual acts were undoubtedly sinful.[19] It was to be quite some time before other denominations were to follow the path blazed by the NSW Presbyterians in the 1960s, but a liberal current within religious circles was to play an important part in the debates within the churches when the gay movement exploded onto the political scene in the early 1970s, forcing Christians, no less than politicians, doctors and other citizens, to turn their minds to the problem of homosexuality. This liberalism, and the distinction between sin and crime especially, was to provide a means by which many churches could meet the movement halfway.

This is certainly what the Anglican Church, for the most part, did. In the late 1960s and early 1970s, inquiries of various kinds were set up in the dioceses of Melbourne, Canberra–Goulburn, Brisbane, Adelaide and North Queensland. These inquiries studied the matter and reported back to synods (annual meetings) with motions for debate. Melbourne's case is fairly typical. After an unexpected motion calling for homosexual law reform produced a bitter and unpleasant debate at the 1970 synod, the matter was referred to the Social Questions Committee. The committee undertook a year of 'extensive reading, participation in seminars and consultation with psychiatrists, lawyers, theologians, sociologists and others' and produced a final report that was primarily concerned with the legal aspects of homosexuality, although there were also brief attachments addressing theological considerations and sociological and psychological research, the purpose of which was explicitly stated as being 'to demonstrate the diversity of possible views'. In the end, although committee members found much on which they disagreed, they were unanimous in recommending that laws 'which render criminal those homosexual acts committed in private between consenting males of 18 years or over, should be repealed'.[20]

In a number of dioceses, reports very much along these lines were received and, except in the case of North Queensland, motions to adopt the reports and their recommendations were passed. The role of gay people in these investigations was minimal, in some cases non-existent – although, in the diocese of North-Western Australia, the mover of the motion sought and received advice from CAMP in Perth.[21] What was at work here was the blooming of the liberal distinction between sin and crime, which is clearly spelled out in all the reports. The seeds of such a position had been sprouting in Australia since the mid-1960s. What brought on this sudden flowering was the way in which the movement had pushed homosexuality and homosexual law reform onto the public agenda. Although activists can claim little direct credit for the Anglicans' interest, without the sudden explosive appearance of the movement it is unlikely that many such motions would have seen the light of day.

In some situations, gays did play a somewhat more direct role in effecting change. In January 1975, the Society of Friends (or Quakers, as they are popularly known) issued a call for 'a change in the law relating to homosexuality...to eliminate discrimination against homosexuals'.[22] This had been the outcome of the group's consensus form of decision making and had, unlike many of the statements and motions of other churches, involved the active participation of all members. It had been initiated by Roger Sawkins, a member of the Society who had been a member of CAMP in Queensland and in contact with the Sydney CAMP since 1970. Sawkins was an active member of Campus CAMP at Queensland University from 1973 and a regular at the clubrooms in the city. He had attempted to set up a telephone counselling service at about the same time. It was as both a Friend and a gay activist that he was involved in eliciting the Quaker statement of 1975.

In contrast to activists' attitudes to the medical profession, which was almost universally hostile, their attitudes towards religion and the churches varied. Most branches of CAMP contained members who were committed to an active engagement with religion, hoping to bring about a change of attitude or policy, and who set up working groups to deal with the churches and clergy.[23] Initially, at least, these groups were politically oriented and operated in much the same way as the other groups within CAMP that concentrated on changing the law or psychiatric practices. Sydney's Working Group on Religion was composed of Christians and non-Christians whose goal, as John Ware saw it, was 'to challenge the church's notion on homosexuality'.[24]

The religion working groups were active in a number of ways. In both NSW and South Australia, statements on homosexuality and religion were prepared and circulated to clergy.[25] Members met with individual clergy and provided speakers to student Christian groups and church committees of inquiry and seminars. When demonstrations were required, activists also organised pickets and protests. A 'Witness, Vigil, Demo, whatever you like to call it' was held outside St Mary's Catholic Cathedral and St Andrew's Anglican Cathedral in Sydney during Easter 1973, at which leaflets were quietly distributed explaining that 'We are Christian homosexuals and are holding this vigil to pray for our sisters and brothers who are being persecuted by the church'.[26] When Cliff Richard, a well-known pop singer, Christian and supporter of Britain's right-wing FOL performed in Hyde Park, a number of members went to leaflet the concert.[27] There was even time for community outreach – Cross+Section, CAMP NSW's church group, held occasional working bees at a Salvation Army boys' home (having been pointedly refused permission to support a home for children with cerebral palsy).[28] This activism was to reach a fuller flowering in the period after 1973.

PSYCHIATRY

If religion was, for many gays, the most ancient enemy, others believed that its hegemony was being supplanted rapidly by the medical profession. Looking back at the early years of the movement, Sue Wills has written: 'Perhaps the most pervasive influence that Camp Inc had to try to combat was that of psychiatry'.[29]

She is pointing in particular to the danger presented by the broad public acceptance of psychiatric definitions of what constituted 'sick' and 'not sick'. The Counter Psychiatry Group of the Gay Liberation Front in Melbourne made the same point, albeit in a more polemical tone, when it referred to psychiatrists as the:

> High Priests of modern society...reinforcing, under the guise of scientific objectivity, primitive Judeo-Christian morality. The only difference between now and then is that what was once regarded as a sin is today regarded as a sickness.[30]

These were not unreasonable charges. When asked, people did, very commonly, identify the causes of homosexuality largely in terms of congenital factors or life experiences of a (pseudo) psychological type.[31]

It would not be true to say, however, that medicalised notions exercised the sort of totalitarian power that activists sometimes assigned to them. In the first place, many gay people rejected such ideas, at least in their most negative form. Lucy Chesser and Ruth Ford have shown that, even in the 1950s and 1960s, very many lesbians lived their lives indifferent to, or in ignorance of, medicalised notions of perversion.[32] And we see something similar in a survey conducted among Society Five members in Melbourne in 1972.[33] Ninety-seven members answered a survey that asked whether or not they had ever sought help with their sexuality from psychiatrists, social workers, psychologists, doctors, clergy or other counsellors. Nearly half of the respondents had never consulted any of these authorities, and many of the remainder had done so only briefly.

Furthermore, members of the medical profession were far from united in their beliefs on homosexuality. The existence of debates and competing schools of thought prevented the emergence of a dominant school and destabilised the various claims to scientific knowledge. More importantly, doctors were by no means merely the passive bearers of social or ideological or occupational positions. As J.F.J. Cade, the psychiatrist superintendent of Victoria's Mental Health Authority, noted, his own views on homosexuality varied according to whether he was thinking about it as an elderly heterosexual happily married grandfather, a Catholic who accepted the teaching of the church in regard to sexual morality or a doctor who believed it irrelevant and mischievous to make moral judgements about patients.[34] Many doctors' politics were tending, at this stage, towards the liberal. By the 1970s, doctors were, as a group, rather more liberal than much of the rest of society, reflecting in part their education and middle-class status, both of which correlated strongly during this period with higher levels of tolerance for procedures such as abortion and behaviour such as homosexuality and drug use.[35] A 1974 ballot of members of the Australian Psychological Association found that approximately 73 percent of respondents wanted the association to condemn discrimination against homosexuals.[36] Psychiatrists, too, even in their professional capacity, were moving rapidly towards opinions that were increasingly accepting of homosexuality. A 1973 survey among psychiatrists and trainee psychiatrists in NSW found that only one-third of the qualified and less than 20 percent of the trainees believed that homosexuality was a neurotic disorder. More than half of both groups saw it as a 'developmental anomaly not necessarily or commonly associated with neurotic symptoms', and a large proportion (14 percent of the qualified and 23 percent of the trainees) viewed it as a normal variant comparable to left-handedness.[37]

Nowhere is this shift more clearly demonstrated than in the adoption during these years of pro-homosexual policies by the psychiatric profession's peak body, the Australian and New Zealand College of Psychiatry (ANZCP). In October 1972, the Federal Council had added its voice to those calling for homosexual law reform, but in 1973, moves were made to extend this to the expression of more liberal professional opinion. Central to this was Dr Ron Barr, then senior lecturer in psychiatry at the University of NSW.[38] Dr Barr was first prompted to have the college adopt a position on homosexuality in May 1973, when he heard of Moss Cass's plan to introduce a homosexual law reform motion into the federal parliament. He believed that, if psychiatrists added their voices to those being raised in support of law reform and tolerance, members of parliament and the wider public might be moved in their views. At his urging, the ANZCP Federal Council established a subcommittee that spent three or four months researching and preparing a draft memorandum. There was a review and evaluation of the relevant literature, as well as the survey of psychiatrists and trainee psychiatrists referred to above. The results of this work gave Barr's group important evidence for its argument that a majority of psychiatrists were not simply in favour of decriminalisation but were, even more importantly, of the view that homosexuality was not, in and of itself, commonly or necessarily associated with neurotic symptoms. The draft memorandum to this effect was submitted to, and endorsed by, the college's Federal Council on 13 October 1973. The point of the memorandum was to give ammunition to those supporting homosexual law reform in the federal parliament, and a copy of the report went promptly to Moss Cass's office. From there, its content found its way into his speech to parliament. The press, too, was informed; on 18 October, on the very morning that parliament was to debate the Gorton–Cass motion, the *Australian* and the *Sydney Morning Herald* reported the ANZCP decision.[39] The interlocking processes of liberalisation and the gay social movement are clear here. Barr wanted to support Cass, who in turn was inspired in his motion not merely by a longstanding liberalism, but by the promptings of Peter Blazey. Blazey was not yet open about his homosexuality but was nonetheless being pushed towards politicisation by the movement around him. There are no easy answers to the questions raised by social change, but the elements at work are often clear enough.

The threat, both social and individual, posed to homosexuals by psychiatric theory had been one of the motives inspiring John Ware to form CAMP, although it was not until early 1972, when Sue Wills joined the organisation, that he had someone else who was willing and able to work on the issue with him.[40] The struggle against the medical profession focused in particular upon aversion therapy – the use of nausea-inducing drugs or electric-shock treatment to 'cure' homosexuality. This technique was practised in Australia by Sydney-based academic-therapists Sid Lovibond and Neil McConaghy. McConaghy, in particular, was an active proponent of the technique and rapidly became the focus of the movement's campaigning.

The campaign involved, as usual, a number of aspects, drawing upon a broad repertoire of activities. There were protests and demonstrations of various kinds. But activists also produced a theoretical critique of the medical model and its various components, and they worked, too, to help those homosexuals whose lives and psyches had been damaged by a vicious and intolerant society. Initially, at least, many imagined that the argument could be won by reasoned debate, believing that, while the medical model was dangerously skewed against homosexuals, medical practitioners themselves did not necessarily hold prejudices. Indeed, the real problem with the professionals seemed to many of the activists to be ignorance rather than hostility. As early as July 1972, Wills had organised a debate on aversion therapy between McConaghy and Robin Winkler, a lecturer in psychology at the University of NSW. Winkler's paper was later produced as a pamphlet by SGL, although it was only one of a large number of writings published by the movement on the topic.[41] The gay critique of the medical model involved a number of elements.

The scientific claims of the profession were questioned. The quarrelling schools of thought, the role of biases and values drawn from prevailing social norms, the inability of the various 'cures' to do their work and the violence inherent in aversion therapies were highlighted. The cumulative effect of these criticisms was to present a profession which, far from its self-presentation as objective, dispassionate and caring, came across instead as riddled with vested interests, carelessness, cruelty and threats to, and breaches of, human rights.

It was never, however, sufficient to argue with the profession, either on its own terms or in the passionate tone that some of the critiques adopted. In August 1973, when Professor McConaghy invited CAMP to provide speakers for his conference on Psychiatry and Liberation, those who had organised the earlier debate with Robin Winkler now refused to participate. Gay Liberation was speaking for all gay and lesbian activists when it angrily declared:

> we're just not prepared to come along and 'rationally' debate our positions with our oppressors. No, we're fed up with that. We're sick of being reasonable any more when the oppressive horrors of aversion therapy, psychosurgery and neo-Freudian bullshit psychotherapy continue to fuck us over.[42]

Now was the time for action. The desire for more direct action superseded the original intention to boycott McConaghy's conference. When McConaghy rose to speak, critics in the audience released balloons and hurled eggs. Chanting and abuse rained down on him.[43] Just as dramatic was an action by members of SGL against Dr Harry Bailey.[44] Bailey was a prominent psychosurgeon (later to achieve notoriety for his use of deep-sleep therapy at Chelmsford) who employed brain surgery as a means of curing homosexuality. In April 1973, a small group distributed a leaflet which denounced Bailey's work as 'Psychobutchery of Gays', outside and within the building where he had his rooms. Then they burst into Bailey's waiting room and noisily dumped a bucket of sheep's brains on the floor.

For those to whom the damage had already been done, help was required. The Homosexual Guidance Service (HGS) was established by Sue Wills and others within CAMP in April 1972 with the short-term aim of helping troubled homosexuals and their families.[45] HGS offered individual counselling, discussion groups and even assertiveness training courses for homosexuals. HGS's contacts provided the service with the ability to help gays who wanted to, or who were under pressure to, seek treatment. It had a number of sympathetic psychiatrists to whom those insisting on treatment could be safely referred. Wills tells of one woman whose parents insisted that she see a psychiatrist. She went to one of the HGS's psychiatrist supporters, who then wrote to the parents advising that a cure was neither possible nor desirable.[46]

By the mid-1970s, it was clear that members of the medical profession were starting to shift their attitudes. One small sign of this may be seen in Brian Davies' book, *An Introduction to Clinical Psychiatry*. Davies was Cato professor of psychiatry at Melbourne University, and three editions of this book were published by his department as a textbook for students. The discussion of homosexuality in the first two editions is identical. The 1977 edition, however, adds a sentence to the section on aetiology: 'It is inappropriate to use an "illness model" in considering homosexuality' and omits the previous editions' discussion of psychoanalytic and behaviour therapy forms of treatment.[47]

More importantly, over the course of the 1970s, medical practitioners found that fewer and fewer homosexuals were reporting for treatment.[48] Neil McConaghy himself estimated that:

> over the last two years, the number of people seeking treatment for specifically 'homosexual urges' was down to about one-third of the average of the years 1964–1976.[49]

In part, this widespread shift was due to a new conviction among doctors that referrals for treatment were inappropriate; clearly, the movement's direct efforts to convince doctors of this must have played a part. But the growing confidence of gay people themselves and the impact of gay pride were important, too.

Gay liberation and liberalism were uneasy bedfellows but, faced with a society in which homophobia seemed deeply embedded, gay activists found themselves working alongside heterosexuals in their struggles for reform. Drawing upon the well-established consensus among liberals in favour of law reform and tolerance, the two currents shared common targets. The division of labour was not a neat one. There were perhaps as many differences as points of agreement. The two groups worked in parallel as often as in active cooperation, but their efforts enjoyed sufficient success to justify the work. By the mid-1970s, the law, the major churches and key sections of the medical profession were starting to shift their positions.

7.

Hastening Slowly, 1974–78

The high point of the first wave of gay and lesbian activism came in September 1973 with the national celebration of Gay Pride Week. Originally proposed by SGL as a way of breaking out of a widespread feeling of deadlock and stagnation, the idea was adopted enthusiastically in Melbourne, Brisbane and Adelaide. Targeted at all 'the institutions of our oppression: the police, courts, job discrimination, the bigoted churchmen and politicians, the media, the psychiatrists, the aversion therapists, the military, the schools, the universities, the workplaces', the week aimed to 'change the mind of the prejudiced, the fearful, the conditioned, the sexually repressed, all those who in oppressing us, oppress themselves'.[1]

Gay Pride Week embraced many of the forms of activism developed over the previous few years: militancy and confrontation, education, coming out and living openly. Melbourne activists organised graffiti paintups, a dance, a talk to high school students and an evening for parents of gays. Gay Liberation members appeared on television and radio programs. About 250 people turned up for the Friday night demonstration, but, in many ways, the centrepiece of the week was the picnic in the Botanical Gardens, attended by 150 lesbians and gay men in almost equal numbers. The picnic was big, bold and splashy and offered an opportunity to 'blow a few straight minds'. There

Digger, a radical and countercultural newspaper, marks Gay Pride Week.

Gay Pride Week – noisy, joyful, national... (The Kiss, Rennie Ellis)

were radical drag dressers, hand-in-hand promenades along the pathways, rowdy gay songs and a game of drop the hankie that attracted the attention of the constabulary. Public response to the picnic was one of 'good humour at least and an easy-going acceptance at best'.[2] In Brisbane, Campus CAMP marked the week with a similar range of activities: turning up in King George Square, at the university and outside Brisbane Grammar to sell badges and fairy floss and hand out leaflets and boiled lollies. Members also made a case for gay pride on several radio programs.[3] Adelaide was lively and vibrant. For 10 days, almost every day was marked by some event – a press conference, a dance, church leafleting, speak-outs, a march and a fair. Will Sergeant remembers it as exciting, uplifting and exhilarating. After a speak-out in the city, a small group who were too hyped to go home took themselves to Myer. They rode the elevators, singing and chanting, and staged a love-in on a double bed in David Jones department store.[4]

In Sydney, however, things turned nasty.[5] After a week marked by a speak-out, a festival in the Domain and a public meeting on the Saturday, about 200 lesbians and gay men and their friends set out from the Town Hall to lay a memorial wreath at the cenotaph in Hyde Park, only to find the police determined to stop them. There were clashes all along the route as protesters, armed with balloons, banners and streamers, broke through police lines and darted through the traffic chanting: 'Ho, ho, homosexual, the ruling class is ineffectual' and 'Out of the beats and onto the streets'. Several were arrested and, when the crowd marched to the Central police station to demand their release, there were further arrests – bringing the total to 18.

It was a stormy end to both Gay Pride Week and a whole stage in the gay movement's history. If gay pride and gay power had never looked more potent than in September 1973, the reality was rather different. Gay politics was about to enter a new phase, a more difficult time in many ways, marked by fragmentation into special-interest groups and a much less visible practice. But it was not, as is often assumed, a less effective period.

It has been widely argued that, after Gay Pride Week in 1973, the gay movement went into a period of decline, even quiescence, that lasted until the police attack on the first Mardi Gras in 1978. In fact, upon examination, it becomes clear that the movement continued its work throughout this period and continued to make progress. A new political period, offering both new challenges and new opportunities, was dawning. It is to the credit of gay and lesbian activists that they found ways of adapting to the challenges and seizing the opportunities.

The opportunities included very much greater access to the powerholders in society. In particular, the Whitlam government's enthusiasm for committees of inquiry (which was taken up by state governments of various persuasions as well) provided gay activists with the chance to make themselves and their demands heard in a variety of quarters. The inquiry did not need to be about homosexuality; it was only necessary that those conducting the inquiry accepted that homosexuals had a right to speak on the issue under examination. During the middle years of the 1970s, submissions on an extraordinary range of issues were prepared and presented. CAMP NSW alone presented papers to the Australian Law Reform Commission's privacy inquiry; federal government inquiries into education and training, the ABC and the intelligence and security services; and NSW government inquiries into sexism in education and prisons. Even the ALP's national committee of inquiry into party affairs was not ignored.[6]

Underpinning this new openness was a striking shift in public opinion. In 1967, Paul Wilson and Duncan Chappell found that a mere 22 percent of the population were in favour of the decriminalisation of homosexuality, 63 percent were opposed, and 15 percent were unsure or declined to express an opinion. In 1974, in a very similar survey, the percentage supporting decriminalisation had leapt to 54 percent, with those opposed reduced to 26 percent. The undecided category was at an unusually high 20 percent.[7] There was, by this time, majority support for decriminalisation in NSW, Victoria and South Australia, in the capital cities (country residents had a 49.5 percent support rate against 32 percent opposition), in all age groups under 50 years and among supporters of the main political parties. Professionals, managers and white-collar and skilled workers all offered better than 50 percent support, as did groups educated to upper high school level and beyond.

On the rather more interesting question of whether people thought homosexual acts were right or wrong (the terms were not defined), 48 percent of people surveyed in 1971 described them as wrong or very wrong; 25 percent as right or harmless. Here, too, there was a shift taking place; and two years later, in 1974, the figures were 39 percent and 29 percent respectively. While most people still thought homosexuality was wrong, this attitude was rapidly losing its hold.[8] What this shift might have meant in practice is revealed in responses to a question posed by an opinion poll in May 1973. Asked what they would do if they discovered two young men were living together in a homosexual relationship, 74 percent of respondents said they would mind their own business. Another 13 percent would disapprove but not otherwise act, and eight percent would tell either the police or other authorities.[9] Most people may not have approved of homosexuality, but they were firmly of the opinion that it was no business of theirs or the law's. These shifts in opinion were quite remarkable in themselves and in their rapidity and in their consistent trajectory towards toleration. Changing attitudes had produced a solid bloc of citizens in favour of decriminalisation and a broad tolerance of homosexuality – which, in turn, allowed politicians and administrators to treat lesbians and gay men as a legitimate part of the body politic.

And yet, there were negative developments in the middle years of the 1970s, too, which had a marked impact upon the work of all the movements. The first of these was the faltering of the radical momentum of the late 1960s and early 1970s. Ironically, the Whitlam government, elected in December 1972, contributed to this process. In the first place, by resolving many of the issues around which radicals had been protesting and luring large numbers of activists off the streets and into myriad consultative and administrative structures, the new government undermined the very forces that had brought it to power and contributed so much to the transformation of Australian life. Even those who were not directly coopted came to depend more and more upon the government to do things for them or, at the very least, to provide resources.[10] For others, the government's rapid descent into disarray, its failure to carry through many of the reforms that it had promised and the shocking discovery, with the crushing electoral defeat in late 1975, that the mass of Australians did not share the vision was a shattering blow to their confidence.

For the gay movement, the first sign of the changing political climate was plunging membership numbers. In Melbourne, Society Five reported a drop from about 500 members at the end of November 1975 to about 270 a year later, and membership was down to 190 in July 1977. In 1975, Melbourne Gay Liberation was claiming up to 20 active members, well down on the scores who had been attending meetings on a weekly basis during 1972. In Brisbane in 1974, the executive of CAMP declared: 'we urgently require a tremendous boost in our membership'. In Perth, CAMP reported a slump in numbers through 1973. The rise of the commercial scene was most commonly noted as the reason, and certainly, given that CAMP and Gay Liberation's dances had been a major source of both membership and money, their decline in the face of the rising challenge from the scene exacerbated the financial difficulties of the groups.

The effect of a broader decline in interest in radical politics is visible, too. When Melbourne Gay Liberation reviewed its mailing list in 1975, it asked those on it to indicate their wish to continue to receive the newsletter. The result was a reduction on the list from 600 to 250 people. In NSW, CAMP's executive, noting the declining visibility of the group in the press, toyed with the idea of writing an anti-homosexual letter to the *Sydney Morning Herald* in an attempt to spark a debate in the letters columns.[11]

For some groups, the difficulties proved fatal. In Adelaide, CAMP's journal *Canary* ceased production in late 1973, by which time the group itself was virtually moribund.[12] GAA's *Boiled Sweets* last appeared in July 1974, and, while the newsletter indicated that a number of groups were still meeting regularly – Radicalesbians and gay men each held weekly meetings, and Gay Liberation fortnightly[13] – there is no evidence that any of these groups survived much longer.

SGL, too, experienced difficulties. Although 1973 opened as its 'most successful year in terms of activities and visibility'[14] with a burst of zaps, by April a crisis meeting had agreed upon a retreat from over-commitment (abandoning the Gay Liberation Centre in favour of shared accommodation with CAMP, for example).[15] The September 1973 Gay Pride Week had been proposed by Sydney precisely as a way to revitalise the movement; for all its noisy, joyful visibility, it failed in its main aim. At yet another crisis meeting in October 1973, it had been decided to dissolve SGL and to form the Gay Liberation Front (GLF), an umbrella organisation for a number of autonomous groups, including a political action group, gay teachers', lesbian liberation, newsletter, campus, police and psychiatric persecution groups.[16] SGL appealed to other gay organisations for help; in February 1974, at John Ware's urging, CAMP NSW responded with a donation of $20 'in order that they [Gay Liberation] will be able to come back to life again'.[17] Despite this, the front passed out of existence shortly afterwards. Many of the constituent groups that had been gathered within GLF continued to operate for some time, however, and many more sprang up.

There was a certain irony in the fact that SGL had been reduced to asking CAMP for help, and it is an indication that the older group was coping better with the new period. We have seen that, in April 1972, CAMP had cast off much of the countercultural organisational looseness advocated by Ware and Poll, electing an executive headed by Lex Watson and Sue Wills as co-presidents. The new structure was not overly bureaucratic – the co-presidents' intention was that the executive should coordinate the activities of 'a formalised collection of groups who set their various aims and go about achieving them'.[18] Even after Wills and Watson resigned, the group remained very active under its new co-presidents, Peter Bonsall-Boone and Margaret McCann. The new leadership's first action was to revive the journal, *Camp Ink*, which had not been published for some months, and they maintained production on a two-monthly and then quarterly schedule until March 1977 – when, with issue number 40, it finally ceased publication. Denise Thompson notes: 'Until 1977 CAMP's political activities not only continued undiminished, but actually increased in scope and intensity'.[19] Craig Johnston, formerly of Gay Liberation, went further than this, arguing that CAMP was filling the space formerly occupied by the now defunct Gay Liberation:

> Since Sydney Gay Liberation has withered to virtually nothing, the CAMP has replaced it as the main gay liberation group in Sydney. CAMP = gay liberation? Yes, the radical rhetoric that was once the characteristic of Gay Liberation, of militant liberalism with a dash of radical feminism, is now put more vocally by the CAMP.[20]

Gay Liberation in Melbourne also successfully weathered this difficult period, perhaps because, just as CAMP NSW had become Gay Liberation, Gay Liberation in Melbourne had become CAMP. In late 1974, John Holden described the group as still active, though 'mainly concerned with outreach' to schools, university groups and churches.[21] The group's newsletter, produced on an irregular basis from July 1973 to December 1975, reported on the activities of a number of action groups within Gay Liberation. Groups concerned with counselling, law reform, the library, a film group and Radicalesbians were loosely affiliated with the umbrella organisation – just as in the model pioneered by SGL/GLF and implemented by CAMP NSW.

This action-group model was to provide a way forward for gay activism in these new, more difficult times, and the mid-1970s saw the establishment of a number of such groups, each of which aspired to deal with a single issue or area of concern, focusing its attention largely, if not exclusively, upon that activity. These groups might have an orientation towards a particular occupation

Gay and Lesbian Media. Too often denied access to mainstream press, or needing a place to discuss sensitive issues, the gay and lesbian media became increasingly important – and increasingly diverse – over the course of the 1970s. [James Spence collection, AQuA]

(such as gay teachers) or politics (such as lesbian feminists or socialist homosexuals); they might work on an ongoing task (such as the gay radio groups, counselling groups or law reform organisations) or a short campaign (such as running a candidate in an election). Sometimes, they operated autonomously within an overarching organisation, such as CAMP NSW or Melbourne Gay Liberation; sometimes, they were quite independent of each other – although, given the overlapping memberships and the relatively small and close-knit milieu, there were few groups entirely unconnected with any others. Over the course of the period 1974–78, literally scores, if not hundreds, of such groups came into being. Some of them have left little more than a name; others were to achieve great things on behalf of their constituencies. Some still exist, but most do not. It was the invention of these action groups that was to allow the movement to continue to make progress during the middle and later years of the 1970s.

There is a commonsense view that suggests that unity is strength and the existence of fewer, larger political organisations is preferable to the existence of more smaller ones. According to this thinking, the fragmentation of the movement after 1973 was something to be regretted. Not all agreed with this viewpoint, however. A number of commentators were inclined to see the coming into being of a large number of groups as a source of strength, rather than weakness. At the first National Homosexual Conference in 1975, Martin Smith suggested that a further fragmentation of the movement might be desirable.[22] He argued that caucuses and action groups were more likely to be recognised by non-gay peers than a more general grouping. For example, Chutzpah, the Jewish group, could access the Jewish community in a way that non-Jewish groups could not. Gay teachers' groups could work within the education system and gay students within student organisations and so on. Furthermore, by appealing to specific areas of interest – more immediate occupational, political or religious interests – such groups could mobilise gays who were

In the late 1970s, activists turned their attention to anti-gay discrimination whenever it existed, acting through the trade unions, in particular, to make the case for acceptance and gay rights (AQuA)

not amenable to the broader arguments for involvement. From the mid-1970s on, the action group looms large in any account of the continuing life of the movement and its work and achievements.

There was a strong emphasis in this period on educational activities, reflecting perhaps the reduced opportunities for protest and demonstrations. Two two-day seminars on female homosexuality were organised for International Women's Year, and over a dozen women delivered papers on various aspects of lesbian life and politics. These papers were later published in two volumes and widely distributed.[23] In Melbourne, David Widdup, one of CAMP NSW's earliest members, organised a homosexual studies course at Monash University called 'The Homosexual in Society'. Weekly evening classes were addressed by a number of prominent activists who delivered gay perspectives on issues such as the family, literature, the law, psychology, religion, the gay movement and its connections to the women's and socialist movements and sexism. Audiences of up to 200 people participated in lively discussions of the material presented. In later years, Melbourne was also the site for an annual adult education course organised around similar issues, conducted initially by Jocelyn Clarke and then for many years by Lesley Rogers and Helen McCulloch.[24]

One of the more interesting education/publicity ideas initiated by CAMP NSW was the 1976 Tribunal on Homosexuality and Discrimination. A four-person tribunal, composed of prominent public figures, including former deputy prime minister Jim Cairns, assisted by legal counsel, took evidence over two days in November 1976 relating to 44 acts of discrimination. The tribunal then prepared a number of recommendations. A litany of discrimination was unveiled at the hearings in areas including religion, government, de facto rights at work, education, family and children, prisons, media, police and everyday life.[25]

The increasing openness of the political arena to gays allowed for frequent interventions during this period. In this, CAMP NSW was the leader, reporting submissions and negotiations with a remarkable range of parliamentary and bureaucratic/administrative agencies over the period 1974–77. Perhaps the group's most important effort was its submission to the federal government's Royal Commission into Human Relationships, established in 1974 to 'inquire into and report upon the family, social, educational, legal and sexual aspects of male and female relationships'.[26]

CAMP's submission was an impressive 40-page printed document that addressed homosexual oppression under the five basic terms of reference. The outcome of this effort could hardly have been more pleasing: the commission's final report devoted 15 pages to the topic of discrimination against homosexuals, and its 14 recommendations on the matter argued for decriminalisation; against discrimination by employers, the public service and the armed forces; for consideration of de facto rights in financial matters; against aversion therapy; and for the recognition of homosexuality within sex education and public health activities.[27]

The commission's report was the coping stone of the liberal edifice regarding homosexuality, going far beyond anything imagined in the 1960s, and owed much to CAMP's arguments. In many ways, CAMP's real achievement was in having its issues addressed at all. In November 1975, a year after the commission began its hearings, the Catholic Education Office in Sydney suggested that the terms of reference did not allow for the consideration of homosexuality. This was in response to advice from the commission that it intended to hear evidence from Mike Clohesy, who had been dismissed from his teaching position at one of the church's colleges in Sydney. In considering its terms of reference, the commission heard arguments from gay activists, including Clohesy and Dennis Altman, that it did in fact have the right to consider such issues. The mainstream media reported the debate in terms that suggested an attack on free speech, apparently to the embarrassment of the church hierarchy.[28] In the end, the commission decided that it had the power to consider such issues and proceeded to do so. This allowed other gay groups and individuals to present submissions and evidence. Thirty-six written submissions (out of a total of 1,264) were identified by the commission as discussing homosexuality. They came from gay organisations, such as CAMP NSW, Campus CAMP in Brisbane and Society Five in Melbourne, and individuals such as Lex Watson. Witnesses for groups such as Radicalesbians and CAMP were heard in Canberra, Brisbane, Perth and Sydney.

Conscious that policy work of this type represented something of a retreat from the radical aspirations and practices of the early 1970s, those involved nonetheless defended it on political grounds:

> preparation of a submission becomes worthwhile when it brings together a group of people…to collectively work out the forces and values causing its oppression and to find ways of changing a society which is not able to cope with more than one lifestyle.[29]

Such work operated to hold people together and provided a focus for meetings, discussions and interventions into the political life of the time. It also served to contribute further to the normalisation of homosexuality as an issue with which officials in numerous government agencies were expected to deal. Such work is indicative of the changing political climate. Policy work had become possible because of the movement's success in making homosexuality a legitimate social and political issue and homosexuals legitimate spokespeople for these issues; it had become necessary because of the decline in opportunities for more radical political action.

The archetypal action group was perhaps the counselling group, and a number of these came into being within various organisations. The HGS, established by Sue Wills and John Ware within CAMP NSW in April 1972, was the first such organisation and, while its long-term aim was 'encouraging people in the helping professions to use their standing in the community to attack the oppression of homosexuals', its short-term goal was to help troubled homosexuals and their families.[30] It was succeeded by Phone-a-Friend, which was established within CAMP NSW in November 1972 by some of those drawn into the organisation by the 1971–72 recruitment drive.[31] In other states, too, counselling services were set up, with a flurry of them in 1974.

The need for such a service was amply demonstrated by the sheer number of calls received. Over a three-month period in mid-1975, Society Five's advice and referral service processed 500 calls. Melbourne Gay Liberation reported about 1,000 calls during the financial year 1973–74. In November 1974, just after it began to operate (offering a seven-nights-a-week service), CAMP Queensland received an average of 100 calls per week. In its first year, it handled 3,000 calls, noting that, because it was able to advertise in the daily press, CAMP Queensland was receiving more calls than CAMP NSW, which had had its advertisements refused by the mainstream press. The range of issues raised fell roughly into three groups: basic information regarding the location of gay venues; help with emotional problems arising from relationships, loss of jobs and so on; and people exploring their sexuality. The logbooks maintained by Gay Liberation and Society Five in Melbourne provide a powerful insight into the needs and concerns of gay callers.

The counselling services offered more than advice and support to homosexuals. They also played an important part in shoring up gay activism and holding activists together around a common task at a time when the difficulties of sustaining morale were high. In late 1974, according to Gary Jaynes, Melbourne Gay Liberation was 'almost defunct', but at a meeting in early 1975, it was decided to keep the counselling service operating, even if everything else fell away. A list of those interested in the Gay Counselling Collective contains nearly 30 names, including all the most important long-term activists.[32]

It seems likely that the counselling service allowed Melbourne's gay liberationists to regroup and enabled the organisation to survive while SGL did not. Although some members soon gave up (Jocelyn Clarke offers an eloquent description of her difficulties[33]), the Gay Counselling Collective persevered in some form until Gay Liberation itself collapsed in 1978. In a similar way, the Befriending Group (which handled counselling and other activities in CAMP Queensland), with its phone service and continuous advertisements in the daily paper, 'produced results far in excess of our wildest dreams'. Because the phone service operated every night, so too did the club rooms, generating one of the liveliest CAMP social groups in the country.[34]

The gay religious groups were another important development of this period, finding their own way towards the action-group model. Although groups oriented towards changing church attitudes had existed within CAMP in most states from the earliest days, this later period saw new developments. Frustrated, often, by their lack of progress in overturning homophobic attitudes in the hierarchy or among the congregations and faced by the decline and fragmentation of the gay movement, many activists with religious beliefs began to discuss the possibility of organising independently, either as gay churches or as action groups. Many of those involved in this process had been active in CAMP in the various states, usually within the church groups. Acceptance (the Catholic Group) was set up in Adelaide by Graeme Harris and in Sydney by Gary Pye, both members of CAMP. John Willis of the Metropolitan Community Church (MCC) had been a member of the Humanists and Society Five. Ken Goodenough had been a member of CAMP NSW before going to Brisbane and starting Cross+Section within CAMP, out of which emerged a branch of a national gay church.[35] As religious activists moved away from involvement in CAMP, they found their way to one of two kinds of organisations. The first of these was the establishment of organisations to support believers and intervene within the established churches. Acceptance, for example, was a group for Catholics who were members of the church, 'loyal to church authority and dogma'.[36] Originally operating within CAMP's church group, it began to meet separately only in February 1973. It followed the activist model of Cross+Section, advertising its existence in *Nation Review* and the *Catholic Weekly*, recruiting members from those who replied and preparing a Statement of Position and Purpose for distribution to Sydney's Catholic clergy. The group participated in Cross+Section's Palm Sunday and Good Friday vigils during Easter 1973, but in mid-1974, it virtually seceded from CAMP, declaring that it wished to control its own finances.[37] Pye attributes this defection (which was followed by the defection of the Catholic group within CAMP SA) to a lack of cooperation and generally poor treatment from other members of CAMP. By 1975, after a visit to the USA where they encountered both the MCC and Dignity (the Catholic homosexual organisation), Pye and Graeme Donkin returned to Australia determined to build Acceptance more actively. A national conference was organised, where groups from Sydney, Adelaide, Canberra and Melbourne were represented. By 1975, Pye was able to report a number of achievements:

> We have broken into the *Catholic Weekly* of Sydney, the most conservative newspaper in Australia. We are in dialogue with the National Commission for Justice and Peace, and Action for World Development, we are in constant contact with State Governments and with the Australian Government... Acceptance/Brisbane, Acceptance/Wollongong and Acceptance/Parramatta are being formed.[38]

Chutzpah, the Jewish gay group, operated in a similar framework. Initiated in Sydney by Martin Smith, a former member of Gay Liberation and editor of *Stallion/Gayzette*, and in Perth by Vivienne Cass, a leading member of CAMP, the group was first mooted during a debate among Jewish leaders after a prominent rabbi had supported the decriminalisation of homosexuality in a statement to the Western Australian Royal Commission into Homosexuality.[39] Ironically perhaps, it was during the visit to Australia of the Reverend Troy Perry, US founder of a church for gay Christians, that the decision to form Chutzpah was acted upon.[40] Within a year, the group was able to report some successes to the National Homosexual Conference: raising the issue of homosexual oppression at the World Jewish Congress, addressing synagogue youth groups and the Jewish telephone counselling service, the publication of articles in *Australian Jewish Times* and providing a way into the gay movement for many Jews who had not previously been involved.[41]

The second model of religious organising involved the establishment of gay churches. The most important of these was the MCC, founded in the USA by Troy Perry in 1968. Perry toured Australia for three weeks in July–August 1974 at the invitation of Graham Douglas of CAMP WA. He received a great deal of attention in both the mainstream and gay press. At the time of his visit, gay churches had already been set up in Melbourne and Adelaide. In the months after he left, these churches and Brisbane Cross+Section formally affiliated themselves to the MCC.[42]

MCC distinguished itself from Cross+Section, Chutzpah and Acceptance:

> our prime aim is to worship Christ; the other organisations ...seem to be concerned with creating an atmosphere where religious gays can meet and discuss mutual problems, or to study and chew over aspects of their religious lives.[43]

The gay churches also became, in part at least, action groups, contributing to the broader movement for change. John Willis, of the Melbourne MCC, remembers that he was an active supporter of the gay rights campaign and involved as a gay church leader in lobbying for homosexual law reform. In 1976, when Graeme Donkin was running as an openly gay candidate for the NSW seat of Bligh, the MCC was among those pledging support for the campaign, and the MCC minister offered to organise a collection during the coffee hour after his service.[44]

Not all organising took place in gay groups. An important resource for the gay movement during this period was the Australian Union of Students (AUS), a national body that had become more and more politicised over the course of the 1960s and 1970s. Beginning in 1975, the presence of lesbians and gay men within the structures of AUS became very strong and included many who had been involved in the movement for some time: Gaby Antolovich, Laurie Bebbington, Jeff Hayler, Craig Johnston, Jude Munro, Peter O'Connor, Ron Thiele and Gay Walsh. A caucus of homosexuals within AUS first met at the January 1975 annual conference. They proposed, argued for and won majority support for a pro-gay policy statement that opposed 'all discrimination – legal, economic and social – against homosexuals', supported the 'struggles of lesbians and homosexual men against heterosexist oppression' and offered active support to campaigns aimed at advancing the struggle for homosexual liberation. The statement recognised the 'validity of homosexual relationships' and committed the union to 'publicly advocate the positive and healthy nature of those relationships'.[45]

The most interesting feature of this intervention by gay activists is that they then offered a series of motions to be placed before the union's affiliated campuses for debate and ratification. Ron Thiele explains that this approach was a deliberate decision by members of the gay caucus who believed that the need for a debate about homosexuality among students was more important than the risk that such a vote might defeat the motions.[46] The motions instructed AUS to approach governments, teachers, trainee teachers, teachers' unions and university administrations to look for, and work to eradicate, signs of 'biased presentation of only a heterosexual nuclear family-oriented life-style' in their educational policies and practices.[47] By eschewing a simple liberal endorsement of law reform, or even of a general argument for tolerance, the union was raising the level of discussion to a new level. Not all the debates went in favour of the motions, but, even when majority opinion was opposed, the student press and campus meetings provided a forum for debate and the expression of pro-gay arguments, just as the caucus had intended.

Even before the debates and votes took place, the 1975 conference policy allowed the AUS to take action on homosexual issues. Central to its activity during this period was the Women's Department, set up in that same year. With a budget of about $12,000, a specific mandate to deal with the pro-gay policy adopted by the unions and Laurie Bebbington, a longstanding lesbian activist, as its organiser, the Women's Department was able to give a great deal of support to the gay movement at a time when the fragmentation and demoralisation of 1974 was creating grave concerns. The victimisation of Penny Short, a trainee teacher whose scholarship had been revoked after she published a lesbian love poem in a university magazine, hung over the AUS during this time. Bebbington was explicit in her reference to this case, arguing that, were such an event to take place in 1975:

> the Women's Department would consider it a major campaign to be fought. Not only would we produce campaign material, but we would pressure governments, education department and the particular institution concerned as much as possible.[48]

This was no idle promise. In August 1976, a controversy at Kelvin Grove College of Advanced Education (a teacher-training college in Brisbane) erupted over whether or not a gay group ought to be allowed to be registered on campus.[49] The group and its spokesperson, Greg Weir, mobilised to put pressure on the college council, which eventually accepted the right of gay students to organise. At this point, the state government – under the right-wing populist premier Joh Bjelke-Petersen – involved itself in the issue and, in early 1977, Greg Weir was refused employment as a teacher. A storm of protest erupted. Civil liberties groups, political parties and trade unions took up the issue. AUS discussed the matter at its January 1977 Council and voted to support Weir, as part of a broader commitment to the right of homosexuals to teach and to organise politically. For the next two years, AUS provided resources to fight the case and to draw attention to its political implications in what was the first ongoing national campaign ever undertaken by the gay movement. In December 1977, a national seminar was organised by AUS in Melbourne. It brought together 16 members – eight men and eight women – of the various state-based Greg Weir Campaign Committees to discuss the campaign, to explore the problems encountered and to plan for 1978.[50]

One other interesting contribution made by AUS to the movement's work was the establishment of the Homosexual Research Project, an initiative of the January 1977 conference meeting (which had also adopted a more wide-ranging policy on homosexuality). An amount of $3,100 was allocated for a part-time research officer and associated expenses. In June, Manda Biles was appointed to the position.[51] Although the project took the form of an information-gathering exercise – seeking out experiences, policies, practices and attitudes of students, administrations and teachers – the project also had an activist motivation and intent. Rather than collect information herself, Biles drew in activists on campuses, getting them to take the initiative around these issues. The final report detailed gay studies courses and suggestions on how to start a gay group on campus. AUS's most important contribution to the movement was its organisation of the National Homosexual Conference in Melbourne on 16–17 August 1975, which proved to be the first of an annual series lasting until 1986. There had been one earlier national gathering, the CAMP national camp held in Adelaide in 1973, and SGL attempted something similar later in 1973 without success.[52] The AUS succeeded mainly because it had the money and the formal networks to turn its plans into reality. The original suggestion had come from the homosexual caucus at the January 1975 AUS Council,[53] although the actual organisation was taken over by a collective that included lesbians and gay men from inside and outside of the AUS. The conference was expressly not a Gay Liberation conference,[54] being open to as wide a range of participants as possible – 'from Christian homosexuals to feminist lesbians, from society five [sic] to effeminists...homosexual activists of many years, and homosexuals for whom the Conference was first contact'.[55] But it was open only to homosexuals, rejecting sympathetic heterosexuals, voyeuristic social scientists and anti-gay activists, in order to ensure that the 'Conference was homosexual territory'.[56] In the end, about 600 people attended from all over Australia – from as far away as Perth and Townsville – among which 'All the "splinter" and "self interest" groups appeared to be represented'.[57] This first conference voted to hold a second, and in later years the National Homosexual Conference was held in Sydney (1976, 1978, 1980), Adelaide (1977, 1981), Melbourne (1979, 1983), Canberra (1982) and Brisbane (1984). The last of the conferences was held in Sydney in 1986, after which the drain-off of activism into AIDS politics finally ended their run.

It would be difficult to overestimate the importance of these conferences. They provided an annual gathering, open to all the fragments of the movement, for discussions, debates and information sharing. They reminded people working in their groups and campaigns that they were not alone and that the work of the movement was continuing, even if it was not as visible as it had been in the early 1970s. They were lots of fun, too (and included lots of sex), and were a means for binding people together nationally. They acted as a beacon in difficult times. And they inspired, too. After staging the conferences, the host cities often found themselves with new levels of enthusiasm and commitment and large infusions of new and/or revitalised activists.

Perhaps the most successful of the action groups was Melbourne's Gay Teachers' Group, which later became the GTSG.[58] Formed at the first National Homosexual Conference by gay liberationists including Gary Jaynes and Helen McCulloch, the group aimed to ensure job security for homosexual teachers, the right of students and teachers to be open about their sexuality, that schools accepted responsibility for educating students about homosexuality and – ultimately – a positive change in attitudes throughout the education system. Its primary interest was political action in the form of lobbying and action research.[59] From the group that was most vulnerable to homophobic fears around the myth of homosexuals-as-child-molesters, this was an ambitious set of goals. That it made considerable progress is even more impressive.

The group provided support to its teacher members and was closely involved in teacher union affairs in particular. Its manifesto, 'School Was the Worst Time of My Life', was published in all three teacher union journals,[60] and news articles and book reviews often addressed the needs of gay teachers and students, usually in the context of debates about sex education courses. The GTSG and its supporters in the unions were firm in their argument that gay rights, tolerance and the provision of accurate information were the responsibility of all teachers. The unions could support these aims by the adoption of policy that legitimated them.

The breakthrough came when the 1976 Victorian Secondary Teachers' Union annual conference voted to establish the Open Subcommittee on Homosexuality alongside a similar committee on women. Initiated by Simeon Kronenberg, a former Gay Liberation member, the committee provided a forum in which gay and lesbian teachers could develop a policy on homosexual rights, which was adopted by the union a year later. This policy went well beyond the protection of gay teachers as employees to affirm that 'homosexual lifestyles should be treated as equal to heterosexual lifestyles' and 'homosexual teachers have a necessary and valid role to play in the education of staff, students and parents about homosexuality'.[61] Similar policies were adopted by the other two teacher unions the next year. The GTSG had provided support for this work, as did the three unions' Elimination of Sexism in Schools project, whose coordinator was long-term lesbian activist Jude Munro. But GTSG did not confine itself to union work; its 1978 publication *Young, Gay and Proud* was a pathbreaking contribution in the provision of supportive factual information for young gay people.

In the mid-1970s, faced with a political climate that was rather different from the one in which it was formed, the gay movement found a new type of organisation through which to carry on its efforts to change society. Fighting small-scale battles on a series of fronts, operating, when necessary, behind what many would have considered enemy lines and working with those who had been damaged by an oppressive society, hundreds of lesbians and gay men struggled on in myriad ways. Often, the successes seemed small compared with the aims of the movement; often, they went entirely unnoticed. But the cumulative effect was impressive.

Young, Gay, and Proud. Conscious of the particular vulnerability of young lesbians and gay men, Melbourne's GTSG produced the first no-nonsense, factual discussion of the issues for young people.

8.

Backlash, Resistance and the Community

In 1977, Lex Watson was quoted as bemoaning the lack of progress by the gay movement:

> It always staggers me that we have really achieved so little in improving the condition of gays in Australia, compared to other movements, like those of women, blacks and migrants. We have achieved really nothing tangible.[1]

While such a view is understandable in the light of the lack of progress on many of the movement's demands, a more accurate assessment was offered by John Holden, of Melbourne Gay Liberation, who said as early as 1974:

> I feel that we are not being an effective radical or revolutionary movement, but I do feel we are being an effective force for social change.

Holden argued that radical movements are generated by pressures in society and that, as these pressures are altered, so, too, are social movements. He suggested:

> Gay lib will continue to be absorbed by a progressively more tolerant society, which via various means of accommodation will relieve the pressure enough to disallow revolutionary change, but permit 'evolutionary' change.[2]

Certainly, by the late 1970s, homosexuality had become a normal (which does not mean uncontroversial) part of the political landscape. In a 1977 submission to the Tasmanian parliament's inquiry into homosexuality, the Tasmanian Homosexual Law Reform Group listed 35 calls for decriminalisation, emanating from sources as diverse as political parties, newspaper editorials, religious organisations and student unions.[3] In the course of the 1970s (it is striking that virtually all of these calls date from after 1973), professional organisations, trade unions, government departments and churches were all – to varying degrees – aware of the needs and demands of their homosexual constituencies, homosexual citizens in general and the gay movement in particular, and were more and more inclined to take account of them. The movement's submissions were received and considered; its lobbying was scheduled by MPs, bureaucrats and professional associations; and its affiliation fees and participation were welcomed by a diverse range of political groups and campaigns. Along with this went a greater awareness of the issues surrounding homosexuality. Although an attempt by the NSW Health Commission to include gay themes in its 1975 awareness campaign on sexually transmitted diseases was blocked by its senior managers,[4] the fact that homosexuals were identified as a target group and having their needs considered is significant.

Outside the ranks of officialdom, there was a growing acceptance of homosexual concerns. The shift in public opinion continued, with a further increase in support for decriminalisation. By 1978, opinion polls were showing solid support (57 percent) not just for legalising homosexual acts, but for treating such acts in the same way as sexual acts between persons of different sexes.[5]

In the late 1970s, Australia was a rather different society than it had been a decade before, and gay people were living different lives. A commercialised subculture, which was flourishing by then, provided entertainment, support and affirmation for those lesbians and gay men who found their way to it. The fledgling gay press created an information network that brought activists and the homosexual subculture into increasingly close contact. The gay and lesbian churches and counselling groups were another point of contact between ordinary gay people and the movement, even if the organisers and their clientele and congregations often saw themselves as apolitical. Under these pressures, the movement, too, was changing. The creation of the action group allowed for a very much more flexible structure, in which the bitter political disputes of the earlier years could be set aside and the tasks of working out theory and strategies, finding targets and goals and developing ways of working could be carried on.

Despite the evidence of progress, however, a fear that, politically, things were going backwards kept many people going. Australian politics remained strongly polarised in the late 1970s, with the emergence of a right-wing offensive, centred on the churches and conservative politicians, and significant setbacks for liberal and progressive forces.

For gays, in particular, things were looking grim. In December 1976, Victorian police used entrapment techniques to arrest dozens of gay men at the Black Rock Beach beat. In 1977, Greg Weir, a trainee teacher in Queensland, was banned from teaching when his homosexuality came to the attention of the conservative state government. (This was discussed in more detail in Chapter 7.) The impact of this case was heightened by events in the USA, where Anita Bryant led a right-wing campaign to remove anti-discrimination laws, fought especially around the threat to children that gays supposedly represented. In Canada, police repeatedly raided *Body Politic*, a gay news magazine of international repute, as it struggled to debate controversial issues such as pedophilia. In Britain, morals campaigner Mary Whitehouse successfully prosecuted *Gay News* for blasphemous libel. The case caught the attention of Whitehouse's co-thinkers in the Australian FOL, and she was invited to tour Australia. In 1978 in Melbourne, GTSG's *Young, Gay and Proud* was effectively banned from distribution in schools. Meanwhile, in Queensland, a campaign against school-based sex education of any kind was in full swing.

For many in the late 1970s, it was not the achievements of the past decade or the possibility of continuing progress that loomed large, but the threat of a backlash. One of the action groups wrote in 1978:

> We're going to be faced with an intensified Right wing back lash. The working class and their allies are being split up. The issues facing us are huge.[6]

In part, this analysis reflected a response to the broader political shift in society. The dismissal of the reforming Whitlam government by the governor-general and the subsequent endorsement of this action by voters boded ill for progressives. Few would have accepted the Maoists' characterisation of November 1975 as a semi-fascist coup, but most liberals and radicals felt that a remarkable shift to the Right had taken place in Australian society, and some were inclined to blame the Left itself, at least in part. Meaghan Morris has written of how she, and others like her, became interested in moderate politics and new French theory during this period:

> in reaction to the excessive zeal which our…autonomous and marginal movements had for ignoring anything tainted with majority politics and economics: a zeal which eventually led to us being taken by surprise at the time of the Constitutional Crisis by, as people used to say in awed tones at the time, 'the real world'.[7]

The apocalyptic tone of some of the writings of this period reflects the way in which many on the Left were operating with expectations set by the experience of the 1930s. As the long economic boom of the 1950s and 1960s came to an end, it was widely expected that the ruling powers in society would turn, as they had in much of Europe in the 1930s, to authoritarian and repressive measures. It was expected that the gains of the 1960s – by the working class, women, gays and minority groups of all kinds – would be rolled back. This model was as strong among gay activists as among other Leftists, exemplified (exacerbated perhaps) by the adoption of the pink triangle as the movement's most prominent symbol. The pink triangle referred unequivocally to the experience of Nazi death camps, where it had marked homosexual prisoners – as the yellow had marked Jews, the red political activists, and so on. The military coup in Chile, with its massacres of homosexuals among others, served as a further reminder that, even in advanced democratic societies, political disasters could occur. Even those who had never embraced the far Left's linking of gay oppression and the structures of capitalism and whose world view was not shaped by these nightmare images were worried by the organisational weakness of the gay movement and by the fragility of its gains. They were acutely aware of the possibility that vulnerable groups – gay teachers, for example, because they worked with children – might well become targets for conservative forces.[8]

If these expectations can now be seen to have been very wrong, it should not be assumed that they were, at least in their more moderate forms, without foundation. A backlash was indeed brewing, and in the USA and the UK, serious reversals were experienced by gay people over the course of the 1980s.[9] The difference is that attempts to produce a similar shift in political and social attitudes in Australia were soundly defeated by a reinvigorated gay movement, as well as other movements. Events overseas, however, should remind us that a positive outcome was by no means inevitable.

The early years of the gay movement had been remarkable for the lack of resistance that was mobilised. Unlike the controversial and unsuccessful attempt to liberalise abortion laws in the federal parliament in 1973, Moss Cass's homosexual law reform motion later that year encountered very little organised opposition. Calls for homosexual law reform by a wide variety of organisations during the 1970s often provoked considerable debate among constituencies, but it was rare for such calls to be retracted. The earliest serious attempt to stand against the tide came from the Anglican Church hierarchy in Sydney, in both its anti-gay *Report on Homosexuality*, endorsed by the synod in 1973, and, more importantly, its attempt to build a movement of its own to resist and roll back the liberalisation of the 1960s and 1970s. The steady advance of liberal attitudes provoked considerable anxiety among conservatives in general and among Christian conservatives in particular. In 1971, John Court, a conservative Anglican psychiatrist and lay activist, noted:

> A mere ten years ago few would have doubted that homosexuality comes under the strongest Biblical condemnation and should properly be the object of legal sanctions for the protection of society. A succession of reports, secular and spiritual, has changed these assumptions for many.[10]

The Whitlam government of 1972–75 exacerbated the fears because it began to discuss, and even implement, reforms that, to the minds of evangelicals, struck at the heart of society. Civil marriage, divorce law reform, sex education and the possibility of law reform in the areas of prostitution, homosexuality and drug use all indicated to conservatives the influence of noisy, secular-humanist minorities. The response was obvious: Christians had to organise politically to combat the threat.

Central to this effort was the FOL, an organisation committed to the defence of Christian moral standards, founded in 1973.[11] Supported by prominent church figures and enthusiastically promoted by the conservative publication *Australian Church Record*, the FOL organised itself very much on the model of the social and political movements against which it was campaigning. It established local branches that recruited and mobilised members. It organised demonstrations, conferences and public meetings. It developed close relations with other organisations such as the Right to Life. Leading lay and clerical church figures, men such as John Court, B. L. Smith (a lecturer at Moore Theological College) and Lance Shilton (the Dean of Sydney), associated themselves closely with the organisation's work. In 1973, a majority of the Sydney Anglican synod voted to 'commend to the attention of church people the programme and future activities of the Australian Festival of Light'.[12]

The movement of which FOL was a part was actively anti-homosexual. B. L. Smith, who in 1969 had actually supported the decriminalisation of homosexuality, was by 1973 chief author of the synod's *Report on Homosexuality*, which was opposed to law reform as well as the acceptance of homosexuality. The *Sydney Town Express*, which described itself as a Christian magazine for youth and was an enthusiastic supporter of Fred Nile, argued that 'gay people are sad people' and denounced the 1973 Gay Pride Week as 'an advertising campaign, a promotional activity' for 'a symptom of the disease of rebellion and sin'. In 1975, during the debate on the AUS' pro-homosexual motions, the Monash University Evangelical Union presented a lengthy statement arguing that homosexuality was 'an abnormal, deviant expression of sexuality'.[13]

Leading church figures were prepared to take extreme measures against known homosexuals in their ranks. In June 1973, Jeremy Fisher was confronted by the Reverend Dr Alan Cole, master of the Macquarie University Anglican residential college, who had found gay liberation material in Fisher's room. Cole demanded that Fisher live a celibate life and seek treatment. When Fisher, an active member and treasurer of the university's Gay Liberation group, refused, he was expelled from his college. But he found support in the student union, the BLF (which placed work bans on a number of university building projects) and the broader gay movement.[14] The *Australian Church Record* defended Cole's actions, pointing to a recent opinion poll that found that only 29 percent of people thought homosexuality was 'right' as evidence (in a startling non sequitur) of 'how widespread the support for Dr Alan Cole is on his stand at Robert Menzies College' and of how little impact the 'noisy avant garde groups who placard the streets and often the media with their opinions' were having.[15] The victimisation of Peter Bonsall-Boone was, if anything, even more serious. It seems, unlike the Fisher case, to have been carried out deliberately and with some thought. Bonsall-Boone had been church secretary of St Clement's parish in Mosman, Sydney, since the late 1960s and an active member of CAMP since 1970. In mid-1972, ABC television researchers at one of CAMP's regular parties asked him and his lover Peter de Waal if they would appear on the Chequerboard current affairs program with Sue Wills and Gaby Antolovitch. They agreed, and the pre-recorded program went to air on 31 October 1972.[16]

Bonsall-Boone mentioned his involvement in the church in passing (though without specifying his parish or even his denomination), but this was all the hierarchy needed. A week later, he was told to take a week's leave and then to resign his position. On 8 November, CAMP issued a statement regarding the church's action, and Bonsall-Boone recorded an interview for ABC radio. Bonsall-Boone was immediately, and retrospectively, dismissed from his position. The press and television took up the issue, interviewing Bonsall-Boone and other gay movement leaders, and B. L. Smith, who carried the issue for the church. In the course of one interview, Smith acknowledged that he had known of Bonsall-Boone's sexuality (he had been present when Bonsall-Boone and his partner Peter de Waal addressed the Anglican Synod's Ethics and Social Questions Committee in June 1972 during its deliberations on homosexuality) and admitted that it was 'a little curious that it [the dismissal] had to wait until the thing became public'.[17]

Given the broad political shift, it is not surprising that, when the FOL announced in mid-1978 that it intended to tour Mary Whitehouse (founder and leader of the British FOL), lesbian and gay activists experienced 'considerable alarm'.[18] Even the MCC announced: 'There has been a declaration of war against gay people. This is a call to arms'.[19] Anti-FOL groups were set up in Melbourne, Sydney, Adelaide and Canberra. In other states, existing organisations often took up the call for action.

The need to alert gay people generally to the threat represented by Whitehouse and the FOL was urgent. A detailed summary of FOL's pamphlet against homosexual law reform was introduced to *Campaign*'s readers with the editorial injunction: 'Your apathy is the FOL's greatest asset'.[20] Part of the problem was that much of what FOL and Whitehouse said seemed to many gays to be either quaintly old fashioned (homosexuality contravenes Biblical law) or simply ludicrous (homosexual babysitters were known to use the suckling reflex of babies for their own pleasure). But the news editor of *Campaign* argued:

> it would be a great mistake to write her off as a crank and a wowser whose opinions represent only a small minority. That may be the case, but it is not the point.[21]

The point was that, in a society where Christianity and the state were 'in cahoots', Whitehouse spoke on behalf of the values and forces that disadvantaged lesbians and gay men.

The threat was not directed just at gay people. There were many groups at risk, and they needed to work together. Ian Malloy identified as targets for the Right:

> the already limited rights of women to control their own bodies, of children to basic complete information about sex and of gays to liberation from everyday oppression.[22]

The organisations set up to oppose Whitehouse's visit grouped gay activists, feminists and civil libertarians of all stripes. In

Melbourne, the groups involved included the Women's Abortion Action Coalition, the Homosexual Law Reform Coalition, Society Five, MCC, Melbourne University Gay Soc, Gay Liberation, the GTSG and the main far Left groups, the Socialist Workers Party and the International Socialists. Even the conservative and usually very cautious lesbian social group, Lynx, wrote to the campaign offering to help distribute its broadsheet.[23]

The slogans and demands of the anti-FOL groups were correspondingly wide ranging: repeal of anti-abortion laws and the provision of free, safe abortion; repeal of anti-homosexual laws and an end to discrimination; acknowledgement of the rights of children; and abolition of all restrictions on sexual behaviour between consenting adults.[24] The demonstrations against Whitehouse were both numerous and varied in their approach. Even before she arrived in the country, 150 people marched in Adelaide, delivering a petition to the state attorney-general. In Canberra, between 80 and 100 people protested. There were smaller but more frequent turnouts in other cities. Most of the activists in most of the groups were keen to avoid conflict, believing that bad publicity would detract from their message and create sympathy for Whitehouse. In Melbourne, those attending the demonstration were handed a leaflet explaining that the organisers had decided to gather on the opposite side of road and would not attempt to prevent people from entering Festival Hall or Mary Whitehouse from speaking. In Sydney, a number of lesbians in the audience rose, unfurled banners and made a dignified exit, two of them waltzing up the aisle of St Andrew's Cathedral. The most confronting behaviour occurred in Brisbane and Sydney, where cream pies were thrown at Whitehouse. All of this was remarkably successful, both in contesting her views and in 'hijacking much of her publicity quota'.[25] Press coverage was not nearly as sympathetic as most of her critics (and, indeed, most of her supporters) had expected, and the restrained behaviour of the demonstrators was favourably noted. The mere knowledge that demonstrations were likely, however, seems to have deterred many. Numbers attending the meetings were smaller than planned for, and FOL reported a significant financial loss as a result of the tour.[26] The anti-Whitehouse campaign has been somewhat overlooked in Australian gay history, but it clearly played an important part in resisting the rise of the Right. In part, this is because it has been overshadowed by the most dramatic moment of the backlash. In June 1978, Sydney police attacked the first Mardi Gras and, in so doing, opened up a whole new period in Australian lesbian and gay politics.

The first Mardi Gras began modestly enough. In response to a call from the San Francisco Gay Freedom Day Committee for an International Day of Action, a group of gay and lesbian activists in Sydney organised a Saturday morning march, a public meeting and, as something a bit different, a fiesta or mardi gras to be held late at night on Oxford Street, in the heart of the emerging gay precinct. A party atmosphere was encouraged, with revellers urged to dress as outrageously as they wished to join the street theatre, bands, singing and dancing that had been arranged. On Saturday 24 June, 1,000 people turned up to the largest gay and lesbian political event yet organised in Australia. Despite the organisers having a permit for the march, it rapidly became clear that the police were looking for trouble, denying the marchers access to Hyde Park and finally seizing the sound system. Defiantly, the crowd broke away, heading for Kings Cross, the historic centre of bohemian and kamp life in Sydney. Here, the police sealed off the roads and started making arrests. Pandemonium erupted, with police, marchers and bystanders slogging it out with fists, banners and rubbish bins. By the end of the evening, 53 people had been arrested. Many of those arrested were badly beaten inside the police cells, and the *Sydney Morning Herald* sank to new editorial depths by publishing a complete list of names and occupations of those arrested.[27] If all this simply served to confirm the Left's expectation that the long period of economic prosperity of the 1950s and 1960s would lead to a backlash against the gay rights gains of earlier years, what was surprising to many was the wave of resistance that took gay politics to heights of activity never reached before and tapped into a hitherto unseen degree of support from the homosexual subculture.[28] In response to the Mardi Gras arrests, a furious campaign was waged, demanding that the charges be dropped. The issue escalated, with further arrests in Sydney on 26 June outside the court hearings and on 15 July at a protest march. In August, when delegates to the Fourth National Homosexual Conference took to the streets, 109 more were arrested.[29]

These demonstrations were the largest seen in Australia for many years, and Sydney's largest ever to that point. The meetings to debate tactics and strategies for the Drop the Charges Campaign occasionally numbered in the hundreds. Smaller protests were staged at Parramatta, at Trades Hall in the city, outside courthouses and at Sydney Airport. Demonstrations in Melbourne, Brisbane and Adelaide turned the arrests into a national political issue and collected money for legal defence funds. In the end, the campaign was remarkably successful. As early as October 1978, the first charges were dismissed in the courts; and on 29 December 1979, the police quietly dropped the last of them. Even before this, the NSW government had changed the law to make it very much harder for police to refuse permits for street marches, which was perhaps the campaign's most lasting legal victory.

Inspired by the surge of anger and by the willingness of so many to take to the streets, activists decided to take the initiative. At the 1979 National Homosexual Conference, Sydney's Gay Solidarity Group arrived with a fully developed proposal for a nationwide Summer Offensive for Gay Rights. Taken up with varying degrees of enthusiasm in various cities, the campaign emphasised both the usual demands (law reform, custody rights and an end to police harassment) and the usual forms of activity (demonstrations, public meetings and media appearances). The organisers were hoping for the 'biggest yet outpourings of people...who mean business when it comes to equality and human rights for gays'.[30] If the results were not quite at that level, the campaign was by no means a failure. One thousand people marched in Sydney, and respectable numbers in other cities, and there was considerable publicity given to the various events and demands by the mainstream media.

What made the Mardi Gras arrests and the subsequent campaign important was not simply the size of the reaction, but the diversity of those who participated in the protests and organising. The Left – gay and straight – was prominent in the campaign, of course. This was the kind of militant resistance to oppression that Leftists lived for. But fully half of those arrested on 24 June were women (which casts further doubt on the belief that they had withdrawn from the movement in recent years), and the campaign also seemed to draw in the kind of people who had, in the past, been impervious to the demands of the movement: the bargoers.

There was a long history of estrangement between the gay movement and the commercial scene. During the earliest days of the movement, the editors of *Camp Ink* had detected a pattern of opposition 'voiced loudly by those who appear to be preoccupied with their obscure security in the gay-bar subculture'.[31] Lex Watson, visiting a gay bar on Oxford Street during the 1972 Sex Lib Week, was, in his own words, 'abused shitless' by a ring of people, including friends, for his part in organising such an event.[32] Sue Wills, who was with him, reported the concerns:

> By drawing attention to the fact that there were very large numbers of homosexuals in Sydney, most of whom were closeted, we were drawing attention to male homosexuals who had hitherto been able to 'pass for straight'.[33]

Out of the Closets and Into the Streets! The mass resistance to the Mardi Gras arrests galvanised thousands and was to launch a new era of gay and lesbian activism. (Geoff Friend)

Police at Mardi Gras, 1970s-style
Credit

Lesbians Ignite, Sydney 1978 (Geoff Friend)

Members of the subculture feared rocking the boat.

By 1978, this attitude seems to have dissipated, although it was not a sudden change. The Mardi Gras campaign acted like a lightning bolt, revealing what had been overlooked until that moment – that gay men and lesbians, even those who eschewed activism, had become much more political. Ten years of activism had changed both society and gay people. It was increasingly possible to be out to friends and family and at work. And, even when there were limitations on this in individual cases, it was certainly increasingly possible to go out to the bars, coffee shops and restaurants catering to a gay clientele – and more and more people did so, finding there affirmation of what was increasingly dubbed their 'lifestyle'.

The new homosexual was increasingly confident and comfortable with his or her sexuality, although by no means a liberationist. As Dennis Altman pointed out, while gays at the end of the 1970s were likely to be nonapologetic about their sexuality, they were no more likely to be revolutionary than anyone else in society.³⁴ These attitudes were illustrated in a 1978 readers' survey conducted by *Campaign*, which indicated a clear preference for articles on relationships and health and a marked antipathy for more political topics such as feminism.³⁵ But there was interest expressed, too, in law reform news. The response from the subculture to the Mardi Gras arrests seemed to indicate that gay people were now prepared to speak out and take action in defence of their rights.

The gay business sector, too, was emerging from its closet. Gone was the fear that Dawn O'Donnell, one of Sydney's earliest gay bar operators, expressed at one stage:

> You've got to understand, if we stick our necks out, it's very easy for someone to change the law in parliament, altering hotel laws and finding noise pollution problems.³⁶

By the late 1970s, a new breed of entrepreneurs was emerging, less fearful and more committed to actively building a gay community as a social and political force. They had 'taken to meeting each other for a social drink once a month; [and] taken a keen interest in providing services for their clients'.³⁷ They were, cautiously at first, opening up to the idea that visibility and even a little politics might be possible.

Alongside these two groups, the social, welfare and religious organisations of the gay scene were also developing a new confidence and a willingness to put themselves forward as community leaders, rather than just service organisations. In doing this, they were increasingly willing to acknowledge and argue for the need for politics. It was not possible to be apolitical, one such leader said in 1980, although gay liberation was obviously an idea whose time had passed: 'The gay movement of the seventies is now the gay community of the eighties', and what mattered was the broadest possible unity and 'political credibility'.³⁸ In early 1979, the social, welfare and religious groups formed the Council of Gay Groups as a means of coming together to discuss issues of common concern.³⁹

The emergence of a new homosexual consciousness grounded in the developing commercial scene had been first detected by John Lee and Tim Carrigan, both long-term gay liberationists and, in the late 1970s, leading members of the Adelaide Homosexual Alliance. Their paper 'Male Homosexuals and the Capitalist Market' was first published in 1978 but drew upon thinking and arguing that went back at least a year or so. In it, they analysed the recent rapid growth of the commercial scene, assessed its significance for the movement and drew quite detailed conclusions about political practice.[40] Coming from leading left-wing gay activists, the kind of people who had hitherto evinced a suspicion of, and hostility towards, both the patrons and the entrepreneurs of the commercial scene, this paper provided an important breakthrough, legitimising an orientation towards the gay scene.

While it was in Sydney in the aftermath of the Mardi Gras arrests, in the midst of 'the new gay radicalisation' as activists called it, that these ideas were to be put into practice, the debate was a national one. In *Campaign*, *Gay Community News* and *Gay Information* and at the national gay conferences and the Socialism and Homosexuality Conference in Melbourne in 1981, activists struggled to make sense of the new environment and to find ways to respond to it.

By 1981, Craig Johnston, for one, was clear. The gay community would replace the movement as the vehicle for improving the lot of homosexuals. Because this community existed only in embryo, the immediate task for activists was to nurture it:

> This is the role for gay radicals: help in the unification/ solidification of the gay subcultures, help them to explore their way politically and to develop clout. That is, build a gay community'[41]

This, in turn, required a revision of political theory and practice. The radical demands of the 1970s had to be dispensed with. John Lee argued that to 'avoid the let-downs of the early '70s, which were often the end product of waging "totalist" demands – "smash sex roles", "smash the family" etc',[42] activists had to change their thinking. Johnston argued that the vocabulary of gay politics had to shift towards one that would be better understood in the less political milieu of the subcultures – from 'oppression' to 'discrimination', from 'liberation' to 'rights', from 'movement' to 'community'.[43]

In addition, the welfare and service sectors and the entrepreneurs were no longer to be treated as obstacles or enemies but, potentially at least, as allies. In order to get to the newly radicalising gays (who could provide both numbers for demonstrations and a new generation of activists), it was necessary to work with the bar owners, especially the new independent licensees, who had a quite different attitude towards gays and gay rights.[44] Activists needed to recognise the fact that the bar owners' old hostility to visibility and politics was gone and seize the opportunities thus opened up. Needless to say, not all Left-wing activists were in agreement with this political shift. A series of sometimes furious debates followed, touching on both the tactical and theoretical concerns of the movement, including the depoliticisation of Mardi Gras, the new masculine style, the possibility of bar owners as allies, attitudes to the 'fringe sexualities' (S&M, pedophilia and pornography) and the relationship between gay issues and other struggles.

It was on the relationship to the commercial scene or, more precisely, on the extent to which gay activists could work with the bar owners and other commercial interests and the extent to which gay politics should be adapted to appeal to the newly politicised bargoers that the whole debate turned. For many gay radicals, the question of how to work with commercial interests did not arise: the gay movement simply should not do so. At the Sixth National Conference in August 1980, the final plenary session endorsed a motion to exclude 'the owners and managers of commercial interests' from the organisation of Stonewall Day,[45] and one of those who moved the motion explained some time later that:

> Proprietors and managers of gay bars and newspapers, whether they are gay or straight, have a vested interest in the maintenance of the capitalist system... They make their living from gays... [P]roprietors of badly ventilated, expensive, police and mafia protected, fire hazard gay bars have a monetary interest in the continuing oppression of gays [and] a material interest in opposing gay liberation. The 'take over' of the Gay Mardi Gras by this interest signifies a clear attack on the gay liberation movement. It represents a cooption of gay liberation into an amorphous gay community with its emphasis on maintaining a gay lifestyle rather than fighting for gay rights.[46]

Over the course of the 1970s, the early contempt that many Leftists had felt for the bargoers had been moderated, and there had even been efforts to appeal to them: 'activists should continue to talk to patrons (rather than proprietors) of gay bars in order to involve them in demonstrations and forums putting forward gay liberation demands', argued some.[47] But, just at the very moment when it seemed more possible to orient to this group, changes in the subculture raised, for many on the Left, doubts about whether it was desirable to do so.

The new homosexual was the object of some suspicion for many activists. In the first place, he was male. Lesbians seemed almost entirely absent from the public scene; and, for those whose politics were deeply informed by feminism and the need for solidarity between social movements, this was a problem. The new homosexual was also comfortably middle class in his lifestyle – employed and enjoying a reasonable disposable income. And he was increasingly masculine in his self-presentation. The clone look, imported in the late 1970s from San Francisco (John Lee and Tim Carrigan returned to Adelaide sometime in the second half of the 1970s sporting the new look, to the amazement of their friends), was unabashedly masculine in appearance: short hair, moustache, jeans, flannel shirt and work boots and the very body language:

> Little smiling, little moving, lots of muscles, no free-form dancing, thumbs in the loops of belts, beer in hand... An aping of all the best traditions of the ocker male.[48]

For many on the Left, masculinity was not a style option, but a political reality reflecting an unthinking misogyny or, at best, an attempt to ride out the right-wing shift in society by concealing one's homosexuality and conforming to the approved models of masculinity.[49] Even those who were arguing for the new orientation to the commercial subculture, and to the clones in particular, did not deny the problematic nature of the new image; it was just that they saw it as being a two-sided phenomenon. For them, the macho clone, far from concealing his sexuality, was, by the adoption of the uniform, proclaiming it, reflecting 'a growing gay consciousness and a positive assertion of sexual identity'.[50] In any case, the issue was not whether the gay Left approved of the look or whether the negative aspects might outweigh the positive. The fact was that the new homosexual/clone was the bearer of a new gay political consciousness, and activists ignored him at their peril.[51]

The Left may not like the new masculinity, one activist argued; but, if it wanted credibility with gay men, it was going to have to adapt to it. The fear of being cut off from this new base is intensely expressed in this line of argument. It was strongly stated that, if activists ignored this 'remodelling' of the homosexual, the gay movement would become 'outmoded and irrelevant to the majority of homosexuals'. It was necessary, it was argued, to dispense with the traditional political analysis (or the 'doctrinaire approach...of neatly applying a formula to solve every problem'), reject 'puritanism and abstentionism' and work with the new cultural redefinitions.[52]

The debate raged in the pages of the gay press and in meetings and at dinner parties for some time; but, in the end, it was not by force of argument that the issue was resolved. In the end, those who directed themselves to the commercial scene were going with the tide. By 1981, Craig Johnston could declare that:

> A new phase of gay politics is in the making. Broader, more diverse, it draws on areas of the gay lifestyle not previously involved in politics: the social groups and the bar scene. These homosexuals are providing a social base for a new gay activism based on the institutions of the gay subculture. It's when this fusion of the gay movement and the subculture happens that we'll see the 'gay community' that Sydney so desperately wants to be.[53]

In Sydney, it was the struggle in the early 1980s against police harassment and for homosexual law reform that would provide a focus for joint work and eventual fusion between radical and moderate activists, entrepreneurs and the new homosexual. In other states, AIDS would bring these groups together in the same way. It was out of this work that the gay community – about which there had been so much talk and debate – would finally emerge as a reality.

Endnotes

Note (2024): The Australian Lesbian and Gay Archives is now the Australian Queer Archives

1: The Scene and the Unseen

[1] John-Michael Howsen, quoted in David Grant, 'John-Michael Tells All', *BrotherSister*, 14 May 1998, p. 12.

[2] Rictor Norton, *Mother Clap's Molly House: The Gay Subculture in England 1700–1830*, London, GMP, 1992.

[3] Robert French, *Camping by a Billabong: Gay and Lesbian Stories from Australian History*, Sydney, Blackwattle Press, 1993, p. 11. See also Robert Hughes, *The Fatal Shore: A History of the Transportation of Convicts to Australia, 1787–1868*, London, Collins Harvill, 1986, esp. pp. 264–72, 529–38.

[4] Garry Wotherspoon, *'City of the Plain': History of a Gay Sub-Culture*, Sydney, Hale and Iremonger, 1991, pp. 78–9.

[5] Interview with 'Bill' by Graham Carbery, 19 January 1983, unpublished transcript, Australian Lesbian & Gay Archives, Melbourne (hereafter ALGA).

[6] On Adelaide: John Lee, 'Male Homosexual Identity and Subculture in Adelaide Before World War II', in Robert Aldrich and Garry Wotherspoon (eds), *Gay Perspectives: Essays in Australian Gay Culture*, Department of Economic History, University of Sydney, 1992, pp. 95–112. On Brisbane: Clive Moore, 'Pink Elephants and Drunken Police: Bohemian Brisbane in the 1940s', in Robert Aldrich and Garry Wotherspoon (eds), *Gay and Lesbian Perspectives IV: Studies in Australian Culture*, Department of Economic History and the Australian Centre for Gay and Lesbian Research, University of Sydney, 1998, pp. 132–63. On Sydney, Wotherspoon, 'City of the Plain', p. 93. For Melbourne, I have relied upon Melbourne Gay History Walk, unpublished paper, ALGA.

[7] Jeffrey Smart, *Not Quite Straight: A Memoir*, Melbourne, William Heinemann Australia, 1996, pp. 46–7.

[8] Lucy Chesser, *Negotiating Subjectivities: The Construction of Lesbian Identity in Melbourne, 1960–69*, BA Honours thesis, History Department, University of Melbourne, 1993, pp. 34–5.

[9] David Hilliard, 'Australian Anglicans and Homosexuality: A Tale of Two Cities', *St Marks Review*, Spring 1995, pp. 12–20.

[10] Graham Carbery, 'Some Melbourne Beats: A "Map" of a Subculture from the 1930s to the 1950s', in Aldrich and Wotherspoon (eds), *Gay Perspectives*, pp. 133 ff.

[11] Paddy Byrnes and Robbie Byrnes, '*La Vie en Rose* 1956 (Our Song, Our Year)', in Margaret Bradstock and Louise Wakeling (eds), *Words from the Same Heart*, Sydney, Hale and Iremonger, 1987, p. 26.

[12] Neville Jackson, *No End to the Way*, London, Barrie and Rockcliffe, 1965.

[13] Jackson, *No End to the Way*, p. 160.

[14] *Commonwealth Year Book*, annual, 1939–1960. NSW Statistical Register, annual, 1946–1960. Victoria Police, Annual Report, 1951–1960.

[15] Wotherspoon, *City of the Plain*, pp. 113, 116.

[16] 'New Vice Squad Work', *Truth* (Melbourne), 17 August 1957, p. 3.

[17] Director-General of Security, 'Memorandum on Security Risks in Commonwealth Employ', CRS M1509/1, item 35, [1957], Australian Archives, Canberra; Director General of ASIO, 'Persons with Serious Character Defects as Security Risks', 15 April 1964 (with associated Cabinet papers), Australian Archives, CRS A5827/1, vol. 7, Agendum 199.

[18] Clyde Cameron, *The Cameron Diaries*, Sydney, Allen & Unwin, 1990, p. 434.

[19] 'Homosexuality–Officers of Department of External Affairs', CRS 1M509/1; Item no. 34, Australian Archives.

[20] Neville Woodbury and John S. Barrington, *A Camera Life Class*, London, Neville Woodbury, 1953.

[21] Alasdair Forster, 'Getting Physical', *Outrage*, October 1988, pp. 15–18.

[22] 'Vice Shock in Army Camp', *Truth* (Melbourne), 23 June 1956, p. 1.

[23] Ruth Ford, 'Disciplined, Punished and Resisting Bodies: Lesbian Women and the Australian Armed Services, 1950s–60s', *Lilith*, Autumn 1996, p. 55.

[24] For NSW, see Wotherspoon, *City of the Plain*, pp. 113–18. For Victoria, see the 1949 debate on the *Crimes Act*, *Parliamentary Debates*, vol. 229, pp. 67ff, 567ff; and the 1966 debate on the *Summary Offences Act* where clause 18 was agreed without debate, *Parliamentary Debates*, vol. 285, p. 3213.

[25] Victoria, *Parliamentary Debates*, vol. 263, pp. 2200ff and 2408ff.

[26] *Report of the Royal Commission Inquiring into the Origins, Aims, Objects and Funds of the Communist Party in Victoria and Other Related Matters*, Victorian Parliamentary Papers, 1950–51, vol. 2, pp. 1–156.

[27] Robert French, *Gays Between the Broadsheets: Australian Media References to Homosexuality, 1948–1980*, Gay History Project, Sydney, 1986.

[28] Collinson's papers may be found in the National Library of Australia in Canberra (MS 6327); the Mitchell Library, State Library of NSW (hereafter SLNSW), MSS 4934; and in the Stephen Murray-Smith Papers, State Library of Victoria, MS 8272, box no. 298, Laurence Collinson File. There is also his ASIO file: Laurence Collinson, ASIO file, Australian Archives, Series A6126/25, item 689, and an oral history interview: Laurence Collinson, National Library of Australia (hereafter NLA), Oral History Collection, De B 473 (interview conducted 1 May 1970). I am grateful, too, to family and friends who have shared their recollections with me.

[29] Letters from A. Hallidie-Smith to Laurence Collinson dated 3 November 1958, 22 November 1958, 20 November 1959, and other papers relating to the law reform effort are in the Murray-Smith Papers.

[30] Zelman Cowan to Graham Willett, letter, 26 September 1996, in possession of the author.

[31] 'Modern Society and the Homosexual', *Sydney Morning Herald* (hereafter *SMH*), 6 June 1959, p. 2.

2: Liberalism and its Limits

[1] Great Britain, *Report of the Committee on Homosexual Offences and Prostitution*, H.M.S.O., London, 1957, especially paras 50–3.

[2] Parliamentary inquiries and legislative action around this model in Queensland (1944), South Australia (1940–45) and Tasmania (1951) are discussed in Paul W. Tappan, 'Legislation Dealing with the Sexual Psychopath', *Proceedings of the MedicoLegal Society of Victoria*, vol. viii, 1957–59, p. 83.

[3] Tappan, 'Legislation Dealing with the Sexual Psychopath', pp. 88–9.

[4] Donald Horne, *Time of Hope: Australia 1966–72*, Sydney, Angus & Robertson, 1980, pp. 4–5.

[5] David Maddison, 'Psychiatry or Social Work?' (review of Richard Hauser, *The Homosexual Society*), *Nation*, 11 August 1962, pp. 22–3; H, letter, *Nation*, 25 August 1962, p. 15; X and Laurence Collinson, letter, *Nation*, 6 October 1962, p. 16; David Maddison, letter, *Nation*, 22 September 1962, p. 17.

[6] 'The Unknown Detectives', *Nation*, 18 May 1963, p. 6; 'Copping It', *Nation*, 21 September 1963, p. 4. (This is certainly the same episode that Anne Coombs reports in *Sex and Anarchy: The Life and Death of the Sydney Push*, Melbourne, Viking, 1996, pp. 186–7.)

[7] On Baldwin, see Geoffrey Dutton et al., 'Open Letter to Senator Henry' and Editorial, *Australian Book Review* (hereafter *ABR*), June 1963, pp. 122ff and R. Fischer, letter, *ABR*, October 1963, p. 203; Beatrice Faust, 'A Humanist View: Sex Education', *ABR*, October 1969, p. 275.

[8] Gordon Hawkins, 'Homosexuality: Australia's "Greatest Menace"?', *Bulletin*, 8 May 1965, pp. 21–2.

[9] Beatrice Faust, 'Ethics v. Morality', *Australian Humanist*, December 1966, pp. 1–2. Ian Davidson, 'Permission and After', *Australian Humanist*, December 1968, p. 14.

[10] Solon, 'Too Timid', letter, *News* (Adelaide), 6 January 1967, p. 3. Craig McGregor, *Profile of Australia*, London, Hodder and Stoughton, 1966, p. 83.

[11] *Viewpoints* (Newsletter of the NSW Humanist Society), May 1965, p. 16.

[12] 'University Journalism', *Australian Humanist*, October 1968, p. 3; Junius, 'The (Student) Press', *ABR*, May 1969, pp. 220–2.

[13] 'The Homosexual Villain', *On Dit* (Adelaide University), 25 September 1964, p. 8; originally published in *Lot's Wife*, 27 August 1964. 'Four Essays upon Aspects of Homosexuality', *On Dit*, 5 August 1969, pp. 5–6, 11–12. 'Survey Vindicated', *On Dit*, 29 October 1963, p. 1; '236 Faceless Men', *Semper Floreat* (University of Queensland), 5 August 1965, pp. 6–7.

[14] 'Union Morality', *Farrago*, 3 August 1964, p. 3.

[15] 'Abortion Survey: Farrago Social Involvement Survey on Student Attitudes to Abortion', *Farrago*, 21 June 1968, p. 13. The survey addressed a number of social issues.

[16] Rupert Cross, 'Unmaking Criminal Laws', *Melbourne University Law Review*, November 1962, pp. 415–32; '"No Reason" Against Change on Homosexuals', *SMH*, 1 March 1968, p. 11. Terry Carney, 'Homosexuality: A Case For Reform', *Ormond Papers*, vol. 2, no. 2, 1969, pp. 21–8.

[17] Reported in *SMH*, 11 February 1965, p. 6. A letter appeared a few days later warmly supporting the judge's views. F.W. Fraser, letter, *SMH*, 16 February 1965, p. 2.

[18] For this and what follows, see the papers collected in *Male Sex Offences in Public Places, Proceedings of the Institute of Criminology*, no. 2, Faculty of Law, University of Sydney, 1970.

[19] NSW, *Statistical Registers*, 1966–71.

[20] The history of the squad was discussed by the NSW premier in response to a question in parliament in October 1969. NSW, Legislative Assembly, 1969, *Parliamentary Debates*, pp. 1854–5.

[21] Peter McGonigal, 'Summary of Discussion', *Male Sex Offences in Public Places*, p. 4.

[22] V. Green, 'The Role of the Police in the Detection of Homosexual Offences', *Male Sex Offences in Public Places*, p. 51.

[23] S. Belotti, 'The Police and Sexual Deviants', *Australian Police Journal*, January 1970, pp. 37–44; Richard Knight, 'The Police Role in Our Permissive Society', *Australian Police Journal*, July 1973, pp. 165–88. For an early statement of police views, see M. Fernet, 'Homosexuality and Its Influence on Crime', *Australian Police Journal*, July 1960, pp. 181–90.

[24] 'Dr Woods Agrees with Legalised Homosexuality', *Australian*, 28 July 1964, p. 4.

[25] Malcolm Cowan, '"Knowing Sodom": Australian Churches and Homosexuality', in Garry Wotherspoon (ed.), *Essays in Australian Culture: Gay and Lesbian Perspectives III*, Sydney, Department of Economic History and the Australian Centre for Lesbian & Gay Research, 1996, pp. 212–3.

[26] The relevant articles in the *Australian* were as follows: 'Students Vote for Legal Homosexuality', 27 July 1964, p. 4; 'Dr Woods Agrees with Legalised Homosexuality', 28 July 1964, p. 4; letter, 4 August 1964, p. 5; four letters, 8 August 1964, p. 5.

[27] On the revamping of the media to capture this new market, see Horne, *Time of Hope*, pp. 90–1. French, *Gays Between the Broadsheets*.

[28] 'New Censorship Deal', *Canberra Times*, 31 September 1969, p. 1.

[29] John Stubbs, 'Influx of Younger MPs Raises Hopes of Social Reform', *Australian*, 11 March 1967, p. 2; 'The Left Turns Right on that Delicate Question', *Australian*, 13 February 1971, p. 3. Bill Hayden, Homosexual Law Reform: A Point of View, unpublished paper, undated [1971].

[30] Mungo MacCallum, 'No Party Line on Morals, Says Whitlam', *Australian*, 1 September 1970, p. 2.

[31] Lex Watson, 'The Non-Politics of Sexual Liberation in Australia', *Camp Ink*, vol. 2, no. 4, p. 6.

[32] Jonathan Gaul, 'Mr Holding Calls for Modern Outlook', *Canberra Times*, 31 September 1969, p. 8.

[33] T.E.F. Hughes, Deviant Behaviour of a Criminal Nature, Paper presented to the Sixth National Conference of the Australian Council of Social Services, Canberra, 27 May 1970; copy in Homosexual Law Reform Society (hereafter HLRS) Papers, NLA. Newspaper reports include Peter Sekuless, 'Deviants Viewed More Liberally, Says Hughes', *Canberra Times*, 28 May 1970, p. 1.

[34] 'A Case for Change', editorial, *Canberra Times*, 29 May 1970, p. 2.

[35] Interview with James Grieve, 21 September 1995.

[36] Unless otherwise noted, the information in this section comes from my interview with Dr Thomas Mautner in Canberra, 22 February 1995.

[37] *HLRS Newsletter*, no. 2, 23 October 1969, p. 2.

[38] Don Aitkin, 'Between the Lines', column, *Canberra Times*, 9 July 1969, p. 2 ; Henry Mayer, 'So Why Can't Australia Modernise Its Laws on Homosexuality?', *Australian*, 21 August 1969, p. 7; Michael Richardson, 'The Last Great Unmentionable', *Age*, 9 August 1969. p. 7.

[39] John Ware and Christabel Poll to Thomas Mautner, letter, 8 September 1970, and James Grieve to John Ware, letter, 22 September 1970, HLRS Papers.

3: Kamping Out

[1] Much of the history of these early months and of what follows is drawn from Robert French and Ken Davis, 'Twenty Years Out', interview with John Ware, *OutRage*, March 1990, p. 48 (hereafter French and Davis, Ware interview).

[2] 'A Short History of Gay Liberation Sydney or Did He Fall or Was he Pushed?', leaflet, n.d. [1976].

[3] Terry Bell, A History of Sydney Gay Liberation Front, unpublished paper, n.d. [1975], ALGA, p. 11.

[4] Denise Thompson, *Flaws in the Social Fabric*, Sydney, Allen & Unwin, 1985. p. 9.

[5] Author's interviews with Dorothy Simons and Berenice Buckley. Interview with John Ware by Robert French and Ken Davis, Full Transcript, Sue Wills Papers. This is confirmed by CAMP's minutes for 1971, which show an extended participation in executive meetings by both women, as well as other Humanists.

[6] John Ware, personal communication with author, 29 September 1999. Author's interviews with Lex Watson and Berenice Buckley. Dorothy Simons, Berry Buckley, letters, *Camp Ink*, vol. 1 no. 1, p. 11.

[7] John Ware, 'Camp Inc', letter, *Nation*, 19 September 1970, p. 17.

[8] French, *Gays Between the Broadsheets*.

[9] 'Homosexual Law Reform', *Viewpoints*, November 1969, n.p.

[10] Dorothy Simons, 'Homosexual Law Reform', *Viewpoints*, June 1970, p. 47. See also later comment by E.C. Fuller, 'Achievements of the HLR Committee', *Viewpoints*, February 1972, pp. 13–14 and a letter in reply by Dorothy Simons, *Viewpoints*, April 1972, p. 25.

[11] *Victorian Humanist*, February 1970, p. 2. Carl Reinganum to HLRS, letters, one undated, one dated 5 January 1970, HLRS Papers. 'The Brisbane Link (Lynx)', Camp Ink, March 1971, p. 7. William A. Lee, 'Removing the Queens from Queensland', *Camp Ink*, July 1971, pp. 7–8.

[12] On the Daughters of Bilitis, see Australasian Lesbian Movement file, ALGA; Lucy Chesser, 'Australasian Lesbian Movement, "Claudia's Group" and Lynx: "Non-Political" Lesbian Organisation in Melbourne, 1969–1980', *Hecate*, vol. 22, no. 1, 1996, pp. 69–91; Graham Willett, 'Making Gay Pride a Reality: The Australasian Lesbian Movement', *Gay Community News* (hereafter *GCN*), November 1981, pp. 27–28; Marion Paull, 'A Letter From Australia', in Joan Nestle (ed.), *The Persistent Desire: A Femme-Butch Reader*, Boston, Alyson, 1992, pp. 169–79.

[13] See, for example, 'The Forbidden Love', *Sunday Observer*, 19 July 1970; Darmody, 'The Women Who Fear No Stigma Speak Out', *Age*, 14 August 1970.

[14] Australasian Lesbian Movement, untitled, undated history, ALM file, ALGA.

[15] Secretary, Australian [sic] Lesbian Movement, letter, Lot's Wife, 27 July 1970, p. 6.

[16] Author's interview with Jude Munro.

[17] Australasian Lesbian Movement, untitled, undated history, pp. 1–2.

[18] Chesser, 'Australasian Lesbian Movement', p. 74.

[19] Janet Hawley, 'Couples', *Australian*, 19 September 1970, pp. 14–15. There had been a smaller article published a few days before in the Sydney edition only: Janet Hawley, 'Homosexuals Form Group Aimed at Ending Aura of Mystique, Secrecy', *Australian*, 10 September 1970, p. 3.

[20] Author's interview with Janet Hawley, 27 January 1997.

[21] Author's interview with Robert French and personal communication, 26 October 1999.

[22] French and Davis, Ware interview, pp. 48–9. Author's interview with David Widdup, who remembers the group being about 30–40.

[23] Terry Bell, A History of Sydney Gay Liberation Front, p. 5.

[24] A Special Reporter, 'Gay Power on the Move', *Bulletin*, 18 March 1971, p. 38. Reprinted in *OutRage*, March 1990, pp. 52–3, attributed to Garry Wotherspoon.

[25] For this and the following: author's interview with David Conolly, 14 February 1996; and Winsome Moore, personal communication with author, 22 January 1998.

[26] John Larkin, 'Out of the Shadows–Rebirth for the 5 per cent', *Age*, 7 May 1971.

[27] This and following from 'Brisbane Link (Lynx)', *Camp Ink*, March 1971, p. 7 and author's interview with Cora Zyp, 19 December 1999.

[28] 'Historic Hysterics (or a Brief Club History)', CAMP Qld Newsletter, February 1980, n.p. See also Dennis O'Flaherty, letter, *Queensland Pride*, no. 10, 1994. O'Flaherty was the president of the Humanist Society of Queensland.

[29] 'Homosexuals Want Own Club Premises', *Sunday Mail* (Brisbane), 14 March 1971, p. 10; 'Brisbane Scene – The Gala Opening', *Camp Ink*, May 1971, p. 10; also 'Camp Inc', interview with Frank and Anna, *Semper Floreat*, 5 July 1971, p. 4.

[30] Graham A. Douglas, 'Perth Scene: President's Farewell Address', *Camp Ink*, vol. 2, no. 8–9, p. 13; interviews with Graham Douglas.

[31] *CAMP WA Circular*, November 1974, p. 6.

[32] Anna Yeatman, 'Adelaide Women's Lib Supports Camp Ink', *On Dit*, 17 March 1971, p. 3.

[33] Interviews with Roger Knight, David Hilliard, Jon Ruwoldt.

[34] P. Stuart Foss, 'Homosexual Law Reform', letter, *Canberra Times*, 17 September 1971, p. 2; 'ACT CAMP: Chicken and Champagne Picnic', *Camp Ink*, December 1971– January 1972, p. 19; 'ACT CAMP', *Camp Ink*, February 1972, p. 11; Paul [Foss] to Dennis Altman, letter, 4 March 1972, Dennis Altman Papers, Mitchell Library, SLNSW.

[35] CAMP NSW Executive Minutes, 15 September 1971; Walter Hillbrick, Secretary, letter, 3 April 1974, Society Five Papers, ALGA. I have found no one who has any knowledge of a functioning branch in Tasmania or even of the names of anyone who might have been associated. It is possible that David Widdup, who was based in Tasmania at about this time, was involved. Unfortunately, I neglected to pursue this line of inquiry with him before his death in late 1999.

[36] John Ware, 'Twelve Months Past', *Camp Ink*, September 1971, p. 4; 'Homosexuals v. Intolerance', *Newcastle Morning Herald*, 27 May 1971.

[37] CAMP NSW, 'CAMP Inc: A Society for the Rights of Homosexuals', n.d. [Sydney, late 1970].

[38] Christabel Poll, 'Gay Liberation', *Old Mole*, 26 October 1970, p. 5.

[39] 'Homosexuals v. Intolerance', *Newcastle Morning Herald*, 27 May 1971.

[40] Alan Mackenzie, 'CAMP Goes to War', *Pix*, 1 May 1971, p. 18.

[41] Letter to *Semper Floreat*, cited in Wilson, *The Sexual Dilemma*, p. 48.

[42] Mackenzie, 'CAMP Goes to War', p. 17.

[43] For a detailed discussion of counter-cultural politics in the movement, see Chapter 4. Interview with John Ware by Robert French and Ken Davis, full transcript.

[44] Sue Wills, *Politics of Sexual Liberation*, PhD thesis, University of Sydney, 1981, p. 96.

[45] Terry Bell, A History of the Sydney Gay Liberation Front, pp. 5–6. Minutes of Seventh General Meeting of CAMP, 18 August 1971, Evolution file, GCS Papers.

[46] Thompson, *Flaws in the Social Fabric*, p. 12; Sue Wills, 'Looking for a Home: Lesbians and the Women's and Gay Movement. In Both But of Neither', Sydney, 1970–73, unpublished paper, p. 7; Wills, *Politics of Sexual Liberation*, p. 98.

[47] CAMP NSW, Press Release, May 1972, Sue Wills Papers.

[48] Ware's last appearance in CAMP's executive minutes is 6 February 1974, Peter de Waal Papers, Mitchell Library. Although Poll remained listed as editor of *Camp Ink* (along with Ware) until the end of 1973 (when production lapsed for some months), beginning with vol. 2, no. 10 (about August 1972), her name is consistently misspelt. Presumably this reflects a lack of involvement on her part.

[49] Wills, *Politics of Sexual Liberation*, p. 102.

[50] For this and what follows see Wills, *Politics of Sexual Liberation*, pp. 101–2 and Editorial, *Camp Ink*, April 1971, p. 2.

[51] Editorial, *Camp Ink*, January 1971, p. 2.

[52] French and Davis, Ware interview, p. 51.

[53] 'A Helping Hand From CAMP', *Bulletin*, 23 October 1971, p. 32.

[54] CAMP NSW, 'CAMP and the Berowra Preselection', leaflet, n.d. [October 1971], Wills Papers.

[55] 'Our Demo', *Camp Ink*, December 1971–January 1972, pp. 16–17.

[56] Graham A. Douglas, 'Perth Scene: President's Farewell Address', *Camp Ink*, vol. 2, no. 8–9, p. 13.

[57] Address to the Members of the Campaign Against Moral Persecution (WA Division), by the 1974 President, Brian Lindberg, unpublished paper, Graham Douglas Papers.

[58] 'Politics and Poofters ("The Dialectics of Liberation")', *Camp Ink*, September 1971, p. 14.

[59] Cora Zyp and Paul Lucas, 'Brisbane Scene', *Camp Ink*, August 1971, p. 7.

[60] Author's interview with David Conolly. Winsome [Moore] to John [Ware], 6 May [1972].

[61] David Widdup, 'Famous Five or Secret Seven', *Camp Ink*. vol. 3, no. 7, pp. 12–3.

[62] The relevant articles are: Trevor Hughes, 'Deja Vu '52: Did Dr Duncan Die in Vain?', *Camp Ink*, vol. 3, no. 1, pp. 15–6; Jon Ruwoldt, 'Adelaide: An Attack on an Attack', *Camp Ink*, vol. 3, no. 2, p. 15; Trevor Hughes, 'A Defence', *Camp Ink*, vol. 3, no. 2, p. 15.

[63] John Ware, 'CAMP WA, A Black Swan Song', *Camp Ink*, vol. 3, no. 6, p. 10.

4: The Challengers

[1] *How Not to Join the Army: Advice for Twenty-Year-Olds*, Resistance, Sydney, n.d. The use of the word 'gay' is not as interesting as it might be: the pamphlet was essentially a reprint of a US pamphlet with minor changes to make it relevant to Australia. I am grateful to Ken Mansell for information regarding the history of this pamphlet.

[2] For a more detailed discussion of the relationship between the far left and homosexual politics in this period, see Graham Willett, 'Minorities Can Win: The Gay Movement, the Left and the Transformation of Australian Society', *Overland*, Summer 1997, pp. 64–8 and Graham Willett, 'Marxists and Gay Liberation', *Reconstruction: A Socialist Journal of Inquiry and Debate*, no. 9, 1996–97, pp. 25–31.

[3] Lyn Donaldson, 'Revolution and the Counter-Culture', *Lot's Wife*, August 1972, p. 10. On the counterculture in Australia, see also Margaret Smith and David Crossley (eds), *The Way Out: Radical Alternatives in Australia*, Melbourne, Lansdowne, 1975, especially Dennis Altman, 'The Quantum Leap', pp. 13–4.

[4] Kenneth Cook, *Wake in Fright*, Melbourne, Penguin, 1967 [1961], pp. 94–6.

[5] Dilys Kevan, Untitled Paper, in *Female Homosexuality Seminar One: Conditioning Processes in Education and Mass Media*, CAMP (NSW), n.d. [1975], pp. 35–6.

[6] On Number 96, see Frank Wells, 'The Sale of No. 96', and 'The Joe Hasham Story, Starring Don Finlayson', *Campaign*, July 1977, pp. 19–22.

[7] Dennis Altman, quoted in Martyn Goddard, 'The Electronic Closet', *OutRage*, September 1990, p. 42.

[8] Martin Smith, 'The "Gay" Guys are Great', *Campaign*, February 1976, pp. 7–8. See the Australian Broadcasting Control Board (ABCB) research reported in its *Attitudes to Television: A Report Based on Surveys Made in Adelaide during 1973, 1974*, p. 11; *Attitudes to Television: A Report Based on Surveys Made in Melbourne during 1974, 1976*, pp. 19–20. ABCB Annual Reports also included mention of Number 96 in the section dealing with 'Broadcasting of Objectionable Matter' in 1972, 1973 and 1974. Interesting earlier research on the attitudes of viewers to controversial material, including homosexuality, is reported

in ABCB, *Attitudes to Television: A Report Based on Surveys Made in Sydney and Melbourne during 1968 and 1969*, July 1970, pp. 21, 89–90; and *Attitudes to Television: A Report Based on Surveys Made in Adelaide and Sydney during 1969 and 1970*, December 1971, p. 13.

[9] Author's interview with Michael Hurley.

[10] Anthony Fitzgerald, 'Come Out!' leaflet, Melbourne University Gay Liberation Front, n.d. [1972?]. Melbourne University Gay Liberation Front, 'Gay Liberation Front', leaflet n.d. [1973?].

[11] 'Homosexuals Told: You Must Become Militant', *Age*, 10 August 1972.

[12] Sue Wills interview with Dennis Altman, 12 October 1974, p. 7, Sue Wills Papers.

[13] Sydney Gay Liberation, 'Gay Liberation', leaflet, n.d. Sydney Gay Liberation, 'A Gay Attack on Sexism', leaflet, n.d.

[14] Editorial, *Camp Ink*, vol. 2, no. 4, p. 3.

[15] Tess Lee Ack, 'Trendy is the New Oppression' in *Female Homosexuality, Seminar One*, p. 47.

[16] Campus CAMP 'It Is Not the Homosexual Who Is Perverted But His Position in Society: A Gay Liberation Manifesto', *Semper Floreat*, 8 June 1973, p. 4. This is a reprint (though it does not say so) of the London Gay Liberation Front Manifesto of 1971.

[17] Sydney Gay Liberation, 'Sydney Gay Liberation', leaflet, June 1972. Sydney Gay Liberation Publications Group, 'The Way Forward', 1972.

[18] Jon Ruwoldt, 'Gay-Proud of What?' *Boiled Sweets*, vol. 3, no. 2, n.p.

[19] Melbourne University Gay Liberation Front, 'Gay Liberation Front'.

[20] Jon Ruwoldt, 'Gay-Proud of What?' See also Terry Bell, 'Homosexuality Is a Valid Alternative', leaflet, n.d.; Melbourne University Gay Liberation Front, 'Gay Liberation Front', Dennis Altman, 'Gay Lib–Come Out!', n.d. [October 1972].

[21] Dennis Altman, letter, *Camp Ink*, August 1971, p. 16.

[22] Interview with Dennis Altman, 9 January 1996.

[23] On the origins and early months of Sydney Gay Liberation, see Wills, *Politics of Sexual Liberation*, pp. 94–5, 110–11; Bell, History of Sydney Gay Liberation, pp. 7–8. Airman's speech to the Sex Lib forum was widely reprinted, most conveniently in his *Coming Out in the Seventies: Sexuality, Politics and Culture*, Melbourne, Penguin, 1980, pp. 16–21.

[24] Sydney Gay Liberation, 'SGL', leaflet, June 1972.

[25] Wills, *Politics of Sexual Liberation*, p. 111.

[26] Interviews with Rodney Thorpe, 12 October 1996, and Sasha Soldatow, 24 October 1996.

[27] 'Gay Lib Stands Up', *Lot's Wife*, 10 April 1972, p. 3.

[28] 'First Gay Lib Meeting', *On Dit*, 28 August 1972, p. 9. Interview with Jill Matthews, 30 November 1996.

[29] Vivianne Manouge, 'Consciousness Raising', *Boiled Sweets*, September 1973, n.p. 'Some Thoughts on GAA', *Boiled Sweets*, July 1973.

[30] 'Camp Perth', *Pelikan*, October 1973, p. 7.

[31] Denise Thompson, *Flaws in the Social Fabric, Part I*; Sue Wills, 'Inside the CWA: The Other One', *Journal of Australian Lesbian Feminist Studies*, no. 4, June 1994, pp. 6–22.

[32] Craig Melmouth [Johnston], The Homosexual Movement in Australia, 1970–75, *Axis*, 18 October 1976, pp. 30–1.

[33] *Patchwork Newsletter*, October 1976, n.p. [Inserted with CAMP Qld Newsletter, October 1976]. Viv Cass, 'First National Homosexual Conference', *CAMP Circular*, November 1975, n.p.

[34] Liz Ross, 'Escaping the Well of Loneliness', in Verity Burgmann and Jenny Lee (eds), *Staining the Wattle*, Melbourne, Penguin, 1988, pp. 100–8.

[35] Author's interview with Helen Pausacker.

[36] For a description of the debates within the Adelaide women's movement, see Sylvia Kinder, *Herstory of Adelaide Women's Liberation*, 1969–74, the author, Adelaide, 1980.

[37] Sue Wills mentions John Ware and Dennis Altman in particular, *Politics of Sexual Liberation*, p. 106. The writings of numerous gay male activists in this period attest to how much support there was.

[38] Christabel [Poll], 'Joe Stalin and the Sisters', *Liberaction*, April 1973, pp. 7–8.

[39] For a detailed discussion of the relationship between women and men in CAMP, Gay Liberation and Women's Liberation, see Sue Wills, 'Inside the CWA: The Other One', and her unpublished paper 'Looking for a Home'. For a report that Christabel Poll attacked women's liberation as a 'bourgeois movement', see Kay, 'Women's Liberation National Conference June 10–12: A Personal Report', *Liberaction*, no. 3 June 1972, p. 4.

[40] Hobart Women's Action Group, 'Sexism and the Women's Movement', *Refractory Girl*, Summer 1974, pp. 30–3.

[41] Gaby Antolovich, 'Women's Commission 1973', *Camp Ink*, vol. 3, no. 4, p. 9; CAMP Women's Association, 'Can You Sexually Love a Woman?' leaflet, n.d. [1973]; Wills, *Politics of Sexual Liberation*, pp. 128–30.

[42] Janey Stone, 'Radical Feminism: A Critique', in her *Perspectives for Women's Liberation*, Melbourne, Redback Press, n.d. [1981], pp. 11–18 [originally published 1974].

[43] What follows is based upon Chris Sitka, 'Herstory of Melbourne Radicalesbians', unpublished paper, December 1988, ALGA; Melbourne Gay Women's Group, 'The Melbourne Gay Women's Group', in Jan Mercer (ed.), *The Other Half: Women in Australian Society*, Melbourne, Penguin, 1975, p. 441; Jocelyn, 'Radical Lesbians – Break Away', *Voices of Vashti Anthology: Melbourne Women, 1972–81*, p. 80 [originally published July 1973] and a number of interviews: Laurie Bebbington, Jocelyn Clarke, Barbara Creed, Sue Jackson, Kay Mosley, Jude Munro, Helen Pausacker and Jenny Pausacker.

[44] Wills, 'Inside the CWA: The Other One', passim.

[45] Jenny Pausacker, cited in Sitka, 'Herstory of Melbourne Radicalesbians', p. 4.

[46] Sitka, 'Herstory of Melbourne Radicalesbians', p. 6.

[47] The papers of the conference are reprinted as appendices in Sitka, 'Herstory of Melbourne Radicalesbians' and available at ALGA.

[48] Melbourne Gay Women's Group, 'The Melbourne Gay Women's Group', pp. 441–6.

⁴⁹ *Melbourne Feminist Collection*, Melbourne, July 1973.

⁵⁰ Lucy Chesser, 'Australasian Lesbian Movement, "Claudia's Group" and Lynx: "Non Political" Lesbian Organisation in Melbourne, 1969–1980', *Hecate*, vol. 22, no. 1, 1996, pp. 69–91.

⁵¹ Author's interview with Chris Sitka, 1 November 1999.

⁵² On the particular difficulties of writing this history, see Sue Davies, 'Writing Her Story: Notes on Feminist History', reproduced as Appendix 4 in Tanya Pietzker, *Toward the Construction of a Lesbian History in Australia: Dyke Intellectuals of the Liberation Movements and Their Influence on Sexual Politics Today*, semester research project, Australian Studies Centre, University of Queensland, 1994. Copy held at ALGA.

⁵³ Natalie Varnish, 'Dykotomies', *Campaign*, July 1989, pp. 57–8.

⁵⁴ Natalie Varnish, 'Gyroscopes and Lavender', *Campaign*, October 1989, pp. 72–3.

⁵⁵ Judith Ion, 'Degrees of Separation: Lesbian Separatist Communities in Northern New South Wales, 1974–95', in Jill Julius Matthews (ed.), *Sex in Public: Australian Sexual Cultures*, St Leonards, Allen & Unwin, 1997, pp. 97–113.

⁵⁶ Jai Greenaway, *Political Acts: Lesbian Theatre in Sydney*, Sydney, self-published, 1990.

⁵⁷ Angelo Rosas, 'An Intellectual History of Sydney Gay Liberation', unpublished paper, p. 5. Copy held at ALGA.

⁵⁸ Craig Johnston and Brian McGahen, 'Draft Manifesto of the Revolutionary Homosexuals of the GLF', unpublished paper, 1974.

⁵⁹ Craig Johnston, '(Ef)feminism', *National U*, 15 July 1974.

⁶⁰ Lance Gowland, 'Homosexuals and Sexism', leaflet, n.d. Copy in ALGA.

⁶¹ Ray, letter, *Melbourne Gay Liberation Newsletter*, October 1973, n.p.

⁶² Michael Hurley and Craig Johnston, 'Campfires of the Resistance', in *Papers and Proceedings of the First National Homosexual Conference*, the Collective, Melbourne [1975], pp. 53–8.

⁶³ Peter Hawkins, 'Effeminism', in *Papers and Proceedings of the First National Homosexual Conference*, pp. 51–2; Angelo Rosas, 'Against a Masculine Society', in *Papers and Proceedings of the First National Homosexual Conference*, pp. 59–61.

⁶⁴ Paul, 'Some Thoughts on the MAS and the Conference', Males Against Sexism, August 1977; 'Males Against Sexism', *Gay Teachers' and Students' Group Newsletter* (hereafter, *GTSG Newsletter*), March 1977, n.p.

5: Lobbing Eggs and Lobbying

¹ Quintin Hoare and Geoffrey Nowell Smith (eds), *Selections from the Prison Notebooks of Antonio Gramsci*, New York, International Publishers, 1971, p. 10.

² Wills, *Politics of Sexual Liberation*, p. 108.

³ Craig Johnston and Pauline Garde, 'The Political Sociology of Gay Activists', *Australian and New Zealand Journal of Sociology*, July 1981, pp. 76–7.

⁴ Miss Lovejoy to Dennis Altman, letter, 29 January 1973, Altman papers, NLA.

[5] David [Widdup] to Dennis Altman, letter, n.d. [1972], Altman papers, NLA.

[6] Gay Liberation Publications Group, 'Queens and Dykes Want Gay Lib Back', leaflet, n.d. [1972]. Rodney Thorpe threw much light on this episode when I interviewed him on 12 October 1996.

[7] See references (including television and radio coverage) in French, *Gays Between the Broadsheets*.

[8] Interview with Rodney Thorpe.

[9] Melbourne Gay Liberation, 'Gay Pride Week News', leaflet, August 1973.

[10] 'Our Gay Demo', *Gay Rays*, December 1972, p. 12.

[11] Cass Radley, 'Our Demo', *Camp Ink*, December 1971–January 1972, p. 17.

[12] Mim and Sue, 'On Holding Hands', *Camp Ink*, December 1971–January 1972, p. 10.

[13] Alan Begg, quoted in George Tavistock, 'Gay Power', *Lot's Wife*, 15 April 1971, pp. 12–13.

[14] Peter K. Cashman, 'Homosexuality', *Farrago*, 26 March 1971, p. 5.

[15] 'Melbourne Scene', *Camp Ink*, vol. 2. no. 4, p. 11.

[16] Lorraine Burrows to Michael Clohesy, letter, 8 October 1974, Gays Counselling Service Papers (hereafter GCS Papers), Mitchell Library, SLNSW, Box 7.

[17] 'Gay Liberation and the CR Group', *Boiled Sweets*, 27 November 1973 [despite the dating of the issue, internal evidence suggests 1972].

[18] Bill Morley, 'Coming Out at Latrobe', *Gay Liberation Newsletter*, October 1973, n.p.

[19] 'A Radicalesbian Lifestyle', *Refractory Girl*, Summer 1974, pp 12–15; Peggy Clarke, 'Women Living Together', *Refractory Girl*, Summer 1974, pp. 9–10.

[20] I am grateful to Reece Plunkett for this fact.

[21] Interview with Rodney Thorpe.

[22] The mailing lists could be quite extensive – Melbourne Gay Liberation's mailing list in 1974 contained over 400 names. Melbourne Gay Liberation Mailing List, box of Cards, ALGA.

[23] For a contemporary discussion, see Nicholas Langton, 'Pamphlets as a Form of Communication on Campus', *Semper Floreat*, 17 March 1969, n.p.

[24] Editorial, *Camp Ink*, April 1972, p. 3; Dennis Altman, 'Gays Abandoned' in his *Coming Out in the Seventies: Sexuality, Politics & Culture*, Melbourne, Penguin, 1979, pp. 58–62 [originally published 1973]; 'If It's CAMP, It's Not News', *Nation Review*, 5–11 September 1972, p. 1203; 'Oppression, Suppression', *Nation Review*, 22–8 July 1972, p. 1143; C.J. Poll and Jill Row, 'Granny Decamps', letter, *Nation Review*, 29 July–4 August 1972, p. 1166; Dennis Altman, 'Forum on Sexual Liberation', *Coming Out in the Seventies*, p. 18; author's interview with David Widdup.

[25] Sue Wills in Bill Calder, 'From the Bars to the Barricades and Back', interview with Lex Watson and Sue Wills, *OutRage*, September 1990, pp. 36–8.

[26] Secretary's Report, Society Five Annual General Report for the Year October 1971–October 1972, p. 3.

²⁷ See, for example, 'CAMP NSW Co-Presidential Report April 1973', *Camp Ink*, vol. 3, no. 4, p. 11; Wills, *Politics of Sexual Liberation* lists others at p. 92. Graham Douglas, of CAMP WA, says that he and other public speakers did their presentations so often that they could do them off by heart. Author's interview with Graham Douglas.

²⁸ This is drawn from Gary Jaynes' speaking notes, Homosexual Counselling Group file, Gary Jaynes Papers.

²⁹ Wills, *Politics of Sexual Liberation*, p. 92.

³⁰ W.H., 'Public Politics and Private Morality', *Camp Ink*, December 1970, pp. 4–5.

³¹ 'Thank You Anne Deveson', *Camp Ink*, vol. 1, no. 6, p. 10.

³² 'Adelaide Scene', *Camp Ink*, May 1972, p. 9.

³³ Letter Winsome [Moore] to John [Ware]; Annual Report from the Membership Committee For the Year Ending November 1973, Society Five Papers, ALGA.

³⁴ Lesley Rogers, 'On Being a Political Lesbian' in Bradstock and Wakeling (eds), *Words from the Same Heart*, p. 110.

³⁵ For the following, see 'Sydney Scene – Forces of Darkness', *Camp Ink*, vol. 2, no. 8–9, p. 19. The letters referred to here are to be found in the Altman Papers, NLA: John Dean, 11 July 1972; Ian Black, 3 July 1972; E.H. Arblaster, 6 July 1972; A.G.W. Keys, 10 July 1972; R. Makula, 3 July 1972.

³⁶ Sandra Dawson, television column, *Australian*, 25 November 1972, p. 21; see also Wills, *Politics of Sexual Liberation*, p. 91.

³⁷ Reported in Peter K. Cashman, 'Homosexuality', *Farrago*, 26 March 1971, pp. 4–5; George Tavistock, 'Gay Power', *Lot's Wife*, 15 April 1971, pp. 12–13. The leaflet advertising the event referred to K.A.M.P. Inc (presumably it was prepared by someone unfamiliar with the group). Debating Union, 'Forum on Homosexuality', leaflet, n.d. [March 1971]. This forum is also discussed in an audio tape made by members of Gay Lib in Melbourne in 1976 in which they recall events leading up to the formation of Gay Liberation. Gay Liberation History, audio tape dated 7 February 1976, ALGA.

³⁸ 'Gay Day', *Farrago*, 15 September 1972, p. 12. Barry Charles, 'Campus Camp Discussion on Legalising Homosexuality', *Camp Ink*, December 1971–January 1972, p. 20.

³⁹ The correspondence and the memorandum are in Dennis Altman Papers, NLA.

⁴⁰ 'In, Out and Around the Syndrome', *Camp Ink*, vol. 2, no. 6, p. 11; the significance of the date chosen for Sex Lib Week is noted in CAMP NSW, Press Release, 10 August 1972, Sue Wills Papers.

⁴¹ 'Our Gay Demo', *Gay Rays*, December 1972, p. 12.

⁴² Michael Smith, 'Gay Lib Protest Leads to Meeting with ABC Chiefs', *Age*, 12 July 1972, p. 3; 'Gay Lib Grows Angry at ABC', *Age*, 13 July 1972, p. 12.

⁴³ Wills, *Politics of Sexual Liberation*, p. 75. See also leaflets: CAMP NSW, 'Demonstration', leaflet, n.d.; Sydney Gay Liberation Publications Group, 'Blatant Oppression', leaflet, n.d.; CAMP NSW, 'Why We Are Here', leaflet, n.d. [all November 1972]. Graeme Vincent, 'St Mary's Sunday Protest: Gay Lib Demo', *Geelong News*, 28 November 1975, p. 1.

⁴⁴ Roderick Byatt, 'Events Leading Up to the Meeting of Pissed off Activists', unpublished paper, 22 November 1974, Sue Wills Papers. On the Domain zap: Sydney Gay Liberation, 'Homosexuality Is a Valid Alternative', leaflet, Sydney, n.d. June 1973].

⁴⁵ Adelaide's zaps are reported (usually in articles without titles) in *Boiled Sweets*: first edition, n.d. June 1973]; 'Zapping Steele Hall', July 1973; September 1973.

⁴⁶ Interviews with Bill Hayden and Moss Cass. Lamond's comments were made during the Mardi Gras television broadcast.

⁴⁷ Author's interview with James Grieve.

⁴⁸ Jack Mundey, *Green Bans and Beyond*, Sydney, Angus and Robertson, 1981, p. 106.

⁴⁹ 'Sexism and Racism', interviews with Cheryl Buchanan and Lionel Lacey, *Axis*, 14 July 1976, pp. 8–9. Gary Foley to CAMP, letter, 8 October 1975, GCS Papers, Box 7.

6: The Three Pillars of Ignorance

¹ This account relies heavily upon Tim Reeves, 'The 1972 Debate on Male Homosexuality in South Australia', in Robert Aldrich (ed.), *Gay Perspectives II: More Essays in Australian Gay Culture*, Sydney, Department of Economic History and the Australian Centre for Gay and Lesbian Research, 1994, pp. 149–92; Malcolm Cowan and Tim Reeves, 'The "Gay Rights" Movement and the Decriminalisation Debate in South Australia' in Robert Aldrich and Garry Wotherspoon (eds), *Gay and Lesbian Perspectives IV: Studies in Australian Culture*, Sydney, Department of Economic History and the Australian Centre for Gay and Lesbian Research, 1998; and my interviews with Roger Knight and David Hilliard.

² Don Dunstan, *Felicia: The Political Memoirs of Don Dunstan*, South Melbourne, Macmillan, 1981, p. 127.

³ This and previous quote from *Boiled Sweets*, September 1973, cited in Reeves and Cowan, 'The "Gay Rights" Movement', pp. 175–6.

⁴ The original is in the HLRS Papers, NLA.

⁵ Unless otherwise noted, what follows is drawn from my interview with Moss Cass. For the debate, see Australia, House of Representatives, *Parliamentary Debates (Hansard)*, (1973), pp. 2327–35.

⁶ Interview with Moss Cass.

⁷ Peter Blazey, 'Big Quakes, Gay Shakes', *OutRage*, March 1994, p. 59.

⁸ Australian Capital Territory, Legislative Assembly 1974, *Hansard*, pp. 102–13.

⁹ Law Reform (Sexual Behaviour) Bill (ACT), 1975; Explanatory Memorandum; Memorandum from Gordon Bryant, Minister for the Capital Territory, to the President ACT Legislative Assembly, no. 1975/57, 28 May 1975.

¹⁰ Lex Watson, 'Old ACT HLR Saga', *Speaking Volumes*, July–August 1976, n.p.; Lex Watson, 'Federal Poofter Bashing Resumes', *Nation Review*, 20–26 February 1976, p. 466.

¹¹ Garry D. Toddam, 'A Gay Christian Is a Contradiction in Terms', *Semper Floreat*, 31 July 1975, p. 22; Garry Souter to Catholic Leader, letter, 24 August 1973, Cross+ Section Papers, GCS Papers, Mitchell Library, SLNSW.

¹² Text of letter accompanying the Statement on Religion by the CAMP NSW Working Group, Sue Wills Papers.

¹³ David Hilliard, 'Australian Anglicans and Homosexuality: A Tale of Two Cities', *St Mark's*

Review, Spring 1995, p. 12. The sole item that Hilliard found was PM [sic], 'The Problem of the Homosexual', *The Anglican*, 9 September 1955, p. 9, a review of Bailey's *Homosexuality and the Western Christian Tradition*.

[14] Philip Strong, archbishop of Brisbane, 'Inaugural Address', Church of England in the Province of Queensland, *Proceedings in Connection with the Eighteenth Session of the Synod, Brisbane*, Diocesan Registry, 1964, pp. 5–32.

[15] Rev. A. North, 'The Responsibility of the Church Regarding Homosexuality', in *The Responsibility of the Church Regarding Homosexuality*, published by the Church and Nation Committee of the NSW Presbyterian Assembly, n.d. [1968], p. 4.

[16] Rev. H.A. Brown, 'The Bible and Homosexuality', letter, *SMH*, 3 August 1967, p. 2. 'Homosexuals and the Law', six letters, *SMH*, 8 August 1967, p. 2.

[17] Cited in North, 'The Responsibility of the Church Regarding Homosexuality', p. 1; and in Cowan, '"Knowing" Sodom', in Garry Wotherspoon (ed.), *Gay and Lesbian Perspectives III*, p. 215.

[18] Rev. W.G. Coughlan, 'The Church and the Homosexual', in *The Responsibility of the Church Regarding Homosexuality*, p. 15.

[19] 'Reform of Sex Law Sought', *SMH*, 19 May 1967, p. 7.

[20] [Anglican] Diocese of Melbourne, *Social Questions Committee, Report on Homosexuality*, no publication details [Melbourne 1971], p. 5.

[21] Correspondence relating to this episode in August–September 1972 is held in the Graham Douglas Papers.

[22] Society of Friends, cited in Roger Sawkins, letter, n.d. [January 1975]. I am grateful to Roger Sawkins for discussing this episode with me and for providing a copy of this letter and other material relating to the society's deliberations.

[23] On Sydney, see Wills, *Politics of Sexual Liberation*, p. 74. On Adelaide, see 'Adelaide Scene', *Camp Ink*, vol. 2, no. 4, p. 10. On Brisbane, see Ken Goodenough, letter, *Camp Ink*, vol. 3, no. 7, p. 2.

[24] John Ware interviewed by Robert French and Ken Davis, Full Transcript, Sue Wills Papers.

[25] Wills, *Politics of Sexual Liberation*, p. 74. 'Adelaide Scene', Camp Ink, May 1972, p. 9.

[26] 'Cross+Section: The Church Group within CAMP', in CAMP NSW Co-Presidential Report, Sydney, 1973, p. 14; 'Christian Homosexuals Protest', *Church Scene*, 30 April 1973, p. 6; 'Dear Passer-by', leaflet, 15 April 1973, Cross+Section Papers.

[27] 'Cross+Section: The Church Group Within CAMP', p. 14.

[28] Cross+Section news sheet, n.d. [late March, early April 1973], Cross+Section Papers.

[29] Wills, *Politics of Sexual Liberation*, p. 76.

[30] Gay Liberation Front [Melbourne], 'The Counter Psychiatry Group of the Gay Liberation Front: Why Its Name; Why It Exists', leaflet, n.d.

[31] See, for example, the letters columns of the *Canberra Times* during the 1969 law reform debate (letters, 5, 9, 11, 12, 15, 16, 17, 18, 19, 25, 26, 29 July and 1, 4, 6, 12, 13, 15 August) and Sue Wills, Eva Cox, Gaby Antolovich, 'Attitudes to Sexuality, Sydney', Research Report No. 8, Royal Commission on Human Relationships, Research Reports, Canberra, 1977, pp. 76–7.

[32] Lucy Chesser, *Negotiating Subjectivities: The Construction of Lesbian Identities in Melbourne, 1960–1969*, Honours thesis, History Department, University of Melbourne, 1993; Ruth Ford, *Deviance and Desire: Meanings of Lesbianism in Post-War Australia, 1946-1960*, BA Honours Thesis, History Department, La Trobe University, 1992.

[33] Survey No. 1, file of returned survey forms, Society Five Papers, ALGA.

[34] J.F.J., Cade, 'An Eclectic Psychiatrist Looks at Homosexuality' in N. McConaghy (ed.), *Liberation Movements and Psychiatry*, Sydney, CIBA-GEIGY Australia, 1974, p. 99.

[35] Robin Winkler and Una Gault, 'Psychiatry and Clinical Psychology' in Paul Boreham, Alec Pemberton and Paul Wilson (eds), *The Professions in Australia: A Critical Appraisal*, St Lucia, University of Queensland Press, 1976, p. 172; Simon Haselton, 'Permissiveness in Australian Society', *Australian Journal of Psychology*, vol. 27, no. 3, 1975, pp. 257–67.

[36] 'Notes from Council', *Australian Psychologist*, July 1974, pp. 207–8.

[37] R.E. Barr, H.P. Greenberg and M.S. Dalton, 'Homosexuality and Psychological Adjustment', *Medical Journal of Australia*, 1974, 1, p. 189; R.F. Barr, 'Psychiatric Opinion and Homosexuality: A Short Report', *Journal of Homosexuality*, vol. 1, no. 2, 1974, pp. 213–15.

[38] Unless otherwise indicated, what follows is based upon my interview with Dr Barr on 16 February 1995.

[39] 'Psychiatrists Back Homosexual Law Reform', *Australian*, 18 October 1973, p. 5. 'Moves for Homosexual Law Reform', *SMH*, 18 October 1973, p. 2.

[40] Wills, *Politics of Sexual Liberation*, pp. 77, 81; also French and Davis, John Ware interview.

[41] Robin Winkler, *A Critique of Aversion Therapy for Homosexuals*, Sydney Gay Liberation, Sydney, n.d. See also Laurie Bebbington and Jocelyn Clarke, 'Psychological and Psychiatric Theories of Lesbianism' in *Homosexuality: An Action and Resource Guide for Tertiary Students*, Melbourne, Australian Union of Students, n.d.; John Ware, 'Psychosurgery in Australia', *Camp Ink*, vol. 3, no. 4, p. 8; John Ware, 'Rat-psychology and the Homosexual', *Union Recorder*, 25 September 1970, pp. 3–4; Sue Wills, 'The Psychologist and the Lesbian', *Refractory Girl*, Winter 1975, pp. 41–5.

[42] 'A Statement From Gay Liberation', leaflet, n.d. [1973].

[43] Wills, *Politics of Sexual Liberation*, pp. 196 ff.

[44] John Ware, 'Psychosurgery in Australia', p. 8. Wills, *Politics of Sexual Liberation*, p. 182.

[45] On the Homosexual Guidance Service (HGS) see Wills, *Politics of Sexual Liberation*, p. 85.

[46] Sue Wills, *Politics of Sexual Liberation*, p. 85.

[47] Brian Davies, *An Introduction to Clinical Psychiatry*, Melbourne University Department of Psychiatry, 1966, 1971, 1977. Compare the 1966 edition pp. 132–3 with the 1977 edition p. 150.

[48] Lex Watson, 'Homosexuals' in Erica M. Bates and Paul R. Wilson (eds), *Mental Disorder or Madness: Alternative Theories*, St Lucia, University of Queensland Press, 1979, pp. 138–40.

[49] Neil McConaghy, cited in Wills, *Politics of Sexual Liberation*, p. 414.

7: Hastening Slowly, 1974–78

[1] 'Gay Pride Week', (Melbourne) *Gay Liberation Newsletter*, n.d. [September 1973].

[2] Rennie Ellis, 'A Gay Picnic in the Park', *Nation Review*, 14–20 September 1973, p. 1516.

3 'Campus CAMP News', *Semper Floreat*, 27 September 1973, p. 14; Brian Day, 'Gay Pride Brisbane Style', *Camp Ink*, vol. 3, no. 7, p. 8.

4 'Gay and Proud', *Boiled Sweets*, September 1973, n.p.; Will Sergeant, 'Gay Pride Week', *Boiled Sweets*, October 1973, n.p. ; Ian Purcell, 'If You Go Out in the Streets Today: Adelaide's Gay Pride March: 25 Years On', *Adelaide GT*, 18 September 1998, p. 7.

5 The following is based on Dianne Minnis, 'Slaughter in Martin Place', *Lot's Wife*, 8 October 1973, p. 3; 'Gay Demonstration', *Tharunka*, vol. 1, no. 1, p. 1; 'Gay Demo', *Scrounge*, 21 September 1971, n.p. 'Gay Pride Week', *Melbourne Gay Liberation Newsletter*, n.d. [September 1973], p. 12.

6 Copies of these submissions (and others) are held in the Peter de Waal papers, MSS 6089, Mitchell Library, SLNSW.

7 Paul Wilson, *The Sexual Dilemma: Abortion, Homosexuality Prostitution and the Criminal Threshold*, St Lucia, University of Queensland Press, 1971, ch. 3. Morgan Gallup Poll, no. 41, 24–31 August 1974, pp. 22–6.

8 'We're Still a Conservative Lot', *Age*, 30 July 1973.

9 Simon Haselton, 'We're Growing Up on Homosexuality and Abortion', *Nation Review*, 1–7 June 1973, p. 1022.

10 Tom O'Lincoln, *Years of Rage: Social Conflicts in the Fraser Era*, Bookmarks, Melbourne, 1993, p. 23; Graham Willett, 'Slouching Away from Bethlehem: Australia and Its Left since 1975, *Reconstruction*, Summer 1995–96, pp. 11–18; Horne, *Time of Hope*, p. 176.

11 CAMP NSW, Executive Minutes, 14 December 1974.

12 Interview with Roger Knight.

13 *Boiled Sweets*, July 1974.

14 Thompson, *Flaws in the Social Fabric*, p. 48.

15 Sydney Gay Liberation Publications Group, 'Dear Subscriber', leaflet, n.d., Sue Wills Papers.

16 *Sydney Gay Liberation Newsletter*, 2 November 1973.

17 CAMP NSW, Executive Minutes, 6 February 1974, Peter de Waal Papers.

18 Lex Watson and Sue Wills, 'Where Are We Going?', *Camp Ink*, May 1972, p. 13.

19 Thompson, *Flaws in the Social Fabric*, p. 19.

20 Craig Johnston, 'Tribunal on Homosexuals and Discrimination', *Red and Lavender*, 1 January 1977.

21 John Holden, 'Radical Days Over', *Nation Review*, 27 September–3 October 1974, p. 1582.

22 Martin Smith, 'The Reason for So Many Gay Societies', *Campaign*, September 1976, p. 8.

23 *Female Homosexuality Seminar One: Conditioning Processes in Education* and *Mass Media and Female Homosexuality Seminar Two: Conditioning Processes in Society and Family*. [Neither has publication details, but both were published by CAMP NSW in 1975–76].

24 'The Homosexual in Society', *Lot's Wife*, 5 August 1974, p. 6; 'Homosexual Lecture Series', *Melbourne Gay Liberation Newsletter*, June 1974, n.p; Jay Watchorn, 'Gay Course to Be Published?', *Gayzette*, no. 16, p. 4. Interviews with Lesley Rogers, 18 November 1996 and

Helen McCulloch, 1 April 1996. See also Lesley Rogers, 'On Being a Political Lesbian', in Bradstock & Wakeling (eds), *Words From the Same Heart*, p. 114.

[25] Peter de Waal, *A Review of the 1976 Tribunal on Homosexuals and Discrimination*, Tribunal Working Group, Sydney, 1994.

[26] Royal Commission on Human Relationships, 'Terms of Reference', *Final Report*, Canberra, AGPS, 1977, vol. 1, p. ix.

[27] Royal Commission on Human Relationships, 'Recommendations in the Report', *Final Report*, vol. 1, p. 124.

[28] 'The Catholic Church as Censor', *Feminist and Gay News*, no. 1, p. 1.

[29] 'CAMP's Submission to the Royal Commission on Human Relationships', *Camp Ink*, vol. 4, no. 4–5, p. 14.

[30] Wills, *Politics of Sexual Liberation*, p. 85.

[31] Wills, *Politics of Sexual Liberation*, pp. 145, 167–72; Christopher Bendall, 'PhoneA-Friend', *Camp Ink*, vol. 4, no. 1, p. 5–6.

[32] Gary Jaynes to Brian Barrett, letter, 23 December 1975, Gay Teachers' and Students' Group Papers, ALGA. Names and addresses list headed 'If you are interested in being involved in Gay Counselling Collective', handwritten, Homosexual Counselling Group Papers.

[33] Jocelyn Clarke, 'On Counselling, or Personal Problems, Mine and Other Peoples', in *Papers and Proceedings of the First National Homosexual Conference*, pp. 67–8.

[34] CAMP Queensland, *President's Report*, 1975.

[35] Garry Pye, 'Homosexual Liberation in Australia, Acceptance', *Papers and Proceedings of the First National Homosexual Conference*, p. 71. Interview with John Willis, 12 February 1996. Details regarding Cross+Section in Brisbane are held in GCS Papers, Box 1.

[36] 'Gay and Catholic', *Stallion*, no. 9, p. 10.

[37] There is an unsigned history of the Catholic group and a copy of the letter to the clergy (as well as many replies) in GCS Papers, Catholic Group File.

[38] Garry Pye, 'Homosexual Liberation in Australia, Acceptance', pp. 71–2.

[39] On WA, see 'Religious Groups', CAMP WA, *Circular*, May 1975, n.p.

[40] 'Same Battle, New Arenas', *Gayzette*, no. 19, p. 20.

[41] Martin Smith, 'Homosexuals in Australia: Past, Present and Future', *Papers and Proceedings of the First National Homosexual Conference*, pp. 74–5.

[42] 'Carlton, Perry Find Australia Really "Camp"', *Gayzette*, no. 19, p. 11. ML, 'MCC Melbourne: The First Years'; 'Gay Church in Adelaide'; CAMP Qld, *President's Report*, 1975.

[43] 'Metropolitan Community Church', *Camp Ink*, vol. 4, no. 2, December 1974, p. 13.

[44] Author's interview with John Willis. Minutes of first meeting held by Graeme Donkin Campaign Committee, 5 April 1976. Craig Johnston Papers, Donkin Campaign File.

[45] 'Vote Yes to Homosexual Motions', *National U*, 28 April 1975, p. 20.

[46] Author's interview with Ron Thiele. 14 August 1996.

[47] 'The Motions', *National U*, 7 April 1975, p. 6.

⁴⁸ Laurie Bebbington, cited in Simon Marginson, 'Women Have Very Little to Celebrate', *National U*, 24 March 1974, p. 9.

⁴⁹ For this and the following discussion, which emphasises the role of AUS, see *Homosexuality: An Action and Resource Guide for Tertiary Students*, Melbourne, Australian Union of Students, n.d., pp. 30–2; AUS, *Homosexual Research Project*, Melbourne, AUS, n.d. [1978], pp. 11–13.

⁵⁰ Report of the Greg Weir Seminar, unpublished minutes, Greg Weir Campaign Papers, ALGA.

⁵¹ 'AUS Policy on Homosexuality', Resolutions Adopted at the Annual Council 13–22 January 1977, Motions Fl–F6, Box 241, File AUS Lesbianism and Homosexuality, AUS Papers, NLA. On the history of the project, see 'AUS Homosexual Research Project', leaflet and questionnaire, n.d. [1977]. The report itself was published as *Homosexual Research Project*, AUS, Melbourne, n.d. [1977].

⁵² Terry Bell, letter, 15 November [1973], Craig Johnston Papers, SOL file.

⁵³ Marginson, 'Women Have Very Little to Celebrate', p. 9.

⁵⁴ 'Statement of the Homosexual Conference Collective', *Papers and Proceedings of the First National Homosexual Conference*, p. 4.

⁵⁵ Mark Kaspryzyk, 'Those Who Came', *National U*, 8 September 1975, p. 10.

⁵⁶ Jeff Hayler, 'National Homosexual Conference', *National U*, 8 September 1975, p. 10.

⁵⁷ CAMP Queensland, *Newsletter*, September 1975, n.p.

⁵⁸ For a more detailed history of the following, see Graham Willett, 'Proud and Employed: The Gay and Lesbian Movement and the Victorian Teachers' Unions in the 1970s', *Labour History*, May 1999, pp. 78–94.

⁵⁹ 'What Now for Gay Teachers?', *GTSG Newsletter*, July 1976.

⁶⁰ 'Presenting the Views of the Gay One's' [sic], *Teachers' Journal*, 22 June 1976, pp. 3, 7. 'Homosexual Rights: Where Do Unions Stand?', *Secondary Teacher*, no. 11, 1976, pp. 9–12. 'School Was the Worst Time of My Life: Comments on Teachers and Homosexuality by the Melbourne Gay Teachers' Group', *Associate News*, 29 April 1977, pp. 7–9. The three articles differ very slightly, reflecting date of publication.

⁶¹ Motions E4, E6, E7, 1977 AGM agenda; amended and approved by Council, VSTA Council Minutes, 7 October 1977, Victorian Secondary Teachers Association Papers, Australian Education Union, Melbourne.

8: Backlash, Resistance and the Community

¹ 'Where Do We Stand? Guest Speaker Lex Watson', *Insight: Newsletter of Acceptance/Sydney*, December 1976–January 1977, p. 2, Society Five Papers, ALGA.

² John Holden, 'Radical Days Are Over', *Nation Review*, 27 September–3 October 1974 p. 1252.

³ 'Homosexuality: Submission on Behalf of the Tasmanian Homosexual Law Reform Group', 18 July 1977, Tasmanian HLR File, Gary Jaynes Papers.

[4] Peter C. Langford, 'V.D. The Valiant Few', *Campaign*, November 1975, p. 6; Jay Watchorn, 'VD', *Campaign*, November 1975, p. 7.

[5] 'Attitudes to Sexual Issues', *Age*, 10 May 1978.

[6] Anti-Festival of Light Melbourne, Minutes 23 September 1978, Anti-FOL file, ALGA.

[7] Meaghan Morris, 'Eurocommunism vs Semiological Delinquency' in Paul Foss and Meaghan Morris (eds), *Language, Sexuality and Subversion*, Darlington (NSW), Feral Publications, 1978, p. 48.

[8] I am grateful to Gary Jaynes for sharing his recollections of this period with me.

[9] On the USA, see Sara Diamond, *Not by Politics Alone: The Enduring Influence of the Christian Right*, New York, Guilford Press, 1998, ch. 8.

[10] John Court, 'Excerpts from *Homosexuality* by J.H. Court', in M.A. Jeeves (ed.), *Behavioural Sciences in Christian Perspective*, to appear in 1973, p. 11, typescript, Mortlock Library, South Australia.

[11] On the FOL, see David Hilliard and John Warhurst, 'The Festival of Light', *Current Affairs Bulletin*, 1 February 1974, pp. 13–19.

[12] 'Resolutions', *Year Book of the Diocese of Sydney, 1974* [Anglican], Sydney, Diocesan Registry, 1974, p. 254.

[13] 'Gay Is a Prison', *Sydney Town Express*, September 1973, p. 3. Stuart Fowler, 'Blessed Are the Straight', letter, *Lot's Wife*, 9 June 1975, pp. 21–2.

[14] Thompson, *Flaws in the Social Fabric*, p. 50.

[15] 'Notes and Comments – Some Opinions', *Australian Church Record*, 20 September 1973, p. 4.

[16] 'This Just Happens to be Part of Me', *Chequerboard*, ABC TV, 31 October 1972. I am grateful to Peter Bonsall-Boone and Peter de Waal for allowing me to view their tape of this program.

[17] B.L. Smith's appearance on *A Current Affair*, November 1972, reported in CAMP, 'Why We Are Here', leaflet, n.d. [November 1972].

[18] 'The Anti-Festival of Light Campaign', leaflet, n.d., Anti-FOL File, ALGA.

[19] MCC, 'There Has Been a Declaration of War against Gay People. This Is a Call to Arms', leaflet, n.d. [1978].

[20] Ron Jacobs, 'This Is What the Public is Being Told about YOU!', *Campaign*, January 1978, p. 8. This article features a detailed summary of Jean Benjamin, *Homosexuality: Its Victims – and the Value of Legal Deterrence*.

[21] Lillian Lowe, 'No Joke', editorial, *Campaign*, October 1978, p. 5.

[22] Ian Malloy, 'Profile of a Morals Campaigner', *Campaign*, September 1978, p. 8.

[23] Assistant Secretary, Lynx, letter, 1 September 1978, Anti-FOL file, ALGA.

[24] 'The Anti-Festival of Light Campaign', leaflet, n.d., Anti-FOL file, ALGA.

[25] Lillian Lowe, 'Hail Mary, Here Come the Pious', *Campaign*, October 1978, pp. 7, 9.

[26] 'FOL Blames "Radicals" for Money Troubles', *Campaign*, April 1979, p. 8.

[27] Graham Carbery, *A History of the Sydney Gay and Lesbian Mardi Gras*, ALGA, Melbourne, 1995, ch. 1.

[28] See John Lee, 'Gays on the March', *Gay Changes*, Spring 1978, p. 5; Craig Johnston, 'The New Gay Radicalisation', Paper to the Socialism and Homosexuality Conference, April 1981; Maurice Blackman, 'Gay Men's Rap: A Space to Breathe', *Gay Changes*, Autumn 1979.

[29] *Campaign* provided regular reports in its monthly issues from June 1978 on.

[30] 'Dawn of the Summer Offensive', *Campaign*, November 1979, p. 5.

[31] Editorial, *Camp Ink*, vol. 2, no. 4, p. 3.

[32] Lex Watson, cited in Bill Calder, 'From the Bars to the Barricades and Back', *OutRage*, September 1990, p. 36.

[33] Wills, *Politics of Sexual Liberation*, p. 103.

[34] Dennis Altman, 'What Changed in the Seventies?' in Gay Left Collective (eds), *Homosexuality: Power and Politics*, London, Alison and Busby, 1980, p. 52.

[35] Larry Galbraith, '*Campaign* and a Decade of Change', *Campaign*, September 1985, p. 14.

[36] Dawn O'Donnell, cited in Frances Round, 'Dawn O'Donnell: 'Hard But Fair'', *Lesbians on the Loose*, no. 25, January 1992, p. 14.

[37] Paul Atreides, 'Sydney Bar Goes up in Smoke', *GCN*, December 1980–January 1981, p. 6.

[38] Terry Goulden, 'The Gay Community: Who Speaks for Us?', *klick!*, December 1980, p. 34.

[39] 'COGs Formation Set', *Campaign*, January 1979, p. 8.

[40] There were two versions of the paper published: Tim Carrigan and John Lee, 'Male Homosexuals and the Capitalist Market', *Gay Changes*, vol. 2, no. 1, Spring 1978, pp. 28–30; Tim Carrigan and John Lee, 'Male Homosexuals and the Capitalist Market', *Gay Changes*, vol. 2, no. 4, pp. 39–42. For a history of the Adelaide Homosexual Alliance and its contribution to the remaking of Australian gay politics in the late 1970s, see Graham Willett, *'In Our Lifetime': The Gay and Lesbian Movement in Australia, 1969–1978*, PhD thesis, University of Melbourne, 1997, ch. 8.

[41] Johnston, 'The New Gay Radicalisation', p. 4; see also Craig Johnston, 'Homosexual Politics: From Gay Movement to Gay "Community"', *Gay Information*, Autumn 1981, pp. 6–9.

[42] Lee, 'Gays on the March', p. 5.

[43] Johnston, 'Homosexual Politics', p. 8.

[44] Johnston, 'The New Gay Radicalisation', p. 2.

[45] Sixth National Conference for Lesbians and Homosexual Men, 'Resolutions for the Final Plenary', unpublished, 1980, ALGA.

[46] Oska Puglisi and Di Minnis, '1981 Mardi Gras??', *GCN* [Melbourne], November 1980, p. 39.

[47] Puglisi and Minnis, '1981 Mardi Gras??', p. 39.

[48] Phil Carswell, 'Life behind Bars', *GCN*, May 1980, p. 31. The 'best traditions' is used ironically here.

[49] See, for example, the letters debate in *GCN*, December 1980–January 1981, pp. 4, 40.

[50] Craig Johnston, 'Clones and the Question of Liberation', *Campaign*, January 1981, p. 17.
[51] Johnston, 'The New Gay Radicalisation', p. 4.
[52] Phil Carswell, 'Clones', *GCN*, November 1980, pp. 24, 25.
[53] Craig Johnston, 'Losing the Battle, Starting the War', *klick!*, May 1981, p. 7.

 **Queer *oz* Folk**

Queer Oz Folk has been established to bring Australia's very queer history into print. It does so in well-produced, affordable editions written with broad audiences in mind. Topics range across the gay, lesbian, bisexual, transgender, intersex and/or queer historical experience in Australia. We will publish both original texts and reprints of significant material from the past. Queer Oz Folk is an imprint of Interventions.

Passionate Friends

Mary Fullerton, Mabel Singleton and Miles Franklin
Sylvia Martin

Mary Fullerton (1868 - 1946) and Mabel Singleton (1877 - 1965) met in Melbourne as suffrage and peach activists in Vida Goldstein's Women's Political Association. They remained together for 35 years as loving friends, raising Mabel's son born in 1911. Through her literary friendship with Miles Franklin (1879 - 1954), Mary Fullerton's last two volumes of poetry were published in the 1940s. Rescued from near destruction, a box of Mary's manuscripts eventually made its way to the Mitchell Library. It contained poems she never sent to Mabel. These poignant poems trace a love story that sheds light on how women of the early twentieth century may have understood their love for each other.

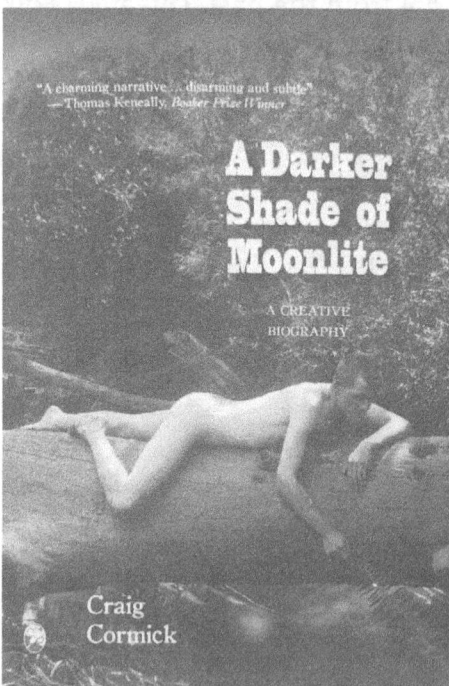

A Darker Shade of Moonlite

A Creative Biography
Craig Cormick

Captain Moonlite (Andrew George Scott, 1842-1880) was an adventurer, fraudster and fabulist who found a respectable post in Victoria as a lay preacher in Bacchus Marsh. Things went haywire after he was convicted of various crimes - at least some of which he probably committed. Long story short he ended up in Melbourne's Pentridge Gaol where he met the love of his life, James Nesbitt. Scott seems to have been a remarkable public speaker. When he directed these skills to prison reform, the authorities put every possible obstacle in his way. The life of a bushranger beckoned, and his gang of young companions set off for New South Wales.

The Mystery of the Handsome Man

The Double Life of John Lempriere Irvine
By Wayne Murdoch

'Hallo, are you working?' John Lempriere Irvine greeted 19-year-old Ernest Smith on the footpath of Grattan Street, Carlton, one September evening in 1897, setting off a chain of events which saw both men in court and Irvine's life in ruins within a week. Ranging from the convict settlement of Port Arthur, to the heights of colonial Tasmanian Society, the goldrush towns of Ballarat and Bendigo, and the ballrooms of Marvellous Melbourne in the 1880s, this book recounts the strange-but-true story of John Lempriere Irvine (1847-?), banker, champion sportsman and bon vivant. He was also a man with a secret – a secret that would occasionally lead him into the half-light of the Victorian underworld and would ultimately lead to his downfall, disgrace, and disappearance.

Survivors and Thrivers

Male Homosexual Lives in Postwar Australia
David Gould

In interviewing 27 men aged between 74 and 95 in the late 2000s, David Gould discovered lives - now rapidly being lost to history - that were lived under the shadow of homophobic prejudice. Their stories reveal how men tried to make sense of their same-sex attraction in an era when homosexuality was defined as a mental illness and criminal. What emerges is a revelation - stories of resilience and, sometimes, joy.

www.ingramcontent.com/pod-product-compliance
Lightning Source LLC
Chambersburg PA
CBHW071958290426
44109CB00018B/2062